AGENTS OF CHANGE

THE STORY OF DC SHOES AND ITS ATHLETES

ReganBooks

An Imprint of HarperCollins*Publishers*

Editor
ERIC BLEHM

Executive Art Director
KEN BLOCK

Art Director
CARL HYNDMAN

Designer
TERRY SNYDER

Senior Editor
LORIEN WARNER

Copy Editor
RITA SAMOLS

Chief Photographers
MIKE BLABAC AND CARL HYNDMAN

The Photographers:
Niko Achtipes, Carlo Bagalini, Michael Ballard, Mike Balzer, Eric Bergeri, Brian Bielmann,
Adam Booth, Grant Brittain, Paul Buckley, Steve Buddendeck, Jason Childs, Nate Christiansen,
Daren Crawford, Simon Cudby, Lance Daws, Dimitry Elyashkevich, Fat Nick, Ryan Gee, Geoff Graham,
Trevor Graves, Cory Grove, Frank Hoppen, Chris Hultner, Greg Hunt, Spike Jonze, Rob Keith,
Mark Losey, Mehring, Garth Milan, Jody Morris, Jamie Mosberg, Keith Mulligan, Jeff Murillo,
Dave Norehad, Luke Ogden, Mike O'Meally, Chris Owen, Markus Paulsen, Sean Peterson, Skin Phillips,
Torey Piro, Scott Pommier, Jeff Potto, Giovanni Reda, Shem Roose, Tom Rulon, Jim Sanderson,
Scott Serfas, Gary Soles, Ethan Stone, Dan Sturt, Dave Swift, Derrick Swinfard, Peter Tankersly,
Pete Thompson, Rich Van Every, Shelby Woods, Andy Wright, Kevin Zacker

The Writers:
Russ Bengtson, Eric Blehm, Nancy Carlson, Davey Coombs, Lee Crane, Ryan Fite, Carl Hyndman,
Eric Johnson, Scooter Leonard, Blair Marlin, Whitey McConnaughy, Harold McGruther, Aaron Meza,
Joel Muzzey, Joel Patterson, Jason Stein, Dave Swift, Miki Vuckovich, Kevin Wilkins

Special Thanks:
Kurt Andrews, Steve Astephen, Matt Baglio, Eric Berger, Liza Bolitzer, Brian Botts, Thomas Campbell,
Nancy Carlson, Chris Carter, Mysun Dean, Curtis Doss, Scott Drouillard, Brian Dvorak, Ryan Fite,
Christy Fletcher, Fox Racing, Jack Gentle, Matt Goodman, Sharon Harrison, Tony Hawk, Lori Hennessy,
Rick Hennessy, Renee Iwaszkiewicz, Dan Janssen, Eric Johnson, Cassie Jones, Thomas Jones,
David Kinsey, Donna Kokinelis, John Kokinelis, Michael Lau, Scooter Leonard, Mark Losey, Blair Marlin,
Pete McAfee, Mary O'Dea, Racer X Illustrated, Fran Richards, Steve Rocco, David "Persue" Ross,
Steve Saiz, Jeff Salgado, Cris Searle, Wendy Snyder, Tim Swart, Mike Ternasky, Tha Liks,
Brian Thompson, Amber Warner, Evan Warner, Kevin Wilkins, Brian Wright, Randy Wright, Pam Zam

FIRST EDITION

Library of Congress Cataloging-in-Publication Data has been applied for.

ISBN 0-06-050560-5

03 04 05 06 07   10 9 8 7 6 5 4 3 2 1

   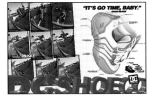   

CONTENTS

This story begins in 1989 with a series of serendipitous events. In that year, twenty-one-year-old Ken Block dropped his budding architectural career to become a snowboard bum, and conceptualized a clothing brand called Eightball. In a 1991 college math class, he became friends with Damon Way, nineteen, a skateboarder who'd suffered a head injury that shattered his dreams of going pro. The following year, I introduced Ken and Damon to my father, Clay Blehm, fifty-eight years old, an unemployed accountant who was broke and living in my sister's garage. The three would create DC Shoes in 1993.

Ken and I had met in 1985 in a high school architectural drafting class. We later forged our friendship as roommates living in an overcrowded flophouse, known as Motel Hell, in Breckenridge, Colorado; we migrated there from Southern California to snowboard powder and tried not to grow up.

Our career paths would follow that same philosophy: to have fun. In the hope that I'd get to see the world and scam heli-boarding trips on somebody else's dime, I took the journalistic route, eventually becoming the managing editor of *TransWorld SNOWboarding Business* and then, until 1998, the editor of *TransWorld SNOWboarding*. Ken Block went on to found Eightball, which turned into Droors and Dub, which turned into DC Shoes, the empire that is the basis for this story.

As early as 1991, word was that a new company had somehow scored the endorsement of skateboarding prodigy Danny Way, younger brother of Damon. While working my way up the ladder at TransWorld (the hub of a highly active rumor mill) in the early nineties, I witnessed the reactions of action sports industry insiders. Nobody knew my link to the company; I just sat in the shadows, enjoying and occasionally jotting down candid and often cynical comments such as:

• "I don't know what they're thinking. That's the ugliest skateboarding shoe I've ever seen."
• "Pretty small company for such a big ego. What's up with all the logos?"
• "There's a formula that works, and I don't think they get it."
• "It's a bunch of hype over Danny. I give it a couple of years before it dies."

A handful of industry visionaries took Ken and Damon's ideas seriously from the start, and nine years later, DC Shoes has become one of the most credible companies in the history of skateboarding and number one among those who really matter: the skateboarders. The company sells nearly $100 million a year in product, and for three years in a row the brand has been voted the "coolest brand of skateboarding shoes." DC's teams of multi-talented athletes are revered by an army of young people that is changing the face of athletics from traditional team sports to individual action sports. Abused DCs worn by professional and amateur athletes alike represent the persistence that has elevated DC and these sports and athletes to house-hold names in less than a decade.

The abused shoes pictured at left were custom-made on short notice as a marketing tool to enhance Danny Way's visual image. The shoes were rushed overseas just in time for Danny to wear them at the 1999 MTV Sports and Music Festival in Las Vegas, where he defended his world record high air. During Danny's warm-up (i.e., bomb-dropping into a gigantic ramp from a hovering helicopter) two days before the contest, he ripped all the ligaments in his shoulder. Despite the painful injury that would later require surgery, he carried on and stuck the bomb drop, then won the contest—apt illustrations of how Danny Way (as do many athletes) drives himself into the ground for the sake of the sport.

DC Shoes is not just a "buy an athlete's endorsement" kind of company. The action sports industry doesn't work that way. If that were the case, big-name shoe manufacturers who make billions off basketball, baseball, and football players would prosper, instead of fail miserably, in the action sports arena. The company is not about success based on deep pockets, because there was no money in the beginning. It's not about following a formula. It's not about a single athlete or a single ad campaign. It's about taking chances and making sacrifices like putting your house up for collateral. It's about living the lifestyle, not just selling it.

When I was contacting various publishers about this book, I touted my idea as a company history celebrated through its athletes. I wanted the book to convey the message that an audience of one is often more daunting and demanding than any crowd, because the only person the athlete is up against is him- or herself. And I wanted readers to understand that the same can hold true for anyone—and any company.

I found that most publishers trying to sell books to "extreme sports junkies" don't want metaphors and prose. They want full-color photos of pros. The editors at ReganBooks, on the other hand, realized that "extreme sports junkies" can actually read. They trusted our judgment to write and design a book for the people we know best: the skateboarders, the snowboarders, the surfers, the BMXers, the motocrossers, and anybody else who appreciates the athleticism and fearlessness associated with these sports.

Agents of Change is a culmination of the work of photographers, artists, and writers who live the lives they document. Without their often-overlooked talents, this book wouldn't have been possible. In addition, special thanks go to designer Terry Snyder, who hasn't slept or surfed nearly enough during the last year, to my devil's advocate and Jedi editor, Lorien Warner, to all of DC's creative employees, who continue to convey Ken and Damon's vision, and to my dad, Clay, who has proven that it's never too late to realize your dreams.

This has been one of my toughest assignments, and one of the most rewarding. May the DC Shoes story inspire you as it has me.

—Eric Blehm, May 2002

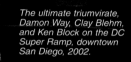

The ultimate triumvirate,
Damon Way, Clay Blehm,
and Ken Block on the DC
Super Ramp, downtown
San Diego, 2002.

"THE HISTORY OF DC SHOES IS, ESSENTIALLY, THE HISTORY OF THE MODERN SKATEBOARD SHOE."

– Miki Vuckovich, former editor, *TransWorld SKATEboarding Business*

Like all success stories, DC's began with a person and an idea.

The year was 1989. The person was Ken Block. The idea was Eightball clothing. That seed evolved into serendipitous partnerships and business plans and a pivotal year—1993—in which Block and his associates pioneered what would become the modern-day skateboarding shoe.

Digging through the layers of DC's relatively brief, yet explosive, history reveals various intricately woven recipes for success, formulated over sometimes seemingly insurmountable odds. The company began with zero—there were no venture capitalists lurking in the shadows. Its original screen-printing factory was a classroom at a local community college. Its warehouse was an apartment. Its marketing? Word of mouth. Its customers? Notoriously critical and fickle skateboarders, who tended to regard anything successful as corporate and uncool: the more product you sold, the less desirable you became.

In the late eighties and early nineties, the economic climate of the skateboarding industry was rocky at best. Skate parks had closed due to insurance issues, skate shops were boarding up their windows because of declining sales, and, as Tony Hawk remembers the era in his book, *Hawk: Occupation: Skateboarder,* "Everybody involved with skating began looking up to see when the sky was going to fall."

But Ken Block, along with his friend and new partner, Damon Way, wasn't concerned that the skateboarding industry was in a downward spiral. That didn't affect their skateboarding. Likewise, their winter fun—snowboarding—was still a fledgling, misunderstood sport, in part for the same reasons that skateboarding was declining: negative or lack of mainstream media coverage. *Time* magazine had even called snowboarding the "Worst New Sport" in a January 1988 issue.

This was exactly the kind of degrading media coverage that fired up Block and Way. They liked being in the wary eye of the public.

They felt comfortable there. So, as hard times plagued the skate industry and businesspeople strategized ways to cut their losses and get the hell out, Block and Way figured out a way to get in.

One problem. Their combined experience in running a business amounted to, roughly, zero. Still, they were having a great time in the process of learning—partying in their tiny warehouse, skateboarding in the parking lot, snowboarding in the local mountains, and selling quite a bit of clothing along the way.

That's when Block and Way were introduced to a down-on-his-luck fifty-eight-year-old accountant named Clay Blehm, who eyed their graffiti-deco warehouse warily and carried with him a healthy dose of skepticism. The three— polar opposites in background, personality, and age—would form an incomparable triumvirate that turned zero into an almost $100-million-a-year business in less than a decade.

This is their story.

THE BEGINNING

Ken Block was born on November 21, 1967, in Long Beach, California, the youngest of four siblings. He was raised by his parents: James, an entrepreneur who owned and operated a successful laminating business, and Geraldine, who handled the traditional role of homemaker in a comfortable, middle-class nuclear family.

His teachers considered him smart and precocious as early as kindergarten. In the first grade, however, Block failed "reading" and his teachers recommended summer school. Block didn't want to relinquish his summer, so instead his folks returned him to first grade the following fall, this time in a private Catholic school. "We thought how much better it would be to be the smartest one in the first grade than the dumbest one in the second grade," says Geraldine Block.

Indeed, from that point forward, Block was at the top of his class, earning mostly A's with a handful of B's. Soon enough, he was excelling in sports as well, the starting pitcher on the all-star Little League baseball team. He had mostly up days, with the occasional down, like the time he walked a bunch of batters and his team lost. When the coach sat the kids down and asked, "Who lost this game?" the entire team yelled, "Ken!" "Stuff like that didn't even rattle Ken," says his mother. "He came back next game and was the star pitcher all over again."

In 1977, Block's brother, Steve, took him to a skateboard shop and helped him pick out a skinny wooden Sims skateboard with big, fat Alva wheels. That purchase led him to the Badlands Skate Park in Long Beach and the Lakewood Skate Park in Lakewood. Ten-year-old Block was one of the youngest kids to frequent these parks. Dropping into the snakeruns and bowls was an intimidating experience that he forced himself through, but eventually, young Block earned the respect of the older teenagers who frequented the popular skate hangouts. That, in turn, led him to an eclectic group of friends, music, and fashion. A BMX bike kept his attention for a short period of time, but his skateboard won out; he used it to explore his neighborhood's street-skating options. This solitary hobby often found him practicing tricks alone by streetlight, a lifestyle he continued into his teens.

When Block was fourteen, his parents moved south to a rural area of San Diego County, Valley Center, where there was plenty of dirt but, unfortunately, not much cement for skateboarding. The skateboard quickly outgrew the confines of his blacktopped driveway, and boredom became the catalyst for bigger and faster toys, like the motorcycle that kept him busy for the rest of his first summer in a strange new place.

He began school at Escondido's Orange Glen High School that fall, and pursued his longtime love of baseball by trying out for the high school

The logo that started it all: Ken Block's first "8ball" logo, 1990.

team. During tryouts, he was the outsider, aware of other players "kissing the coach's ass"—something Block refused to do. He figured his talent would speak for itself. When lesser players made the team and he didn't, Block's view of "team" and "coached" sports was soured. He turned back to his skateboard and, to fulfill his competitive nature, started amateur motocross racing. He also discovered partying, and his grades dropped.

Block's parents had always supported their son's "athletic endeavors," whether they be baseball, soccer, skateboarding, or basketball. But upon learning that their home had become a popular party zone when they were out of town, they abandoned sponsorship of their son's motocross racing career. The infamous Block parties scaled back considerably (as did Block's high school income, since he'd charged admission to the parties), and motocross was replaced by a new passion: architectural drafting.

When Block was in his junior and senior years, architecture evolved into a career aspiration and upon graduating high school in 1986, he immediately dove into continued education at the Phoenix Institute of Technology, a technical college in Arizona known for its architectural programs. One year later he had graduated, was working as an architectural draftsman in San Diego, and was on his way to becoming a full-fledged architect.

Block had spent his young life jumping from one hobby to the next, so it was no surprise when he got bored with drafting. "I'd sit there and stare at the clock," he says, "and look at the stressed-out people I was working with, and I realized, this isn't for me." That's when a friend named Tom Russell introduced him to snowboarding, and Block ditched his architectural career to become a snowboard bum—perhaps a step backward in the eyes of society, but a leap forward as far as Block was concerned. Life was fun again.

He moved to June Mountain, California, for the 1988/89 season and progressed rapidly in the sport, loving the lifestyle and working first in the ski rental shop and then as a snowboard instructor. California, however, was experiencing a poor winter, so after three months, Block traveled east to Breckenridge, Colorado, where some of his high school friends were living.

"When you look at how big DC has become, I think the craziest thing is where it came from. It all started with Ken Block and Eightball. Most people don't know that."
– Jim Ruonala, owner, Pacific Drive skateboard shop

One of those friends, Matt Goodman, a talented surfer/skateboarder who'd grown up skateboarding in Southern California parks with the likes

Ken Block snowboarding in Arapahoe
Basin, Colorado, 1990.

Skateboarding legend Kevin Staab
started 90 in the late eighties.

of Tony Hawk and Danny Way, introduced Block to Kevin Staab, another well-known pro skateboarding icon from the eighties, who was marketing his successful new skateboard apparel company, 90. Even when he was in grammar school, Block had been very particular about what he wore—shoes, pants, shirts, everything "had to be picked out by Ken," says his mother. He'd already developed a keen fashion sense at an age when most kids were content wearing whatever their parents had bought for them, and by the time he met Staab, it took a lot to pique his interest. He was intrigued, however, by Staab's simple black-and-white circular 90 logo and the fact that only skateboarders and in-the-know snowboarders wore it. Staab's 90 became a life-altering inspiration for Block, who coveted the T-shirt and sweatshirt hand-me-downs he'd score from Goodman.

"I thought, 'How could anybody make money selling T-shirts?' Of course, I'm eating my words now."

– Geraldine Block, Ken Block's mother

The following winter, Block returned to Breckenridge to live as a mountain bum, working in ski shops, riding, and consuming massive quantities of Eightball malt liquor (a beverage that was popular with rap music artists like N.W.A.) with roommates Goodman and Will Newland. That's just what he was doing one night when the creative lightbulb came on. A black eightball was a simple, highly recognizable logo. It sounded cool. He pondered, "Would Eightball T-shirts sell as well as 90?" Using his drafting skills, he drew a few logos, but the creative drive was short-lived, the sketches soon forgotten in a drawer.

Block spent the winter riding the Breckenridge halfpipe with superstar snowboarders like Andy Hetzel, Brett Johnson, and Shawn Farmer, all friends of Goodman, who was on the road to becoming a pro snowboarder himself. In the humbling company of greatness, Block could keep up, but he soon came to the realistic conclusion that he would never make it as a pro.

Kevin Staab's 90 logo was the inspiration for Eightball.

Regardless, a California summer of skateboarding and keg parties was enough to convince him that he liked the snowboarding/skateboarding lifestyles despite their bad rap as subversive and shady subcultures. He just needed a way to turn his interests into a career. Anything was more appealing than going back to college, getting married, and buying a house, mainstream prospects that terrified him. Then he had a hunch: maybe Eightball would be the ticket.

Back in 1991, the Blocks loaned their
son $10,000 to fund a T-shirt company.
He paid them back in full.

THE DC OWNERS

Name: KEN BLOCK

Title: President
Date of Birth: November 21, 1967
Location: Long Beach, California

Education:
- Orange Glen High School (Escondido, California), graduated in 1986.
- Phoenix Institute of Technology (Phoenix, Arizona), completed a one-year architectural drafting certificate course in 1987.
- Palomar Community College (San Marcos, California), course work in computer graphics, photography, screen-printing, and general education.

Hobbies/Interests:
- snowboarding
- skateboarding
- basketball
- wakeboarding
- buying expensive cars and doing ridiculous things to them
- product design and development
- motocross
- architecture
- traveling with friends
- being outdoors . . . hiking, mountain biking, etc.
- annoying others
- hurting himself by accident
- advertising and marketing
- pool parties

Business Philosophy:
"Honesty. Integrity. Hard work. Study every angle to make the best decisions. Look at both sides of every situation. Think through your enemies' eyes. Be creative no matter what the situation . . . there's always a better, creative solution."

Life Philosophy:
"I'm bored . . . what's next?"

LEFT TO RIGHT: Larry LaLonde (guitarist of Primus), Carla Alaponte, Ken Block, Jen Wolfe, and DC snowboard/BMX team manager Brian Botts at a 1999 X Games qualifier, Lake Havasu, Arizona.

Mike Bisbee

Garth Milan

Former supercross and motocross champion Jeff Emig (left) and Ken Block having a little fun during a magazine photo shoot in San Bernardino, 2001.

Ken Block enjoying some powder during the DC Decadence Tour in Utah's Wasatch Range, 2001.

Carl Hyndman

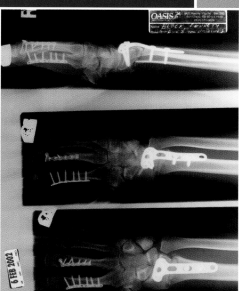

RIGHT: You've got to pay to play . . . just a little reconstructive surgery from when Ken Block crushed his hand between his head and some boulders at Snowbird, Utah, in 1999, and a broken wrist from a 2001 MX race in Anaheim Stadium, California.

Ken Block with one of his best friends and DC team rider Rob Dyrdek at another infamous DC trade-show party.

Though tempted to return to Colorado that fall, Block instead stayed in San Diego and headed off to Palomar College, the local community college—a "high school with ashtrays," as snooty pals who attended prestigious universities called it—to pursue artistic aspirations, with Eightball in mind. Block also took to skateboard/snowboard shops, bookstores, magazine racks, libraries, and anywhere he could go to educate himself about the business he was formulating in his mind, a tireless self-teaching approach he would incorporate into his marketing plans for years to come.

Another one of his high school buddies, Mark Bealo, urged Block to take it to the next level via computer classes. Block was already comfortable behind a keyboard: his parents had bought him a RadioShack computer when he was eleven, and a year later he'd graduated to one of the first Apple computers. He was addicted to computer games and graphics, which made the prospect of learning how to design computer graphics very appealing.

> ### "You know, sometimes the best time to start a company is when your world is falling down around you. That was skateboarding in the early nineties."
> – Fran Richards, VP of sales and marketing; publisher, *TransWorld SKATEboarding*

Block met graphic design and computer instructor Neil Bruington, a mentor of sorts who taught him the fundamentals of designing logos and artwork on the college's new Macintosh computers and transferring the designs onto T-shirts and other mediums by screen-printing. In his first screen-printing class Block used photos of fellow Breckenridge snowboarding buddies Goodman and Eric Blehm to create basic one- and two-color T-shirts. He sent a sample T-shirt to an acquaintance he'd met in Colorado, the owner of First Tracks snowboard shop in Breckenridge, who liked it enough to order a few more. The capitalist seed had been planted.

Ken Block used this classic 1988 photo of Eric Blehm, taken off Peak 8 in Breckenridge, Colorado, as the artwork for his first screen-printed T-shirt (below), which he sold to First Tracks snowboard shop in 1990.

> ### "I had to push Ken out the door so I could go home at night. He'd spend twenty, thirty hours a week at the college sometimes, and it always seemed his 'student' projects had a commercial slant. Little did I know..."
> – Neil Bruington, professor, Palomar College

His next designs would incorporate the long-nurtured Eightball logo.

Eric Blehm was working at Hobie Sports (now Surf Ride) in Oceanside at the time and introduced Block and his debut Eightball T-shirts to Hobie's manager and buyer, Dana Hill, who immediately took a dozen shirts on consignment. In a few weeks, Hobie had sold out and wanted a dozen more, which Block hand-delivered within a week.

> ### "The first time I heard it was going to be called Eightball, I thought the name was horrible—just a bite right out of hip-hop. They had sick skaters, though."
> – Aaron Meza, editor, *Skateboarder* magazine

While continuing to use Palomar College as his mini screen-printing factory, Block also took a retail job at Hobie. It was the kind of work he didn't much care for, but he needed a paycheck for rent, car insurance, and expanding his "line" to include sweatshirts. Block was working in Hobie's snowboard department when then-nineteen-year-old Damon Way came in to get his snowboard waxed and tuned. After he'd left, another employee informed Block that he'd just met the older brother of the young pro skateboarder Danny Way.

CREDIBILITY SKATEBOARDS INTO THE PICTURE

To fully appreciate the serendipity of the moment when Ken Block and Damon Way first met, we must rewind nineteen years and envision Way as a baby crawling around in the dirt outside his hippie parents' tepee home in a Northern California commune, not long after he was born on September 23, 1971.

His parents, Mary and Dennis Way, lived life the vegetarian Whole Foods way: growing their own food, practicing daily yoga; and for Dennis, a musician and maker of Gibson guitars, writing songs. When Damon Way was three (his brother, Danny, had been born six months earlier to the sounds of Neil Young, BB King, and Jefferson Airplane— groups that Dennis Way had jammed with or done studio guitar work for) his parents moved the family back to Southern California, where they'd met. Peace, love, and happiness were abruptly shattered when Dennis Way was taken to court by his ex-wife for having missed a child-support payment for the half sister the Way brothers never knew. The judge reportedly gave the ex-wife an option: to have Dennis Way pay the delinquent fifty dollars immediately, or have him spend sixty days in county jail.

Damon Way (age three) with his mom, Mary, and little brother, Danny, in 1974.

She chose the latter, and nine days later Dennis Way was found dead in his county jail cell—a mysterious case, ruled (but not accepted by family and friends) as suicide and, according to Mary Way, "surrounded by a shroud of foul play and cover-ups."

Twenty-four-year-old Mary found herself alone raising an infant and a toddler. She found work first as a landscaper and then delivered auto parts. A

Damon Way and his father, Dennis Way, 1974.

couple of years after her husband's death, she met Tim O'Dea, a jack-of-all-trades who measured his life out among odd jobs, sailing, and surfing. He was great with the Way brothers.

The two married, and O'Dea assumed the role of father. He built a skateboard for five-year-old Damon Way, who took to it immediately, skating around his neighborhood and jumping off curbs, becoming a role model for his younger brother. When Way was eight, O'Dea introduced him to skateboarding transitions—vert and pool—at the Del Mar Skate Ranch.

O'Dea and Mary divorced around this time. She found a new boyfriend shortly thereafter, a relationship that relocated her sons to upstate New York, then back to the West Coast in time for Way to enter the fifth grade at Santa Fe Elementary School in Vista. The boys continued to spend time with O'Dea, who took an active interest in both their lives, which for Damon revolved around sports: team ones like baseball and football (which he'd taken up in New York) and skateboarding and surfing.

"When you're younger, everybody does it all," says Way. "We all skated, played football, surfed, played baseball; there wasn't a separation when I was in elementary and middle school. It was all about discovery and having fun with your friends."

> *"Damon was pretty much the leader of the Vista Skate Locals, jump ramps and stuff. Nobody could touch him. We all figured he'd be the first to go pro."*
> – Steve Ortega, former pro skateboarder; current DC sales

The Ways skateboarded at the Del Mar Skate Ranch and also hung out sessioning mini ramps in friends' backyards. When Way was twelve, he and his brother added to the ensemble by building a quarterpipe in front of their house. Nobody could get to the top of the poorly designed ramp, which was eight feet high with four feet of vert. The tranny was rough and sent more than a few neighborhood kids home with bruises, but the Way brothers persisted in skating it, for hours and hours every day. At night, they'd go into their garage and breakdance on cardboard. Within a few years Damon Way joined the California Amateur Skateboard League (CASL) and started winning contests in his "1A" division, including one held in the notorious combo pool at the Upland Skate Park.

It was the early eighties. The family was surviving on unpredictability: wages from Mary O'Dea's low-paying jobs and, during a particularly difficult time, help from welfare and

Damon Way, backside air at a Vista skate hangout: Davey Lach's backyard, 1985.

a church. His mother had one "really cool boyfriend," according to Way. That the boyfriend had money made everything easier for the three years he and Mary were together. That he also happened to be a drug dealer meant that the relationship wouldn't last and Mary would continue her search for stability, while her sons led increasingly independent lives.

Way admits that he was sometimes ashamed that he and his family didn't have much—especially in his teenage years when he wanted to bring a girlfriend over. He envied friends like future pro skateboarder Matt Hensley, whose family Way considered perfect, and pondered what it would be like to have a stable and nurturing environment. "My mom was and is very, very loving, extremely loving and good-hearted," he says. "She did something right. I mean, with all the chaos that me and my brother grew up with, we actually turned out okay. My childhood was pretty unique and unpredictable. It just wasn't very stable."

Tim O'Dea, who turned his stepsons Damon and Danny Way onto skateboarding and surfing, takes his son, Lane, surfing in 1998.

But Way understood that life outside normal parental guidelines had its benefits, too. He had the freedom to do "pretty much whatever" he wanted, including street skating until three in the morning. "We'd get in trouble if we really pushed it, but we never got into really bad things. Never got into drugs. Never ran with the wrong crowd or were violent or anything like that. Skateboarding was our savior."

Damon Way's days revolved around skateboarding with the Vista Skate Locals, the self-named group of friends that consisted of his brother, Matt Hensley, Steve Ortega, Mario Rubalcaba, Brennand Schoeffel, Tim Tillman, Jay Hit, Matt Lorenz, Mike Crum, and Tommy Grihalva. Many of them would go on to become skateboarding superstars, but in the beginning it was all about skating and leaving behind their VSL mark—usually a spray-painted tag—at every skateable spot within the Vista city limits; listening to punk rock while learning new tricks; camping out in sleeping bags at the bottom of a halfpipe during the amateur Rock Socks vert contest in Ramona (Way won his division, taking home a Dave Hacket Skull Skates deck and some checkered socks); and building numerous portable street ramps and a halfpipe in the Ways' backyard. They pillaged from nearby construction sites simply because they needed wood for the ramp and "there was a bunch of wood."

"We took around a hundred sheets of four-by-eight plywood and four hundred eight-foot two-by-fours. We'd load the wood on our skateboards and ride it down a long hill to my house and then quickly transfer it into my backyard. It was probably the worst thing we did."

– Damon Way

Around this time, Way was "discovered" by Alexander's, a beach shop in Pacific Beach that sold skateboards and was the place to hang out when the brothers were visiting O'Dea, who lived on a boat in adjacent Mission Bay. Jim Ruonala and Milo Myers, shop managers at the time, sponsored Way, giving him stickers and T-shirts. Ruonala also looked into ordering smaller skateboards for Way's tagalong little brother, but it was Way who was "the leader of the pack at that time," says Ruonala. "These were the jump ramp days, and we were hyped on him. All his Vista crew were good, too, but Damon stood out."

By the time Way was fifteen, skateboarding was giving him everything he needed: confidence, friends, and fun, and most importantly, an identity and a goal. He was poised, and reasonably so, to make professional skateboarding his career.

That was brutally ripped away at a Friday evening high school football game.

"November 16, 1986," Way rattles off as easily as if it were a birth date, "I got hit in the head." Stories vary, but the theme remains: a fellow Vista High student had heard a rumor that Way had been "talking shit" about him, and Way had heard the same rumor in reverse. Even though Way wasn't the fighting type, a confrontation ensued and punches were thrown. He returned home with a bad headache, but figured he'd feel better in the morning and went to sleep. That was the

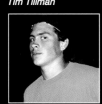

THE DC OWNERS

Name: DAMON WAY

Title: Executive Vice President
Date of Birth: September 23, 1971
Location: Portland, Oregon

Education:
- Vista High School (Vista, California),
  graduated in 1989.
- Palomar Community College (San Marcos,
  California), general education classes from
  1990 to 1991.

Hobbies/Interests:
- music (listening, playing, recording)
- art (buying, collecting, appreciating)
- design (product, fashion, interior)
- collecting records
- road-racing Ducati motorcycles
- combing cities for new things
- skateboarding
- snowboarding

Business Philosophy:
  "Enjoy what you do or do not do it."

Life Philosophy:
  "Same as business philosophy."

Damon Way and his
guitar, circa 1996.

Willow Springs

Laying it over on a
Ducati road bike.
Damon Way in
Willow Springs,
California, 2001.

Damon Way in his home
music studio. Leucadia,
California, 2001.

last thing he remembered until three days later, when he woke up in the hospital.

"I woke up and Damon was on the floor in seizures. I thought I was watching my brother die right there in front of me."

– Danny Way

A main artery in his head had burst as the result of a blow to his temple, causing a hematoma—the accumulation of blood—between the brain and skull. Way's life was saved by an emergency procedure in which the swelling was relieved via a hole bored into his skull. Had Danny not discovered Damon having seizures early on November 17, the older Way brother would have died.

The first written representation of Eightball, a logo that Damon Way drew for Ken Block during an algebra class.

The trauma caused partial paralysis to the left side of Way's body, a condition similar to a stroke, but almost immediately he vowed to skate again. Skateboarding became the driving force behind a two-year battle with depression and physical therapy that included learning how to put on his socks and tie his shoes.

And there was Danny Way.

"Danny would come into his brother's hospital room and show him new tricks on his skateboard," says Mary O'Dea, recounting the six weeks Damon Way spent in the hospital. "The physical therapists saw the fire in Damon's eyes and eventually incorporated the skateboard into his therapy." The skateboard was a successful tool for relearning balance and movement, and eventually Way could shakily carve the skateboard on a treadmill between two parallel bars that he used for support.

"Danny became a professional skateboarder as much for Damon as for himself—he did it for both of them."

– Mary O'Dea, Damon and Danny Way's mother

Throughout his grueling rehabilitation, Way overcame physical and emotional hurdles, reentered high school, caught up on missed credits, and

eventually was able to drop in on a vert ramp with relearned tricks that included backside airs, fakie rock 'n' rolls, and mute body jars. He graduated on schedule in 1989, but his dream to become a professional skateboarder was out of the question.

A lawsuit filed by the Way family eventually yielded a fair cash settlement that covered the massive medical expenses and damages resulting from the injury, and Way made a conscious decision to use the money as a springboard to finding success and stability. He began by making more conservative investments that included buying the small home he'd been renting, as well as riskier ventures involving the stock market and "those 'get rich in ninety days, send two dollars' kits." He read through moneymaking schemes, kept on skateboarding for fun, took a few commercial art classes, and tried to figure out what his career should be. Then, four years after "the accident," Way, who'd also taken to snowboarding, went to Hobie Sports to drop off his snowboard and met Ken Block for the first time.

A few weeks later Block was sitting in the back of a Palomar College algebra class when Way sauntered in, late. By chance, there was an empty seat next to Block, and a friendship was forged.

"It's amazing that Damon was able to take such a gnarly incident and turn it into such a positive thing."

– Brennand Schoeffel, former Vista Skate Local; current real estate broker

Their conversations tended to focus on snowboarding parks (a new development at ski areas), music, and Block's aspiring clothing line, Eightball. Way was immediately interested in his friend's endeavors and even drew a graffiti-inspired rendition of the word "Eightball." Within weeks, that drawing had made it into Block's next round of screen-printing.

At the time there weren't many clothing companies that sponsored skateboarders, so Way gave a bunch of Eightball T-shirts and sweatshirts to his brother, who'd worked his way up into the pro ranks while Way recovered from his injury, and to his friends. The young pros, members of the very popular Plan B team, liked both the designs and the vibe of the fledgling business and made it a point to wear the clothing during magazine photo shoots, while being videoed, and when simply hanging out.

boyz in our hood.

sean sheffey | sal barbier | danny way | jordan richter

clean. hard. funky.

8 eightball

770 sycamore #J471
vista, ca 92083
(619) 598-5450 phn
(619) 598-4241 fax

legit clothing

The first Eightball advertisement: Sal Barbier and an injured Danny Way, 1992.

*Damon Way and Ken Block selling product in their first trade-
show booth: a ten-by-ten for the 1992 Action Sports Retailer.
Notice the first Droors logo in the upper left corner.*

The immediate acceptance was exciting for Block, who attributed much of the good luck to Way's connections. Way also had contacts with various skate shops and offered to help Block out as a sales representative working on commission from any sales he could muster up. Quickly thereafter, Eightball's retailer base escalated to a few small skateboard shops that included Pacific Drive, a surf/skate shop that Jim Ruonala (the manager from Alexander's) had opened in 1987. The shop sold out of the small Eightball consignment, "though not as quickly as the big brands," says Ruonala. "These guys had no advertising, and most of the skateboarders didn't know the Plan B guys were wearing it. Kids were buying it because they were cool designs that nobody had seen before."

*The first Eightball ad appeared
here, the March 1992 issue of
TransWorld SKATEboarding.*

Way never got around to negotiating a commission. He and Block had been entertaining the idea of a partnership just as Eightball outgrew the loosely drawn limitations of a "student project." After Palomar College had provided the screen-printing utilities for an estimated three hundred garments, instructor Bruington broke the bad news: Block would have to find a new production facility.

Having maxed out a $5,000 credit card (and the storage capacity of his two-bedroom San Marcos apartment), Block was faced with the dim prospect of forging ahead with scant funds or calling it quits. He decided to take his business to the next level and hit up his parents for a loan.

James Block, a successful businessman himself, insisted that his son draw up a detailed business plan, highlighting exactly how and when he intended to pay back the proposed $10,000 loan. His parents accepted the plan, and Block rented a 750-square-foot warehouse/office that he and Way moved into in December 1991.

Way did his part by selling his remaining stocks, which had declined rapidly since the 1990 stock market fall instigated by the Iraqi invasion of Kuwait. With the last of his money ($10,000), he became Block's equal partner.

"Damon amazes me because he has none of the killer instincts that I think are necessary for business. Patient, philosophical, analytical, and basically just too nice for corporate warfare."
– Steve Rocco, owner, World Industries

The two opened a bank account and hired their first vendor, Aaron Lovejoy, a fellow student from the Palomar graphic arts department who had bought some used screen-printing equipment and turned his garage into a mini production facility. They next met with Fran Richards, TransWorld Publications' marketing manager/ad sales rep/in-house marketing genius, as well as a fellow skateboarder and snowboarder. Their common interests broke the ice and they got down to business in a low-key conversation in which Richards candidly explained the ins and outs of getting exposure in magazines, the costs of advertising, and crucial marketing strategies.

Says Richards, "They told me about their idea, which was basically selling T-shirts. I'd had a lot of meetings with kids who started companies by selling T-shirts, and I can't remember most of them. That should tell you something."

Block and Way both remember that first meeting as a critical primer in marketing. They discussed larger advertising campaigns and grassroots stickers (which they'd already been plastering all over the place) and mailers, the only significant option within the Eightball budget. Back at their tiny office, Block and Way designed a flyer—a one-page catalog with order information—on a Macintosh computer owned by their friend Andy Davis. Davis, who was also starting his own clothing company called Free, had agreed to buy the computer and leave it at the Eightball headquarters if Block would help design his logos and artwork. Block and Way then rented TransWorld's shop list (the addresses and phone numbers of four hundred skateboard/snowboard shops in North America) for a nominal fee. They mailed the flyers and waited.

After the Christmas holiday, Block and Way returned to TransWorld and saw Richards for a third time. "I asked them how the mailing went," says Richards. They told him they'd gotten two hundred orders. Richards says, "My eyes bugged out of my head," and he confirmed, "There were only four hundred addresses on that list, right?" Block and Way nodded. "So you got two hundred responses?"

Block replied, "No, we got two hundred orders."

To this day, Richards says that that initial mailing was the most successful response rate he's ever encountered: "Better than Vans, Burton, Quiksilver, Airwalk, Stüssy, any of the big-name brands. None of them ever got that kind of response."

Block and Way set their sights on another Richards recommendation: the February 1992 Action Sports Retailer (ASR), a Southern California trade show where surf and skateboard retail shops buy merchandise for the following year. Bikini models, athletes, journalists, buyers, and international distributors crowd the same aisles as Hollywood stylists who are keeping an eye out for the next trend in youth culture. Since Danny Way and other Plan B team members were showing up in magazines wearing the Eightball logo, Block hoped they'd get enough orders to offset the price of the ten-by-ten-foot booth he'd reserved at the last minute.

"Ken said he was going to shave his head if they got $120,000 in orders at their first trade show. He's always been very ambitious."
– Geraldine Block, Ken Block's mother

Even though *TransWorld SKATEboarding* magazine's advertising schedule had been finalized weeks before, Richards offered to slip a last-

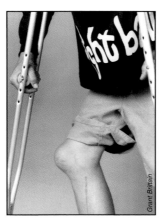

Danny Way's cantaloupe knee prevented him from bearing his own weight in the premiere Eightball ad, 1992.

The second Eightball ad: circa 1992.

minute Eightball ad into the March 1992 issue, which would hit newsstands just before the ASR show. He sweetened the deal by requiring no money up front. Block and Way quickly designed their first advertisement: a small black-and-white photo of Sal Barbier and Danny Way, with the header "Boyz in Our Hood." It was luck of the draw that the same magazine issue had the cover blurb, "Danny Way Wins NSA Pro Mini-Ramp Comp," the ultimate endorsement for their debut ad and debut trade show.

"I think Damon has an intense sense of style, personal style that's not necessarily derived by watching other people. It's sort of innate. And I think Ken has that sense of what's right in the market and isn't afraid to go for it, even if it's something unproven."
– Fran Richards, VP of sales and marketing; publisher, *TransWorld SKATEboarding*

Block and Way constructed the Eightball booth from two-by-fours and corrugated plastic sheets at Block's parents' home, then finished it off by ceremoniously spray-painting it. By show's end, they'd received $300,000 in orders. The partners were at once blown away and absolutely perplexed at the prospect of producing and delivering such a massive amount of clothing in just a few months' time. According to their calculations, they were about $200,000 short of being able to pay for materials and production. The classic line—it takes money to make money—never made more sense. The two found themselves so "desperate for money" that they considered loan sharks and other risky quick-money schemes, before settling on a high-interest loan for $40,000 against Way's one remaining piece of security: his home.

A few international distributors intent on discovering hard-core underground brands had written substantial orders. Block and Way knew, in theory, that distributors would sometimes prepay manufacturers in order to help with production costs—but Eightball was hardly worthy of this sort of treatment. Or was it? They had no choice but to try to appear "big" by bluffing Japanese and European distributors, threatening to cancel their sizable orders without partial payment up front.

That was when the partners remembered that Block's friend Eric Blehm had a father who was some sort of businessman. Blehm had mentioned his dad on more than one occasion, telling the two that if they ever needed any honest business advice, he thought his dad would talk to them and probably for free.

Free business advice intrigued them, but at this point they needed money. And fast. Perhaps Blehm's father could help them find it.

THE DEVIL'S ADVOCATE DROPS BY

Clay Blehm, then fifty-eight years old, received a telephone call in March 1992. On the other end was a friendly and polite Damon Way, who introduced himself as "a friend of Eric's" and requested a meeting concerning some business issues.

Blehm was an entrepreneurial businessman/certified public accountant who had dabbled in businesses ranging from the music industry to the pharmaceutical industry to child care to a family-owned Christmas tree farm. Creative by nature, he modified and produced such inventions as wind-up extension cords and eyeshades (without lenses).

"I think the critical thing that made Ken and Damon so successful is they knew what part of the company they wanted to run. They knew they wanted to find someone who could help them do the business. It let them each concentrate on what they really enjoy."
– Fran Richards, VP of sales and marketing; publisher, TransWorld SKATEboarding

But although Blehm was a workaholic who tirelessly strove for success, his persistence was paid off by relentless bad luck, and in December 1990, he had hit rock bottom. "I lost everything. My business, my home, my wife had passed away a few years before, and if it weren't for my daughter offering me a place to live, I could have been homeless on a park bench at fifty-eight," says Blehm. "Everything I'd ever planned and built for the future always got ripped out from under me." In this dark time, Blehm read about Ray Kroc, who, at fifty-two, had grown an empire out of a hamburger stand in San Bernardino, California, called McDonald's. Inspirational story, but Blehm was too depressed to entertain such remote possibilities. "Honestly, I thought my life was over," he says.

One of Clay Blehm's early entrepreneurial ventures: the first independent drug store with groceries in Alhambra, California, 1963.

Work had always been his salvation, and without it, just getting through the day became a struggle. Blehm created a routine, one in which he'd wake up and drive to the same breakfast shop for coffee and a doughnut, check the classifieds, and try to find a dream. Even though he'd been self-employed since 1958, he sent out a hundred résumés—and never received a single response. His life continued to spiral downward until he was breaking into a piggybank he'd been filling for his grandkids' upcoming birthdays because his bank account was empty.

Born November 3, 1932, the youngest of four brothers and two sisters, Blehm had been working since he was a child growing up on the Kingfisher County, Oklahoma, family farm that didn't have modern electricity, plumb-

ing, or heat. His parents, Ben and Amelia Blehm, were divorced when Blehm was seven and he assumed his father's duties, learning to drive a tractor and plow fields, pumping water from a well, cutting firewood, feeding the chickens, and milking the cows. This was better than his terrifying younger years during which he witnessed his alcoholic father repeatedly beating his mother.

That same year his sister Ruby headed to Los Angeles with dreams of becoming an entertainer. Ruby knew her little brother had both smarts and musical talent (at age four, he had memorized and could sing twenty-seven songs) and wanted to get him out of Oklahoma, so she struck a deal with their mother. "I needed glasses," says Blehm, "and my mom couldn't afford them. Ruby said she'd buy me glasses if she could take me to California with her and her husband."

Despite his mother's need for a "man" around the house, she agreed, and the seven-year-old went to live in California for the fall and winter—the beginning of an Oklahoma/California lifestyle in which he bounced between the two places and in and out of eight different schools. He experienced things like the Los Angeles air-raid blackouts in World War II, while learning the ins and outs of farming: obtain-

Clay Blehm's 1951 Big Four high school graduation photo, Kingfisher County, Oklahoma.

ing an Oklahoma "farming" driver's permit when he was eleven and joining harvest-threshing crews at thirteen. By age fifteen, he'd learned enough to farm his mother's land.

In order to make extra money during his junior and senior years at Big Four high school in Kingfisher County, Blehm rented, plowed, and planted 130 acres of wheat. The first year, "the green bugs ate the whole thing." His senior year, "a hailstorm hit and smashed the entire crop into the mud." He graduated from his tiny high school (twelve graduates) with none of the money he'd hoped to save. That's when Blehm's sister Violet, a bookkeeper, sat him down and asked him what he wanted to do with his life. "I know I don't want to be a farmer" was his response.

He also didn't want to leave his mother alone on the farm, but Violet, who recommended that he pursue an education in business, told him that his other siblings would take care of their mother and that he deserved his own life. He took her advice, attending a small Oklahoma business and ministry school called Phillips University before he transferred to the University of California, Los Angeles, paying his way by working odd jobs at grocery stores and the freight docks.

By his final year at UCLA, Blehm was already landing accounting-related jobs. He'd also fallen in love, and immediately after graduation he became both a husband and a father (his new wife, Jacqueline, had a son from a previous marriage). Jacqueline was an equally driven entrepreneurial pharmacist, and the couple opened one of the first independent food-and-drug stores in California: Blehm's Drugs in Alhambra and San Gabriel. The business thrived for a number of years until corporate superstores moved into the prescription business in the late sixties and forced the Blehms to close shop. Things got tough, especially because their family had expanded to two more boys and a girl, and when an accounting job opportunity opened up in San Marcos, near San Diego, they moved south.

As they battled to rebuild finances, a new foe presented itself. Jacqueline was diagnosed with terminal cancer and given a fifty-fifty chance of living six months. It was a war she fought for four years before succumbing to the disease in 1986, when Blehm was fifty-three, his stepson, John, was thirty-three, son Steve was twenty-eight, daughter Lori was twenty-two, and the youngest, Eric, was seventeen.

By this time, his accounting job wasn't panning out, and each of his children had become independent by either age or necessity, enabling Blehm to focus on a new business in the realm of child care. Eventually, he'd nurture another relationship that turned rocky about the same time he lost his new business and his home. In 1990, he found himself destitute in a remodeled garage bedroom, living with his daughter's family.

The highlight of the following year was eventually securing employment as controller for a vending machine company and winning the Chili Cook-off at the company's annual picnic. It was nice collecting a regular paycheck again, but Blehm's mind was still swimming like a college graduate's. He was neither content nor happy about what he considered a depressing job. Then he received a fateful phone call.

Clay Blehm with his mother, Amelia, on their farm in Kingfisher County, Oklahoma, 1939.

Blehm, who knew full well the struggles associated with start-up businesses, maintained a healthy skepticism when his son urged him to meet his friends Ken Block and Damon Way. "The last thing I wanted to do was join a fledgling company owned by a couple of young kids, who also happened to be friends of my son," says Blehm. "I'd had several businesses go flat, in some cases, I felt, because of bad luck. I actually thought I might be jinxed."

> **"My biggest challenge was working with two young and inexperienced associates whose perception of personal creative genius had to be reconciled with a practical and workable business application to ultimately achieve profitability."**
>
> **– Clay Blehm**

He wasn't against a meeting, however; plus he knew the company's name was Eightball, a good omen, perhaps, since one of Blehm's favorite pastimes was shooting pool, and "eightball" had been a game he'd learned as a boy from farmers in Oklahoma pool bars. So he drove from his daughter's Escondido home to the San Marcos warehouse to meet Block and Way for the first time.

The "warehouse" had a couple of rows of cardboard boxes, stacked and cut to form shelves and bins that were filled with T-shirts sporting logos and artwork that Blehm neither understood nor liked. There were skateboards, snowboards, and bikes cluttering the workspace, making it seem more a storage facility for youthful hobbies than a business. To Blehm, Block and Way were just boys. "They weren't smart-aleck, they were both nice," remembers Blehm. "They had nice demeanors and seemed relatively clean-cut, except for Damon's long hair, and, you know, their clothing was definitely geared toward skateboarding."

Block and Way explained their predicament—not enough money to produce the goods for an abundance of orders—and asked Blehm if he thought they had any chance at a loan. Blehm's response was blunt: Theirs might have been the best kind of problem, but "generally speaking, my experience is that a bank won't spit on you until you've had three to five years' positive operating experience." The fact that they were young didn't help, either. He told them, "to grow, you're going to have to make it out of your own working capital. It's going to have to come out of your own profits."

Although Blehm hadn't told the two what they wanted to hear, they were nevertheless impressed by his keen, if not cynical, business language. Blehm, likewise, was intrigued by the demand their T-shirts were getting and anxious for anything that might help pass the time, even if it paid next to nothing. After all, Fortune 500 companies weren't exactly knocking on his door. He agreed that for a couple hundred bucks he'd come in twice a month to help out.

Blehm showed up for work the following week and discovered that his "office" consisted of a folding table, a floor heater, and a Macintosh computer inside the cement-walled warehouse. He preferred IBM accounting software and eyed the Mac with suspicion. Says Damon Way, "We should have known right there we'd be clashing. We were the creative kids wanting to play with graphics, and he was the numbers guy. Those lines were drawn right off the bat."

Little did any of them know that this conflict would be a critical ingredient in their company's success.

THEN THERE WERE THREE

Blehm took on more duties in measured amounts, championing the business and accounting side of things. He encouraged the owners to concentrate on what they did best: marketing, graphics, and apparel design.

Way had taken to designing Eightball apparel, which expanded from T-shirts and sweatshirts to beanies and flannels and a pair of baggy jeans. While researching the fine art of clothing manufacturing (something he knew nothing about), he met Toni Darling, a freelance pattern maker who used the facilities at the clothing company Life's A Beach in nearby Vista.

THE DC OWNERS

Name: CLAY BLEHM

Title: Chief Financial Officer
Date of Birth: November 3, 1932
Location: Guthrie, Oklahoma

Education:
- Big Four High School (Kingfisher, Oklahoma), graduated in 1951.
- Phillips University (Enid, Oklahoma), general education and business classes from 1951 to 1953.
- University of California, Los Angeles, graduated in 1956 with a bachelor of science in business administration with a specialization in accounting.

Hobbies/Interests:
- travel
- making friends in countries visited
- singing
- listening to music
- movies
- blackjack
- shooting pool (eightball)
- dining out

Business Philosophy:
  "Work first, play later (learned from my mother), and do not cheat others. When I get old I want to play first and work later and I am learning to do that now, thanks to all the competent backing from our DC staff."

Life Philosophy:
  "It is more blessed to give than receive (also learned from my mother)."

Mike Blabac

Clay Blehm in his office at DC's headquarters, 2001.

Clay Blehm sings on the radio, age four (1936) in Oklahoma City, and at DC's Christmas party in 2001.

Eric Blehm

Sightseeing in 2001. Clay Blehm on Cheju island, South Korea.

광명사

Eric Blehm

Playing his favorite game, Eightball. Clay Blehm in The Office, a bar in Cardiff-by-the-Sea, California, 2002.

"We were so small back then, Life's A Beach didn't even mind me going in there and talking with Toni," Way says. "She taught me everything about making clothes."

"The business guys [at DC] never thought they were cool and the cool guys never thought they knew too much about the nuts and bolts of business. A lot of businesses can't figure that out; DC did early on."
– Jeff Harbaugh, business editor, TransWorld SKATEboarding/SNOWboarding Business

Block continued to master the computer and be mesmerized by all the cool things new software was enabling him to produce. He hung out with the skateboarders on the loosely designated "team," making them laugh with funny artwork that often showed up, along with his logos, on Way's apparel—sometimes in uniquely odd locations like at the waist or off-center on the back.

Both Block and Way shared sales duties along with Will Newland (the first Eightball sales/warehouse employee), but calls and orders were beginning to come in on their own. Blehm marveled when the foreign distributors Block and Way had bluffed earlier actually came around and handed "these two young kids $20,000 to $30,000 or more, and then waited months for production and delivery." The line expanded and the Eightball headquarters doubled when a twin 750-square-foot warehouse opened up next door. So much Eightball gear was being sold to the populace that Danny Way began to notice many nonskateboarders wearing the brand. By mid-1992, swap-meet pirates were copying the popular logo at an alarming rate and selling it on everything from T-shirts to beer mugs.

HABITS FOR SUCCESS

Throughout the late eighties and early nineties, the skateboard industry experienced extremely hard times, yet in the summer of 1992, Blehm did some overall calculations and found that Eightball had pulled in a very slight profit. At a time when most companies were surviving on credit, this new venture was sustaining itself with consistent orders. The secret seemed to be a combination of the continued output of fresh advertising and clothing designs by Block and Way and the team that included Danny and most of his Plan B friends: Sal Barbier, Colin McKay, and other prominent pros during this era.

Says Block, "The team was so important, especially in the beginning. If I showed them something and they liked it, we'd go forward. If they didn't, it got canned." Block and Way were especially grateful because they couldn't afford to pay

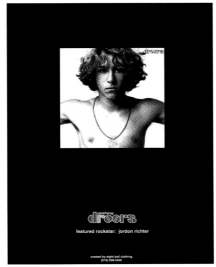

The first Droors ad: Jordan Richter's spoof of Jim Morrison appeared in the June 1992 TransWorld SKATEboarding.

the skateboarders. "It was a barter system sponsorship; free clothes for exposure," says Way.

"Danny's been a critical ingredient since the beginning, not only as a team rider but also as an incredibly perceptive decision maker in the skateboarding industry."
– Ken Block

The company's owners were surviving, barely, on meager savings accounts. Their recreation consisted of skateboarding (free) and snowboarding when they could clip lift tickets at ski area parking lots from people who were leaving for the day (shady, but also free). But despite the seriousness of their business and finances—or lack thereof—Block and Way had no problem screwing around every chance they got, especially because Blehm encouraged them to let him worry about the bills while they focused on creative angles.

ENTER DROORS

Despite the steady demand for Eightball, Block and Way heeded Danny Way's warnings that the brand might eventually become too trendy for skateboarders and/or snowboarders. Since retailer consensus was that Eightball Jeans were "much more durable than their competitors' cheaply made versions," the two partners considered them a good starting place for a new brand. (Early on, they'd made the conscious decision to maintain high quality over cheaper materials and processes, a policy that sacrificed higher short-term profits but gained a return customer base.) Block took a synonym for jeans, "drawers," and played with different spellings of it. He liked the double O for logo purposes, and the name "Droors" stuck.

"Straight up, I've never had more fun than when we were shooting some of the Droors ads. It was all over the map."
– Rob Dyrdek

As a restless and bored skateboarding community cried out for change, Block and Way headed into a fun and inventive period that was, for them, fueled by Droors. Skateboarding's vert days had fizzled out in the late eighties with the closing of skate parks, and was replaced by street skating, which brought with it the need for continual invention. Tricks born from urban influences—curbs, gaps, and rails—incorporated themselves seamlessly into the billboards, paint, and sex appeal of the Droors advertisement era that forged forward with a confident and eclectic mix of the unexpected, sarcasm, and spoof.

The first Droors advertisement, a shirtless Jordan Richter, arms outstretched like Jim Morrison

The Droors/Doors-inspired logo.

RUMORS AND TRUTHS

In 1992, Ken Block and Damon Way held small parties with close friends at the warehouse. This escalated into the false industry rumor that Eightball was being funded by all-night raves at its industrial park. The rumor that there'd been a drive-by shooting at the Eightball office was also false. Way, who owned a shotgun for protection at his home "out in the boonies," brought it into their ten-foot-by-ten-foot office late one night to clean it while Block was working on an up-and-coming ad. The gun accidentally went off in Way's hands, and the deafening round bounced off the cement floor and went through the front window and over a truck parked outside. Needless to say, it was the last time guns were allowed on the premises.

In 1992, Block and Way never even dreamed of the false rumors that would abound when shoes came into the picture—such as the popular one that has Nike owning 50 percent of DC or the one about the first all-synthetic skateboard shoe being created to attract vegan/antileather skateboarders (a falsehood that ended up being a fringe benefit of this design).

Poking fun at that relentless rumor machine named the "action sports industry," DC handed out a thousand sardonic T-shirts at the spring 2000 Action Sports Retailer trade show. The front of the shirt read: "Don't say anything but ..." On the back:

"I heard DC ...
• was sold to World Industries
• was bought by Quiksilver, Ken got all the money, fired Damon so Danny quit
• is going public
• now sells at Footlocker
• is going out of business because they lost the whole team
• sold out to everyone
• is making a new shoe co. with Jamie Thomas
• fired Danny due to inability to skate because of arm injury from jumping out of helicopter
Believe nothing you hear and only half of what you see."

Some truths: Way has been in two bands that played variations of pop punk and indy rock. One band, Tilt Wheel, did have a song in Plan B's first video. His other band, Norwalk, practiced at high volume beneath Clay Blehm's office, and Blehm retaliated by singing Sinatra-esque Christmas carols at company holiday parties. Various megacorporations in the athletic shoe business do investigate DC Shoes as a possible link to the tough-to-crack skateboarding market and some have even made offers—to no avail. And although Block won't admit it, he once appeared on the cover of a 1991 Denver newspaper wearing a one-piece neon-green Sims jumpsuit and "blasting an air" at Loveland pass. Yes, Block did have a solid gold front tooth; no, it wasn't a gift from Ice Cube.

on *The Best of the Doors* album cover (1985), debuted in the June 1992 *TransWorld SKATEboarding* issue. Follow-up ads incorporated everything from cartoon characters with bulges in their pants (header: "Remember Your First Woodie?") to comedic spoofs utilizing a willing cast of skateboard-team characters. But Block and Way still had an initial uncertainty about the brand, apparent in early Droors ads and catalogs that carried tags like "created by Eightball" or "another fine product by Eightball Clothing."

ENTER MUSIC AND SNOW

The partners didn't forsake the popular Eightball, however. Come winter 1992, they used it as a springboard to enter a snowboarding market that—unlike skateboarding—was picking up momentum as the fastest-growing winter sport. They were sick of the bright colors and ski-influenced outerwear available at the time and wanted to try something more urban, so Way asked Toni Darling to make one of the baggiest Droors patterns, the Utility Jean, out of Supplex nylon. The first "snow jean" was born.

In order to learn more about the snowboarding industry (and to ride powder) Block and Way attended the TransWorld Snowboarding Industry Conference at Wolf Creek, Colorado, that December, wearing snow jeans and Eightball hooded sweatshirts. What they didn't realize was that this casual fashion debut had a lot of snowboard outerwear manufacturers taking notes.

Outerwear manufacturers weren't the only ones interested. Eightball was experiencing a kind of cold-call marketing success—Block had been sending Eightball products to rappers like Cypress Hill that would show up in magazines and videos. Upon

Danny Way wearing the same Droors "Ravers Suck" T-shirt that was popular with musicians like the Beastie Boys in the early nineties.

returning from Wolf Creek, he learned that the Droors clothing he'd sent to the Beastie Boys had also been well received: Mike D liked the lowercase "d" logo so much that he began to religiously wear Droors baseball caps, while other Beastie Boys were seen sporting hoodies and "Ravers Suck" T-shirts. In addition, Pam Wiedmann, the merchandiser for the Beastie Boys' record label, called Block, whom she'd assumed was the Droors public relations person, to request more apparel and stickers for up-and-comers Beck, Foo Fighters, and Sonic Youth. Block had a surprising end-of-year realization: "I was like, whoa, the Beastie Boys and Cypress Hill like our stuff!"

In January 1993, a month after the snowboard industry conference, the Eightball/Droors brands had outgrown their warehouse space and the company moved into a 3,300-square-foot facility in Carlsbad, California. There was room for four offices, a reception area (though not enough money for a receptionist), cheap furniture, and a quarterpipe in the warehouse that Blehm eyed warily as an insurance issue.

NOT ENOUGH HOURS IN A DAY

The best way for Block to keep the brands fresh was to immerse himself in the world he loved: frequenting bookstores, surrounding himself with friends and athletes he both respected and liked, and asking questions and listening to the answers. He often found himself back at the magazine rack and not totally content with what was available to the snowboarders: the magazines were too "clean" and conservative for the skateboarding standards of modern snowboarding.

In addition to Eightball and Droors, whose advertisements, artwork, and logo designs remained his sole responsibility, Block's always active mind was already conceptualizing another brainchild: a magazine. But first he'd have to chew on the idea, gear up, and most importantly, make time for it, which meant hiring freelance help. He knew exactly what he wanted, but there just weren't enough hours in a day.

Former Droors team rider/current DC shoe designer Alphonzo Rawls skating in the Circus warehouse, 1993.

Dave Swift

"When the opportunity arose, Ken went after it. He gave his life to the company. He worked his ass off."
— Matt Goodman, director/cinematographer, 900 Entertainment

The business side—inputting orders, banking, accounting, and office duties—was equally needy and Blehm quit his vending machine job to work "part-time," at well over forty hours a week, for Block and Way. He became the filter for expenses, letting the owners know what was available for spending and what was needed to pay the bills. Checks crossed in the mail as Blehm perfected the fine art of trying to expand the business using zero credit. His strategy was to form solid vendor relationships with the intention of hitting them up for lines of credit down the road when orders (he hoped) would increase.

Blehm renegotiated to full-time (eighty-hour weeks) when the sun came up one morning, "and I hadn't left yet." He wasn't alone those late nights and long hours: for years, he, Block, and Way chose vinyl office couches based on their body sizes, because more often than not, said furniture served as beds while a late-night *ampm* minimart around the corner on Palomar Airport Road provided dinners and midnight snacks.

Droors and Eightball on equal ground at the second trade-show booth in 1993.

Way, who had continued his clothing-design education with Toni Darling, was also in charge of textile buying. He combed fabric outlets and manufacturing options from the Los Angeles garment district to Mexico looking for the highest quality denims, flannels, and other materials. He then transported the large rolls of fabric in the company's first car, a used 1992 Toyota minivan, to sewing facilities in San Diego. Simultaneously, he, too, was scheming a brainchild: a small but complete Eightball snowboarding outerwear line inspired by those early Supplex snow jeans. From crude sketches, scrapbooks of pictures, and clothing items that looked like nothing made for snow country, Darling sewed a set of samples for the fast-approaching March 1993 Ski Industries of America (SIA) trade show in Las Vegas, Nevada.

More than a few booths in The Ghetto (the snowboarding section at SIA) were showing baggy jean–styled snowboarding pants that looked suspiciously similar to those Block and Way had worn at the TransWorld Snowboarding Industry Conference a few months before. Speculation about who had come up with the idea first ran rampant through the show, but Way considered the attention a compliment. Besides, as various distributors sniffed out the trend, many of them ended up at the Eightball/Droors booth. The Japanese, in particular, ordered hefty amounts of the snow line, because the Eightball/Droors names had already proven their skateboarding clout among the always trendy Japanese youth. In fact, the first Droors Japan tour was quietly planned during this show, solidifying the overseas pull of a Droors team that included Danny Way, Sean Sheffey, Sal Barbier, Ronnie Bertino, Lance Conklin, Frankie Hill, Mario Rubalcaba, Wade Speyer, Josh Swindell, Pat Duffy, and Colin McKay. Rob Dyrdek, Kelly Bird, and Alphonzo Rawls would later join the Droors movement.

By the end of SIA, life was good and only getting better. Block and Way had seen their silver-dollar-sized Eightball stickers plastered on urinals, slot machines, taxis, even covering—just barely—the breasts of a friend and fan who volunteered her ample billboard space for a photo (which was never used for an ad). Large orders guaranteed the continued growth of the company, or at least that the bills would be paid for another year, Way wouldn't lose his liened home, and the partners might even be able to work salaries for themselves into the operating budget.

The partners returned to their new offices and barely had time to finish making them cozy (i.e., graffiti the walls) before things spun out of control. Almost overnight, business doubled, then tripled. The phone rang off the hook. They needed help and now had the money to increase their employee count to four, so they

b.l.u.n.t.
m a g a z i n e.

VOLUME 1

Jeff Brushie Interview
Jay Nelson Interview
Del Tha Funkie Homosapien Interview

$3.95 US

BLUNT
SKIBOARDING
M A G A Z I N E

Volume II
$3.95 US

READ THIS.

BLUNT
ENTERTAINMENT FOR SNOWBOARDERS

VOLUME 2.1 • $3.95

Dave England on *fire*
Turquin Robbins at *home*
talking nookie with Ron Jeremy

Covers, layouts, and memories—a tribute to the crazy days that surrounded the Blunt era (RIP). The magazine, inspired by Big Brother *skateboarding* magazine and created by Ken Block, catered to the subversive nature of snowboarding.

Blunt.
SNOWBOARD MAGAZINE

ISSUE 3.3

Fun With Logs!

Mike Ranquet
Nate Cole

Sweden
Mt. Hood
Superchunk
Pete Line Profile

Mortal Combat II —
Preview and Moves!

BLUNT
SNOWBOARDING BIBLE

ISSUE 3.4

• STEVIE ALTERS
• NEW ZEALAND
• SWITZERLAND

1994 VIDEO

snowboard magazine

ISSUE 4.0 $3.95

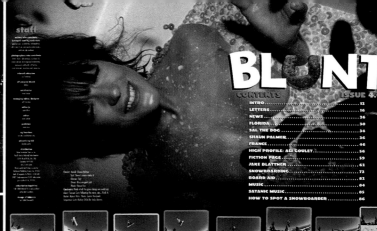

BLUNT
CONTENTS   ISSUE 4.0

BLUNTSNOWBOARDINGMAGAZINEDECEMBER1994

Blunt.
ISSUE 3.5

"I read *BLUNT* for the same reason every other snowboarder does— because it's about us."
—*Jeff Brushie*

Mike Ranquet
Interview page 22

Nate Cole Interview page 54

BLUNT MAGAZINE
GET INTO THE COLD

☐ intro
☐ small talk
☐ products
☐ video awards
☐ new zealand
☐ switzerland
☐ stevie alters
☐ hot pants
☐ junk
☐ high profile
☐ training
☐ fast page

40 OUNCES

BLUNT
CONTENTS
"88" PAGES

MALT CONT

hired Aaron Regan, a surfer/skateboarder studying graphic design, and Jeff Salgado, who'd worked at Life's A Beach and had previously expressed interest in being part of Eightball and Droors.

"Ken is like a sponge for information. Once he's educated himself, he knows exactly what he wants, whether it's the look of a new ad or a shoe design or a television commercial."
– Steve Astephen, founder of the action sports marketing agency The Familie

Regan and Salgado ran the warehouse—folding jeans, packing and shipping boxes, and the like—and took some of the stress off Block and Way, who still taped boxes when big shipments had to get out. Truth be told, they were in over their heads. They'd tricked everybody by appearing to be big, glossy, flashy, and organized to the retailers and distributors of the world, yet small and struggling to young cynical skateboarders and snowboarders. Now they were running like rats on a treadmill, trying to maintain both images while keeping up with the UPS trucks that pulsed in and out of the back doors of the warehouse. Always a glutton for punishment, Block meanwhile continued to think "magazine."

ENTER *BLUNT* SNOWBOARDING MAGAZINE

Inspired by the hard-line editorials and risky content of a skateboarding 'zine called *Big Brother* that debuted in April 1992, Block explained to Way that publishing a rebellious magazine that showcased their own products—for free—would be a fun and profitable way to shake up the snowboarding market. Way liked the idea but knew he had little time to invest in the project. Blehm, on the other hand, predicted that the magazine would become a "cash-sucking hog."

Block and Way decided to publish anyway.

It was spring of 1993, and the snowboarding industry was being inundated with upstart businesses, many of them offshoots from skateboard companies. Block and Way decided to let only smaller, nonmainstream brands like Luxury, Division 23, Evol, and Type A advertise in the magazine. They reserved the coveted back cover advertisement page for Type A, which was an offshoot of Mike Ternasky's skateboarding company, Plan B. Type A's partnership included, coincidentally, the Way brothers, Block, and Carl Hyndman, a Plan B photographer and art director. Hyndman would eventually write articles for and help lay out the pages of *Blunt* (and become DC's director of advertising and marketing), but first Block learned the computer programs and did it himself; spending hours and days and weekends on top of his chief marketing and branding duties in order to assign articles, collect photos, and design a shiny new issue in less than a month.

The issue debuted in 1993 with a cover that featured a dark, smoky profile of rapper Del the Funky Homosapien (Ice Cube's cousin) smoking a rolled cigarette. The title, *Blunt,* said it all. The issue was raw, filled with stories written by snowboarders, loosely edited, if edited at all, and considered an immediate menace to the mainstream snowboarding industry that was trying to present snowboarders as proper mountain athletes.

Blunt provided a forum for independent-minded jibber or freestyle-oriented snowboarders, who in turn appreciated the smaller brands that advertised. This "status" circulated around the snowboarding world, inspiring a Luxury Snowboards ad that ran in *TransWorld SNOWboarding* under the headline "Blunt Lets Us Advertise."

The kids loved the magazine, and conservatives (both in publishing and snowboarding) hated it but still read every issue cover to cover. Behind the how-tos on clipping lift tickets, no-holds-barred gossip columns, and interviews with porn stars, was passionate snowboarding. *Blunt* corrected other snowboarding magazines for mislabeling tricks and was the first to use "video grabs" in order to show (however blurry) complicated snowboarding trick sequences. In essence, *Blunt* represented a side of snowboarding that wasn't seen in any other snowboarding magazines.

THE DEATH OF EIGHTBALL

It was during this era of living dangerously in business, marketing, manufacturing, designing, and publishing that the company's owners learned an important lesson.

In mid-1993, Block received a certified cease-and-desist letter: the Eightball name was owned by a businessman in Seattle, Washington. Block had in fact been researching all his brand names in order to register them, but he was too late. When they met with the man in Seattle, Block and Blehm discovered that he wanted big money and a piece of the action in exchange for continued use of the Eightball name. "Clay absolutely refused," remembers Block with a laugh. "He said this guy was delusional. I think he called him a bloodsucker. He basically said, 'Look, you guys are creative, why don't you think of another name?'"

"The death of Eightball was an absolute blessing in disguise because it got them focused on Droors, which was really the beginning of the significant impact that Ken and Damon have made on the industry."
– Jim Ruonala, owner, Pacific Drive skateboard shop

Eightball was more than half of Block and Way's business and it was a scary prospect to let it go, even with Droors doing so well. But they didn't have much of a choice, so they canceled hundreds of orders, including ones for Way's refined Eightball outerwear line. The only upside was that the "bloodsucker" didn't own the trademark internationally, and Block was able to preserve the Japanese orders from SIA.

THE ERA OF MAYHEM

Block and Way found themselves juggling three different calendars—cyclical selling schedules for summer, back-to-school, and winter—for two successful lines. As if that wasn't enough, they'd agreed to use their facility as a distribution center for Type A snowboards (they had partial ownership in the company) and began to produce clothing for Danny Way's newest venture, the XYZ skateboard shop in downtown Carlsbad. Block was also spearheading *Blunt* and managing the team, which still wasn't really being paid, at least not in a traditional sense. The members received free gear and photo incentives: if a photo appeared in a magazine or video with the skateboarder wearing (or sporting on his board) a distinguishable Eightball or Droors logo, he'd get paid.

But Droors had become the main focus of the company and was gradually getting more attention from kids and the industry, thanks in large part to its ads. Skateboard shop demand grew, as did the same problem of not being able to keep up. In fact, Blehm was deleting about 70 percent of each order he received for Droors because there wasn't enough product in the warehouse. "The brand was hot," he says. "I'd joke with Ken and Damon, 'You guys could put a Droors logo on a dog turd and we'd sell out.'"

Until 1993, Block and Way were the bosses, and Blehm was the accountant sitting in the shadows crunching numbers who didn't know anything about skateboarding or snowboarding. But, Blehm says, "I had built businesses in the past, and I knew all too well the pitfalls. I wasn't going to let that happen this time." By late 1993, he'd gotten involved with production, helping Way to find more reliable vendors and negotiating contracts that would hold them to delivery dates, which weren't being met. Orders began to be filled more quickly and on time, but it was still feast or famine while awaiting the payments that would fund the next round of production. The business would make money one month and lose it all in two.

That attitude was exactly why Block and Way had hired Blehm in the first place, so they agreed wholeheartedly when he suggested organizing all the brands under one corporate entity. Blehm incorporated the company on October 3, 1993, and Way named it Circus Distribution, Inc., a sort of metaphor for what their lives and business had become. Its unofficial logo, a hobolike clown holding a water pistol, was designed by new warehouse employee and talented artist David "Persue" Ross.

Despite the so-called corporation status, day-to-day duties were about as corporate as a well-organized garage sale. And not many corporations have a president who picks up lunch for the warehouse guys and meets after work hours (or during) for one-on-one basketball, using a portable hoop in the parking lot. Ross and Block were actually in the middle of one such heated game when the latter had a front tooth knocked out.

Playing off the gold chains and jewels of hip-hop and rap groups, Block thought it would be funny to get a gold tooth, a spur-of-the-moment decision in the dentist's office that earned him a sort of notoriety:

The Circus Distribution clown, artwork by David "Persue" Ross.

his mug shot ended up in various industry magazines and skateboard and snowboard gossip columns. Some speculated that his action was based on cockiness about his company's growing success. Only the friends who knew how broke Block really was appreciated

the irony. As Block says, "There were times I had to think pretty hard at the ATM machine. Taking out a twenty was a big deal."

"Ken Block had the gold tooth before he was even rich. Now he's rich and the gold tooth's gone. What's up with that?"
– Aaron Meza, editor, *Skateboarder* magazine

So it was a significant loss when the company minivan, which had already taken a beating, was "lost" somewhere in Mexico by Droors team member Josh Swindell. The events leading up to the vehicle's disappearance remain a mystery.

BREAKING THE SEVEN-FIGURE BARRIER

But things were still looking up. By Christmas, Block and Way had paid themselves and Blehm $17,000 each in yearly wages plus an additional $1,000 bonus. Then they offered Blehm the ultimate payment: one-third ownership in the company. Grateful yet wary, Blehm took a rain check. He knew that an owner who was also an accountant would take the full brunt of any future financial downfalls.

"Straight up, we would be out of business if it weren't for Clay. Damon and I were just kids in the right place at the right time having fun, but I personally was in a fantasy world with some of the things I wanted to do. He was there to tell me the right way and the wrong way. Clay made us a profitable company."
– Ken Block

Block moved out of his parents' house and into a rental apartment with Danny Way in Carlsbad, and Blehm also moved, out of his daughter's garage and into an apartment. The three further celebrated the productive year by taking a few days off. Block and Way went snowboarding and actually bought lift tickets, though they still couch-surfed instead of paying for hotel rooms. Likewise, Blehm drove one of his sons to Las Vegas on a spur-of-the-moment trip, the first time he'd been able to afford such a luxury in years. They sat at two-dollar-limit blackjack tables, ate dinner at an all-you-can-eat-for-$4.99 buffet, and slept in his car in the casino parking lot.

Gross sales for 1993 had just topped one and a half million dollars.

SHOES ENTER THE BIG TOP

Blehm was quick to clarify: "Gross sales aren't profits." Nearly all the income was funding the company's operating and production costs and being sunk into new ways to expand the business—like shoes.

Block, who had always been passionate about shoes, began to consider making them. His confidants, the Ways, agreed that skateboarding shoe designs were stagnant and that there was plenty of room for improvement. In addition to Vans and Airwalk, the only significant shoe manufacturer in the industry was Pierre Andre Senizergues, a world champion skateboarder from France, who had started competing against the two skateboarding powerhouses with his Etnies brand a few years before.

The most significant event in 1993 had been a meeting in which Blehm gave the green light, financially, for Block and Way to make some sample shoes to test the waters. Block's potential names included Droors Shoes, DC Shoes (for Droors Clothing Shoes), and Grey. Both the Droors and DC names were researched for trademarking, and Block commissioned Vans to make a small run of Droors shoes.

JUGGLING BRANDS

The shoes were delivered in the beginning of 1994. Simply Vans with Droors logos on them, they were expensive and their quality was poor: glue dripping across seams that weren't sewn properly and other flaws that were obvious even to the rookie eyes of Block, Way, and Blehm. The three were so unimpressed, they decided to look elsewhere for manufacturing, and the shoes, although displayed in the catalog and a few random advertisements, never went into mass production.

The first (and last) Droors casual shoe, which never went into mass production, 1994.

Meanwhile, Way, who had invested a great deal of time and effort designing the Japanese Eightball outerwear line (which included pants, shell and insulated jackets, and beanies) wanted to sell his popular line in America under another name. Potential names like Devious and Petrol lost out to Dub, which Block named after a genre of music that came about in the late sixties/early seventies. This hybrid of reggae mixing pioneered by musicians like King Tubby was later incorporated into everything from punk rock to hip-hop.

The word was symmetrically pleasing—simple, clean, and original. The new brand appeared on North American slopes in winter 1994/95, eventually phasing out Eightball outerwear in Japan. It also targeted urban lifestyle trends.

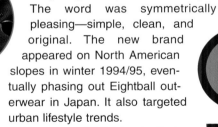

A highlight of Dub outerwear was its technical weatherproofing.

But Block and Way were still itching to find a shoe manufacturer. Block contacted Senizergues of Etnies and asked if he'd be interested in producing a line of shoes named DC. Senizergues liked both the name and idea, and despite his own busy production schedule, he accepted the challenge. Confidentially, he was told that the first shoe would be a Danny Way signature model, the direct result of Danny's willingness to quit—along with Colin McKay—his shoe sponsor at the time, Airwalk.

DC TAKES SHAPE

In the spring of 1994, *Blunt* was going into its second year, Dub's identity was being forged, Droors was going strong, but there were two significant elements missing from the picture: a shoe design and a shoe designer. Block stepped up to the plate. For a few weeks, he collaborated with Danny Way, designing three-dimensional shoe outlines on his computer and hand-coloring the printouts with colored pens and pencils. They finally agreed upon a look and forwarded the printouts to Senizergues.

The original DC logo designed by David "Persue" Ross and Ken Block in 1994.

"Rather than starting a company and hiring someone to design the first shoes, Ken is sitting there with a vision and figuring out what works and what doesn't. That's as hands-on as you can be with the company."

– Colin McKay

As planned months in advance, the second DC model to be released would be Colin McKay's first signature shoe. McKay remembers beginning the design process in a Pacific Beach restaurant. The fine-tuning continued in the office, with Block manning the computer. "To this day, every shoe that DC ever made has his input," says McKay.

Under Block's art direction, David "Persue" Ross had been working out different logo designs for DC. He'd come up with a rounded configuration of interlocking letters, which would later be dropped because of a likeness to the Champion logo—the first in a string of controversial logos.

DUB PICKS UP SPEED

The middle of 1994 arrived and Block and Way had yet to receive a sample shoe from Senizergues. This waiting game did provide extra time for Dub branding and putting together a team of unpaid snowboarders that would allow Dub to truly compete with other outerwear lines. As with skateboarders, enough top snowboarders liked the clothing and wanted to be affiliated with the growing company, and a team with a freestyle focus that represented Dub's urban feel was born: Daniel Peterka, Russell Winfield, Ian Ruhter, Nathan Yant, and Gabe Crane. Peterka's debut advertisement was scheduled to appear in the October 1994 *TransWorld SNOWboarding*.

DUB™ BRAND WEATHERGEAR

The Dub logo as it was released to the public in 1994.

Dub's first ad (October 1994 TransWorld SNOWboarding) featured Daniel Peterka.

SIDEBAR 003
THE INFAMOUS DROORS ADS

"People at TransWorld looked forward to seeing the Droors ads," says Fran Richards, publisher of *TransWorld SKATEboarding*. "They were funny. They even did a Matt Hensley ad and he wasn't sponsored by them."

Droors team member Alphonzo Rawls (who would later join DC as a shoe designer) spoofed the fashion industry's models with his signature boxer shorts ads and the United Colors of Droors via a Got Milk-esque billboard. Spoofs on Calvin Klein had Danny Way with a female model whose tank top was more or less revealing depending on a particular magazine's advertising guidelines. *TransWorld* equaled less skin, *Big Brother* equaled more. Lance Conklin lay in some Playland-style balls with an ominous and very politically incorrect gun pointing outward. Rawls later spoofed this ad by peering out of a bathtub full of marshmallows, pointing a banana instead of a gun, a photo that was never used.

The "Quitter" ad saw Rob Dyrdek taped to a brick wall, a cigarette in one hand, lighter in the other. (Dyrdek has since officially quit the filthy habit.) The Ronnie "Bush Magnet" Bertino "safe sex" ads in *Big Brother* featured an inflatable starlet in various, ummm, poses. Danny Way's "underaged drinker" donned the ever-popular Ravers Suck T-shirt and attracted lots of parents, while Sean Sheffey's AmeriKKKa's Most Wanted was a blatant rip-off of the Ice Cube album of the same name, which was released in May 1990.

Other popular ads, though not as controversial, included Dave Swift's *(TransWorld)* and Jeff Tremaine's *(Jackass)* all-time favorite: Dyrdek having blue paint dumped over his head.

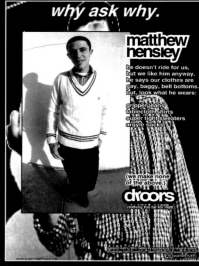

Remember your first woodie? Fall 1992.

Matt Hensley, winter 1993.

Rob Dyrdek, winter 1996.

Bill Weiss, fall 1994.

Sean Sheffey, summer 1992.

Lance Conklin, summer 1994.

Droors brand ad, summer 1997.

Alphonzo Rawls, fall 1995.

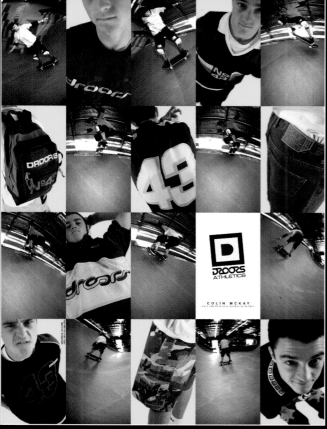

Colin McKay, summer 1997.

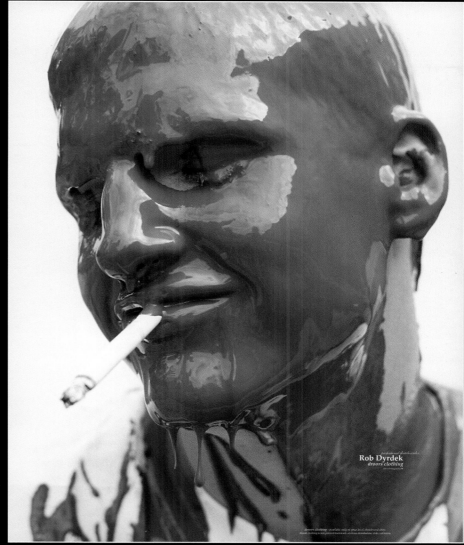

Rob Dyrdek, summer 1994.

Josh Kalis, summer 1998.

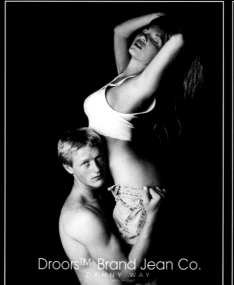

The Danny Way Calvin Klein spoof ad campaign, published in winter 1996. A more conservative version (on the left) was shot for TransWorld SKATEboarding; a more revealing one for Big Brother.

TAKING DC TO THE PUBLIC

It had taken more than half a year for Senizergues to provide three samples for Danny Way's signature shoe, but finally DC's first shoe was ready to be unveiled to the public via an advertisement in the February 1995 issue of *TransWorld SKATEboarding*. The advertisement didn't adhere to the common skateboard ad equation: an action shot under a big logo. A serious neck injury sustained in late 1994 prevented Danny Way from pulling a T-shirt over his head, much less go skateboarding, so for the photo shoot, he instead stood (a bit stiffly) alongside posters of his shoe.

"DC's print ads have brought a highly stylized fashion look to the skate industry. The successful use of team riders as icons to promote the product is proof that ads can be slick and core at the same time."

– Grant Brittain, photo editor, *TransWorld SKATEboarding*

Virtually every skateboard shop contacted wanted to try the shoes, sight unseen. In preparation for the upcoming truckloads of shoe boxes, Circus Distribution was moved to a 16,000-square-foot warehouse in October 1994, about the same time the aforementioned advertisement was designed. Although Senizergues had taken a long time to deliver the samples, his production proved to be faster. Nevertheless, the waiting was painful. Block, Blehm, and the Way brothers couldn't wait to hear the public's response.

EXPANSIONS AND OMENS

The new location, adjacent to the Carlsbad Raceway, seemed perfect. It was also next door to where skateboarding icon Mike McGill's public skate park had been years before, the first of two good omens.

Upon visiting her son's new office, Mary O'Dea was taken aback: it was built on the site of a farmhouse where she had lived with the Way brothers' father at the beginning of their relationship. In fact, this spot was where Damon Way had been conceived twenty-four years earlier. "Talk about coming full circle," she says. "I'm into that sort of thing, signs and omens, and I just knew this was a good thing."

The spacious building allowed for accounting, marketing, and design offices overlooking a hangarlike warehouse, so big it was like a ghost town at first. But then more warehouse employees (mostly skateboarders) were hired, Toni Darling came on full-time as a pattern maker, and to streamline production issues and take some of the workload off Way's shoulders, Jeff McCall—a San Diego businessman who owned a sewing and screen-printing manufacturing business—was brought on as consultant. The warehouse was filled with Droors and Dub inventory, and Circus Distribution seemed poised for something big. Fingers were crossed.

Not skating due to a neck injury—Danny Way in his first DC Shoes advertisement, which ran in the February 1995 TransWorld SKATEboarding.

DC's first mass-produced shoe, the Danny Way model in 1994.

DC's second mass-produced shoe, the Colin McKay model in 1994.

DC from the air, across from the field that once held the famous McGill's Skateboard Park. The original building is at the far right. The two buildings on the left were added as DC expanded.

BIG BROTHER BUYS BLUNT

Grant Brittain

Steve Rocco
admonishes the law.

Throughout its two seasons of production, *Blunt* magazine provided Block with an education he'd never expected. *"Blunt* gave me the opportunity to see things through so many different eyes," he says. It showed him the kind of things he had to do with his own team members in order to get them into magazines. He learned about design, printing, press releases, and, probably most importantly, how to appeal to his audience by taking chances.

But although it was satisfying in a creative sense, *Blunt* had taken a toll on finances and time, and Block was ready to part with it. In 1995, Steve Rocco, ex-pro skateboarder and one of the founding fathers and the financial backer of *Big Brother,* bought the magazine, largely because of its momentum in the snowboarding community. His Dickhouse Publishing now had two titles.

Dickhouse Publishing eventually sold *Blunt* and *Big Brother* to Larry Flynt Publications in 1997—yes, that Larry Flynt, the controversial publisher of *Hustler* and other constitutionally protected publications. *Blunt* lasted another year and was laid to rest in 1998 due to a number of reasons that included an identity crisis of sorts: distributors and advertisers wanted mainstream readers, while mainstream readers' parents wanted a more subdued, politically correct publication. *Big Brother,* which Flynt originally purchased as an afterthought, continues to prosper in that gray purgatory between skateboarding and "adult entertainment"—or at least makes enough money to keep Larry Flynt's accountants happy.

THE SHOE PUZZLE TAKES SHAPE

Giant shipping containers of Danny Way's shoes filled the warehouse, just long enough to be processed and shipped back out. Colin McKay's model was delivered shortly thereafter, coinciding with a request from Senizergues for a "licensing agreement" if he was to continue producing shoes for DC—a sound business move, considering the DC brand was competing with his own line.

As with all business decisions, Block and Way discussed the option with Blehm, who flatly refused the request. The end of 1994 was fast approaching, and Blehm estimated that sales would increase 103 percent from the previous year, thanks in large part to the massive number of shoe orders in the last quarter. If the shoe production dilemma could be solved, he foresaw the trend continuing in the next year.

"When I first saw DC, I had my own shoe company called Duffs. We were pretty good, but it reminded me of when I saw Rodney Mullen at Oasis. You could buckle down, work twice as hard, and still get an ass-whooping. Or you could graciously step aside and make way for the new champ. I immediately sold Duffs."

– Steve Rocco, owner, World Industries

One day around this same time, Way was walking in Pacific Beach, checking out random shops in the neighborhood where Alexander's, his first and only sponsor, had been located. He noticed a small shoe shop and struck up a conversation with its owner, Jai Baek. Way learned that Baek was a Korean-born certified orthopedic technician who had spent the majority of his life in the shoe business and had various shoe-manufacturing contacts in Asia. Way promptly invited Baek to a meeting with Block and Blehm.

In the meeting, Baek proved his expertise in shoe construction. He confidently dissected Danny Way's model and suggested ways to improve upon it, a mind-set that fit in perfectly with Block and Way's intention to change not only the look of skateboarding shoes but also the durability and

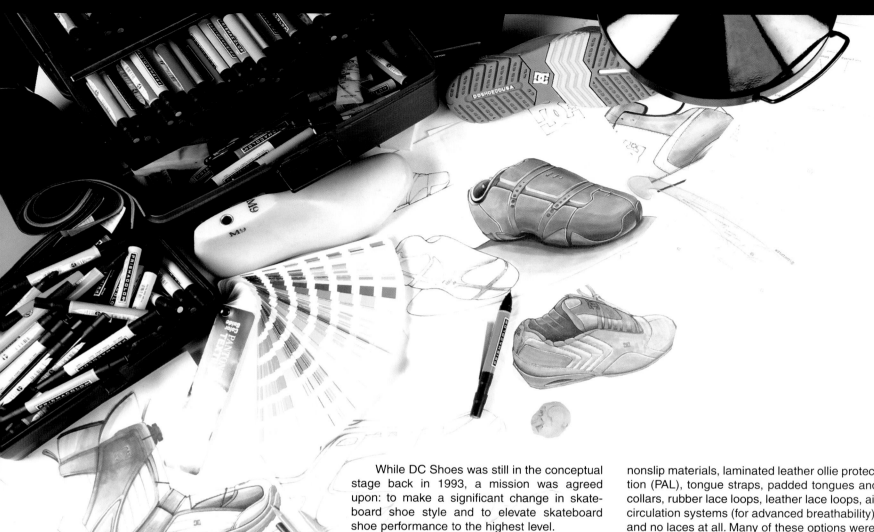

While DC Shoes was still in the conceptual stage back in 1993, a mission was agreed upon: to make a significant change in skateboard shoe style and to elevate skateboard shoe performance to the highest level.

Rob Dyrdek joined the DC team in mid-1995. An amazing street skater and one of Droors' most popular personalities, he trained relentlessly, thus demanding a durable shoe. Although it seems simple in retrospect, one of the most common problems street skaters experienced was laces that wore apart from griptape abrasion during ollies and kickflips. The answer Ken Block and Dyrdek came up with was incorporating nylon lace loops to protect the lace in key contact areas, the first technical feature that was adapted specifically for skateboarding. That feature, and a first-ever athletic shoe appeal, made the shoe, the Dyrdek, an immediate standout.

This marked the beginning of a long list of DC-pioneered skateboarding shoe advances that continued into the millennium: heel cushioning (gel, air, and other padding materials), nonslip materials, laminated leather ollie protection (PAL), tongue straps, padded tongues and collars, rubber lace loops, leather lace loops, air circulation systems (for advanced breathability), and no laces at all. Many of these options were, and continue to be, incorporated into forward-thinking designs that were at first scoffed at. However, nearly all of DC's breakthroughs—both aesthetic and technical—have eventually been copied by competitors.

"DC has impacted skateboarding shoe design more than any other company," says Steve Douglas, president of Giant Skateboard Distribution. "The entire DC operation has built upon this and strives for perfection at every level, but at the same time they're not afraid to experiment with new ideas. That's where they get their strength."

DC continues to stay true to its original mission—pushing style and performance to a level one step ahead of the competition, from the drawing board, to the computer, to the factory, to the concrete and Masonite of skateboarding's proving grounds.

LACE PROTECTION

DC was the first skateboarding shoe company to do battle with lace burnout. Since lace breakage is a common problem for street skaters (practicing repetitive kickflip and/or ollie tricks) and vert skaters (knee-sliding while learning tricks) alike, Ken Block and street skater Rob Dyrdek incorporated protective lace loops into DC's third pro model, the Dyrdek1, in 1995. This feature is now an industry-wide standard in skateboarding shoes.

HIDDEN NYLON LACE LOOP: For maximum protection against abrasion.

DUAL LACE LOOP: Metal eyelets along with hidden lace loops for outer layer protection.

TPR LACE LOOP: Durable Thermoplastic Rubber protects laces and reduces wear and tear.

PAL AB

Because of constant contact with Masonite, concrete, metal, and other hard surfaces, skateboarding shoe uppers must be bomber. In traditional shoes, rubber uppers were strong but too stiff, while leather was flexible and durable, but not indestructible. The perfect anti-abrasion material turned out to be the DC-named PAL AB—a polyurethane-coated leather. This flexible yet durable science was first used in the 1998 Lynx and has since been added to many DC models in varying textures.

AEROTECH VENTILATION SYSTEM

Skateboarding shoes get hot. To cool things down, DC introduced a state-of-the-art airflow system named AVS (Aerotech Ventilation System) in the 2002 Aerotech pro model. Relentlessly tested and abused by Danny Way, the shoe has AVS embedded in a lightweight polyurethane midsole that channels air through a clear thermoplastic urethane shank, helping to lower temperatures without compromising durability or support.

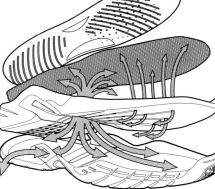

DYNAMIC GRIP TECHNOLOGY

DC's designers took on gravity itself, or at least the critical issue of keeping a skateboard stuck to a skateboarder's shoes, with the revolutionary formula, Dynamic Grip Technology (DGT). This combination of materials and construction methods incorporates three different durometers of rubber, used in different parts of a shoe's sole. Shoes are grippy where needed but durable where grip isn't an issue—the perfect skateboarding-specific design.

DURABILITY: The hardest rubber is located in the DURABILITY section to make it more wear-resistant.

CONTROL: The CONTROL section is made of the softest durometer rubber. It is super grippy and helps provide superior feel and control for ollies and flip tricks.

TRACTION: The medium-durometer rubber makes up the TRACTION section for the perfect combination of traction and durability. This area wears out slower, yet remains grippy.

CUSHIONING

The seemingly obvious benefits of sole cushioning had long been overlooked in the skateboard industry when DC introduced the first advanced heel padding—a gel pocket made from rubber and polyurethane—in the 1996 Clocker. DC improved upon the Clocker's design by incorporating a heel airbag via the Legacy in 1998. The Impact Response System, an impact-absorbing heel cushion that disperses pressure yet still retains its original shape, will debut in Danny Way's 2003 model, the Omen.

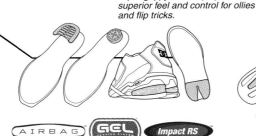

LIGHTWEIGHT INNOVATIONS

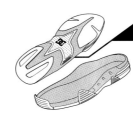

Lighter is always better as long as durability isn't sacrificed. Injected ethyl-vinyl acetate (EVA) is an extremely light molded foam that provides supreme cushioning and overall weight reduction, but is also highly wear- and tear-resistant, and has a high-memory system that allows stretchability while retaining its original shape. DC also utilizes Performalite, which is a slightly different composition of polyurethane that still rivals featherweight EVA.

Following Ken Block and David "Persue" Ross's original DC logo came three logos that are still in use today:

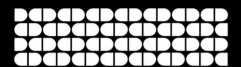

The Pill Pattern: Born from the culmination of designs by various artists working to come up with a pattern for the shoe sole that represented the DC name and was highly functional as traction. It emulates an oval pill shape but is broken in the center by the capital letters D and C, a configuration that satisfies both elements.

The Star Logo: In-house artist Dave Kinsey utilized more symmetrical "squared" interlocking letters, and Block added a five-pointed star. The logo's star was too similar to the Converse star, so its points grew to seven.

DCSHOECOUSA

DCSHOECOUSA: Created by Block, who was inspired by ESPN's *Sports Center* show that uses the Helvetica font in headlines. The font is still used today in DC advertisements, press releases, the Web site, and even this book. Since the days of Eightball, "USA" has been and continues to be incorporated into designs for one simple reason: "American pride," says Block.

---

athletic elements of their design. Block had been spending hours in shoe stores and taking a new interest in the battered shoes of his skateboarding team, especially in the areas that seemed to wear out first. "Skateboarders are athletes," Block explained to Baek, "but there are no athletic skateboarding shoes."

MANUFACTURING THE MODERN SKATEBOARDING SHOE

A major key to the success of DC shoes would be the ability to quickly produce samples using high-quality materials. When Jai Baek was hired in December 1994 as a shoe production consultant, the doors to creative freedom in shoe design were flung open. On his first overseas journey as a DC employee, Baek held a meeting in Pusan, South Korea, with Hwang Young Sun, an entrepreneurial business consultant who specialized in shoe manufacturing. The meeting was straightforward. Baek showed Hwang one of the Danny Way models made by Etnies and asked, "Can you make this shoe?"

DC Shoes' sole iron in action. Pusan, South Korea, 2001.

Hwang answered by taking Baek to a couple of factories, one of which was owned by businessman Lim Bong Gyu, whose Samil Tong Sang Company specialized in small runs of very high quality shoes. Lim studied the DC shoe and said that he couldn't make it. Puzzled, Baek urged elaboration. "I cannot make this exact shoe," said Lim, "but I can make a better shoe." Baek ran down the list of requirements, the most important being "how fast can you make them?" Lim answered, "very quickly," exactly what Baek wanted to hear, because orders for Danny Way's increasingly popular shoe were backlogged.

During the winter of 1994/95, Lim's factory turned out 20,000 pairs of shoes in record time. Hwang and Lim's network also exhibited an amazing ability to provide quick "top secret" samples on demand, within days.

BUSINESS BREAKTHROUGHS

In early 1995, Blehm felt the company was ready to gamble a little via a $100,000 line of credit that he easily secured, because the company had sustained itself for four years on profits and advances alone. This, plus extended lines of credit from vendors, helped take some of the strain off cash-flow issues but made Blehm all the more cautious in keeping the books. If a bank reconciliation was off by even a penny, he wouldn't hesitate to spend an entire weekend finding and correcting the mistake.

After four years of many seven-day workweeks and the weight of accounting proficiency solely on his shoulders, Blehm sought an employee for his department. His first choice didn't work out, so he recruited his daughter, Lori, who was a successful bank manager. Blehm had always been leery of sharing the company's financial issues with anyone, but with a close and professional family member on board, he felt comfortable delegating confidential duties that included payroll, accounts receivable, and collections.

Lori became the company's thirty-seventh employee, more than half of whom worked in the frenzied warehouse trying to keep up with orders that were still delivered and filled on paper, an archaic system by most standards. Blehm fantasized about an all-encompassing computer system that would link each department to a central accounting core and keep track of inventory, pending orders, deliveries, marketing and manufacturing expenses, payroll, credit—the possibilities were endless.

A DIFFERENCE OF OPINION

By the end of 1995, Blehm had become more impressed with the shoe operation and disillusioned with the Droors and Dub lines, which were labor-intensive and less profitable. Block and Way, who had poured their hearts and souls into both the clothing and its image, thought differently, reasoning that the additional costs and lower profits were balanced out by the credibility the brands enjoyed in the fickle skateboard and snowboard communities.

Though the three had experienced many differences of opinion, this was the first one they couldn't reach an agreement on, a futile argument with passion on one side and paper on the other. It was an especially difficult sell for Blehm because overall the company was profitable. The three lines (DC, Dub, Droors) combined were poised to gross almost $7 million that year, a 123 percent increase from the year before, but Blehm's calculations showed that the shoe profits were partly funding the marketing and production costs for Droors and Dub, despite their popularity. The industry seemed healthy, however, so Blehm didn't push the point.

The skateboarding industry was actually gaining momentum, and more shoe companies were sprouting up, theoretically threatening the market share in that category of their business. With the increasing youth demographics and interest in action sports, Blehm sensed there were sleeping giants out there gearing up to cash in on the expanding industry. He also knew that Circus Distribution, with its current operating and production costs, was in no position to compete. But Block and Way were the owners and although they respected Blehm's judgment, they were not yet willing to downsize Droors or Dub—even though the DC skateboard team, which had gained third and fourth team riders, Rob Dyrdek and Rudy Johnson, was standing on its own.

The 1995 ad that introduced DC's powerhouse team: Danny Way, Colin McKay, Rob Dyrdek, Rudy Johnson.

In 1995, the need for shoe production capacity had continued to increase, and Baek's Korean business consultant, Hwang Young Sun, rose to the occasion. Rather than lose business to another factory, he decided to build his own. DC orders alone would keep both Hwang's new factory and Lim Bong Gyu's factory busy year-round. An exclusive manufacturing deal that guaranteed quality control was struck, and containers of DC shoes continued to be shipped from South Korea's largest port city to distributors around the globe: in virtually every European nation, most Asian countries, throughout South America, and even parts of Africa.

"It was like those maps in the back of an airline magazine. There are all those little lines shooting out, with destinations all over the world, and you're like, 'I started that?'"

– Ken Block

Despite their difference of opinion regarding the brands they were producing, Block, Way, and Blehm were proud of what they had built up to this point. Every time they saw someone wearing one of their logos, be it DC, Droors, or Dub, it put a smile on their faces. Still, Blehm was nervous about his lack of authority and felt it was time he officially accepted Block and Way's offer from two years before. He became one-third owner of the company on New Year's Eve, 1995.

FIVE YEARS AND COUNTING

There had been those who felt DC's success was a result of Danny Way's popularity alone, and that the brand would eventually be squashed by bigger players with larger lines, marketing budgets, and business infrastructures. By 1996, however, any industry speculations that DC was destined for

SIDEBAR 007
WHY 07 AND 43?

DC often uses numbers on its jersey, T-shirt, hat, and sweatshirt designs. The athletic-styled numbers were born from a sarcastic emulation of team sports. But why always 07 or 7 or 43?

Ken Block originally chose the number 43 for Droors because he'd heard somewhere (he figures at a party) that it was the most common number in the world. Soon enough he realized that the idea of there being a most commonly used number sounded ludicrous, but nevertheless, something about 43 piqued his interest. He began to sift through random letters, rearranging and respelling the words "four" and "three" and "forty-three," a practice that had led him to logos in the past. And that's how he discovered that the fourth and third letters in the alphabet were D and C. How convenient.

DC is always associated with the number 07.

Number 43 was a Droors mainstay.

With this revelation came another: add four and three together and you get seven, which is widely considered a lucky number and became the standard number associated with DC. Both 43 and 7 looked good in design samples, although the single 7 didn't always work. Easy fix. Add a zero in front. No harm, no foul.

failure were extinguished. To the contrary, the two-and-a-half-year-old brand was expanding in leaps and bounds, taking over adjacent warehouse space and doubling its team size to eight gifted skateboarders, including Keith Hufnagel from New York, Carl Shipman from England, Scott Johnston from Washington, D.C., and Caine Gayle from Florida. With McKay's Canadian roots, Rudy Johnson's and Danny Way's SoCal influences, and Dyrdek's Dayton, Ohio–bred street-skating prowess, the company was well-represented by a range of skateboarding talents with international appeal.

"DC's impact as a truly global brand within the skate industry is clear. Both mainstream and skate, DC leads skate shoe fashion within Europe, no question."
– Marc Ball, international distributor, New Deal Skates

With the new riders came a need for a dramatic advertising campaign, which Block directed. He settled on a style that kicked off with Carl Shipman's huge frontside transfer at an undisclosed indoor skate park. Dramatic logo usage and a unique font combined with a long-lens black-and-white photographic image was voted *Thrasher* magazine's "ad style of the year."

The advertisement also marked the simultaneous release of DC's first two non–pro model shoes, the Clocker and the Boxer. The Clocker was a fairly simple-looking skateboard shoe with a twist—a visible arch, big logos, and an exaggerated padded tongue that looked fat and bulky. The Boxer went one step further. It had all the innovative details of the Clocker plus big rubber lace loops and a thicker sole, making it so radically different that Block feared the reaction when he showed the shoe at the Action Sports Retailer trade show. "I was seriously scared," he says. "I thought people might laugh at it as a skateboarding shoe." The general reaction was doubtful at first, because after all, skateboard shoes had always used flat soles, and what was up with those huge tongues? But as retailers and skateboarders examined and skated in the shoes, word of mouth spread: DC was making serious breakthroughs in design.

Meanwhile, Droors and Dub continued to require equal attention, which in turn required the need for delegating duties, and Block and

The DC advertising campaign that won Thrasher's *1996 "ad style of the year" kicked off with this Carl Shipman frontside transfer in England.*

Way simply couldn't keep up. Instead of continuing to design the bulk of all logos, ads, shoes, and T-shirt and sweatshirt prints, Block began to loosen the reins on his do-it-yourself mentality. It was more difficult for him to trust others with his ideas than it was for Way, who was happy to accept assistance with locating fabrics and materials.

Along with Blehm, they carefully surrounded themselves with a team of employees who, while invisible to the public, proved themselves to be just as important as the athletes. Managing these employees, however, became one of the most difficult aspects of their jobs. "The worst thing about this job is when I've had to let friends go because they didn't work out," says Block. "If there's one duty I could erase, it would be the need to fire people. I hate it."

A MILLION-DOLLAR LOAN

With multiplying orders and the increased personnel required to run an expanding company came the frightening reality that massive credit would be required. Massive credit meant massive debt, and even though Blehm was a gambler by nature, he hated putting what was now a third of his company in the hands of a fickle customer. He had no choice but to seek out a million-dollar line of revolving credit.

"We were really excited about getting our first million in credit, but Clay kept it in perspective by warning us that it didn't mean we had all this money to spend. Instead we had all this money we had to pay back."
– Damon Way

Despite its rapid success and flashy appearance, Circus Distribution continued to operate as a frugal business. The owners agreed to award employees and athletes with bonuses when profits allowed, but sunk the majority back into the company. Most importantly, they paid their bills and wouldn't allow debt to grow beyond manageable levels.

Operating within the realm of budget constraints, Block kept the team as happy as possible while continuing to send out cold-call boxes of free clothing and shoes to various celebrities, mostly in the music industry. He was still spearheading the marketing duties when he sent such a box to the Beastie Boys' merchandiser Pam (Wiedmann) Zamoscianyk, whose husband was a set lighting technician on *Bulletproof,* one of Adam Sandler's early film projects. She introduced Block and Way to Adam Sandler, who became a staunch supporter of Droors and DC during his upward spiral to comedic success. Zamoscianyk also discovered via a business card that Block was the company's president, not the head of public relations, and she immediately informed him that he needed a publicist. Within weeks, Pam "Zam" became Circus Distribution's first full-time media relations and marketing employee—she would become director of media and advertising for DC.

Year's end, 1996: Block and Way examined reports that Blehm had checked, double-checked, and triple-checked before divulging the good news to his associates. The company had increased sales 199 percent since the previous year. In just over two years, Circus Distribution had grown from a tiny three-brand corporation with five employees, two pro riders, and two shoe models into a fifty-person operation with ten team riders and a complete line of six non-pro and four pro-designed shoes.

Skateboarding as a sport had also continued to grow, and alternative "action" sports began to garner attention in the way team sports had once dominated the consumer marketplace. The anticipated influx of shoe companies occurred, and the consensus was that DC inspired many of them—not only in shoe design, but also in advertising styles and apparel ideas such as numbered jerseys and camouflage.

THE UPS AND DOWNS OF BUSINESS AND LIFE

Big Brother *dedicated an issue (October 1997) to DC's European Super Tour.*

In 1997, the DC skateboard team, which had expanded to include Mike Carroll and Rick Howard, invaded the Southern Hemisphere via an Australian promotional minitour. Later that year, the team performed for thousands of cheering fans in venues across the European continent. In the course of two weeks, this DC Super Tour traveled to Stockholm, Amsterdam, and Frankfurt, ending at a highly publicized party in London hosted by DJ Goldie, a pioneer of the drum 'n' bass scene and a hard-core DC fanatic. *Big Brother* devoted its entire October 1997 issue to the tour's coverage, while the finer "moving pictures and partying moments" could be viewed via the September/October 1997 *411 Video Magazine*. The only team member not present was Danny Way, who had other plans for the summer: his top-secret intention to break the world record for highest air on a skateboard.

And then again the following year.

"Honestly, I don't remember a whole lot about the Super Tour because I was inebriated the whole time, but the photographs documented all the sick skating going on. Photographers are great for clearing the fog—DC never disappoints."
– Jeff Tremaine, founding editor, *Big Brother*; co-creator, *Jackass*

Block spent the early summer months planning Danny Way's event. When Block and Damon Way approached Blehm with the idea for the ultraexpensive Super Ramp endeavor, Blehm's first concern was for Danny Way's safety, something he's "always worried about," according to Block. Once Block and Way convinced him that it was "ummm, relatively safe," Blehm brought up insurance questions and legal issues and finally agreed to the "crazy stunt."

"Are you going to put up air bags in case he misses the ramp?"
– Clay Blehm on Danny Way's first Super Ramp

In August 1997, Danny Way achieved his record (see page 246), cementing himself as an icon in the sport and distinguishing the Super Ramp as a pivotal DC marketing tool. A ramp of this size had never been constructed; it was so huge in scale that Danny had an oversized skateboard built to his (and the ramp's) specifications.

At the same time Block and Way were planning Danny's world-record attempt, Block's father fell ill with what ended up being an incurable lung disease. In the

Ken Block and DC's skate team on Big Brother*'s first Euro Supertour in London, England, 1997.*

(see page 246)

SIDEBAR **008**
DUB'S SUBCULTURAL CROSS-BRANDING

Ken Block and Damon Way's initia intent was for Dub to be an urban-feeling yet technically functional snowboarding outerwear line. Dub Brand Weathergea went the extra mile with detailing and innovations that included hand gaiters built with snowboarders in mind and waterproof/breathable fabrics for foul-weather protection.

Many Dub designs—thickly insulated jackets, beanies, and large-numbered jerseys—were commandeered of the mountains and into urban zones o music and skateboarding, and Block and Way decided to simultaneously advertise in skateboarding magazines and hip-hop magazines like *The Source.* In 1996, Block and Way collaborated with DJ Greyboy to create a CD called *Dub Breakbeats, Volume 1.* A review of the CD in *Jazzmopolitan Magazine: On The One* stated: "You'll find this CD lurking in snow/skateboard stores across the world, to be given away with purchases of Dub Brand Weathergear. If this sounds a bit out of your way, then let me encourage you to make the effort . . . "

An early Dub advertisement that ran worldwide in The Source *(left), and Dub's collaboration with DJ Greyboy:* Dub Breakbeats.

In addition to having advertisements in *Big Brother, Blunt, Slap,* and other so-called action sports mainstays Dub ended up in the gear and produc review sections of such high-profile magazines as *Playboy, Paper,* and *Outside,* and virtually all snowboarding and skateboarding publications in Europe and Asia.

midst of encouraging young superstar skateboarders like Josh Kalis (and getting him on the team), he tried to console his mother and spent time with his ailing father. The month after the Super Ramp record, his father's health took a dramatic turn for the worse, and he passed away. It had been six years since Block had borrowed the seed money for his business, and "when his father passed away, Ken had long since paid off the loan, with interest," says Block's mother. "Ken's father was extremely proud of him. He saw his son's business plan flourish more than we ever dreamed."

Not long after his father's death, Block was called into a meeting with Blehm and Way. The subject: Dub and Droors. "We can keep producing these lines and struggle, maybe even go out of business," Blehm told his two associates, "or we can let them go and concentrate on what's going to be profitable for the long haul—DC shoes." Block and Way thought long and hard before they agreed to the sale of Dub and Droors, which came as a shock both to the team that had wholeheartedly supported the brands and also to the industry that saw them as very successful.

When Dub and Droors were transferred to a holding company that Steve Rocco and others had formed, called Diaxis (technically, Dub and Droors did not become part of the World Industries family), Block and Way kept a small interest in the brands. A few of the Dub and Droors athletes remained with their lines (the rest of the team was dropped), which maintained momentum for a short period, then took a slight downward slide in popularity that industry insiders attributed to the transfer of ownership and subsequent lack of focus on the brands' health.

The sale was a sore spot for some Dub and Droors athletes, who speculated that, like DC, the brands would have become powerhouses. Virtually every business-oriented opinion on the subject, however, stood behind the decision as a difficult but critical move for the continued growth of DC.

NEW SPORTS,
CONTINUED PROGRESSION

Blunt, Snowboarder, *and* TransWorld SNOWboarding *ran the first DC snowboard team ad in February 1998.*

While expanding their business, Block and Way discussed what other sports they liked and which ones to support. Already firmly entrenched in the snowboarding world, Block had begun sketching designs of what would become the first DC snowboarding boot in early 1997. Using detailing DC had pioneered with its skateboard shoes, DC's boots became an instant success, though initially a small-time player in the snowboard boot world. This standing would change, however, as designs and production practices were refined and a revolutionary air bladder was patented and incorporated into future models.

"DC is an innovator that's pushed snowboard boot designs to new dimensions. They've stayed true to their skateboarding and freestyle roots, something that ski companies that try and get into snowboarding can't figure out."
– John Stouffer, editorial director, *TransWorld SNOWboarding Business*

The first DC snowboard team included five of the most talented freestyle snowboarders of the time: Nate Cole, Gabe Crane, Bjorn Leines, JP Walker, and Devun Walsh.

At a marketing level, other sports or athletes would have to complement DC's growing image and unofficial mission statement: not only to strive for progressive products but also to support the progression of a sport. Before the end of 1997, Block and Way had added two other teams, motocross and surf. Two top riders from the supercross circuit, Jeff Emig and Ryan Hughes, received custom-colored shoes to match their motocross team colors. Eventually, Kevin Windham and rising star Ricky Carmichael joined the motocross flow team, receiving free DC products. The first surf team consisted of Shane Dorian, Andy Irons, and his brother, Bruce.

> ## "I like the fact that DC hasn't sold out the skate-boarding side in favor of snow, motocross, surf, or BMX, or whatever. Skate still seems to be their primary focus and I respect that."
> – Dave Swift, editor in chief, *TransWorld SKATEboarding*

Jeff Emig's Kawasaki green custom Plug. Another example of how DC goes the extra mile for its athletes.

In 1998, DC introduced PAL AB2000, a revolutionary hybrid composite of polyurethane-coated cowhide leather that flexes like leather but is highly resistant to a skateboard shoe's worst enemy—abrasion. Advertisements for the first shoe to use this material (the Lynx) featured the newest member to join the DC skateboard team, Josh Kalis.

The owners also dropped the name Circus Distribution in favor of its current name, DC Shoes, Inc. With the name change came a determination to take DC to the next level: a complete in-house team was assembled to work on new products such as sandals and children's and women's shoes. Sales strategy was reorganized to include (in addition to an in-house sales team that had, up until now, accounted for virtually all North American sales) outside sales representatives who would handle retail accounts by geographic region. International sales, via nearly fifty distributors in fifty different countries, continued to supply a constant demand.

The first DC surf team—Shane Dorian and the Irons brothers—was seen in 1998 Surfer *and* Surfing *magazine ads.*

A NEW MILLENNIUM APPROACHES

When 1999 rolled around, DC grossed just under $43 million (Block's magic number)—a massive amount by all accounts, but a 3 percent decrease from the year before. Was the skateboarding industry beginning its once-a-decade death march, or were there simply too many competing shoe companies? From 1993 to 1996, sales had increased by over 100 percent each year, with 1996 blowing up to nearly 200 percent. This sudden leveling off was more than a little scary. Everybody in the industry felt the same unease, but what to do about it? While many of its competitors had regional sales representatives making face-to-face contact with retailers across North America, DC had been relying on in-house sales. Now DC was playing catch-up with its own reorganized sales force.

> ## "DC was founded upon exceptional skateboarding and incredibly talented skaters. Sure, they've expanded their brand to other sports—but have never faltered on their strict quality control. The action in DC ads is always top-notch."
> – Tony Hawk

Still, before year's end, Board-Trac—a syndicated market research group that studies the lifestyles and purchasing habits of young people between the ages of eight and twenty-four—announced that DC was voted the number two "coolest brand of shoes" among skateboarders. The study additionally revealed what consumers predicted would be "next year's hottest brand of shoes,"

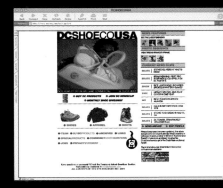

DC AND DJ CULTURE

In the early nineties, DC supported the hip-hop explosion that became a fixture of skateboarding. Electronic music has picked up speed on a parallel plane, particularly the drum 'n' bass movement, whose DJs around the globe have introduced their beats to the worlds of skateboarding and snowboarding.

Goldie, Ascent shoe ad.

Triple Threat, Reason shoe ad.

Philly's Dieselboy, Tekron shoe ad.

eeBee, Dash shoe ad.

DJ Sage, Women's Vectra shoe ad.

Disco D, Williams shoe ad.

ne of DC's former in-house designers, Dave Kinsey provided his distinctive look to DC's J advertising campaign, which ran in music and lifestyle magazines beginning in 2000.

DC has always supported these cultural music trends by establish-ng relationships with numerous hip-hop talents, including SoCal's Greyboy and Philly's Dieselboy. Forming alliances with drum 'n' bass DJs Goldie, Philly's Dieselboy, TeeBee, Empress, Abstract, Sage, and UFO as twisted skate culture around the nuances of electronic music both tateside and abroad. This effort is just the beginning: the company con-nues to forge bonds with underground dance communities like Detroit's asty ghetto tech scene and with DJs like the infamous Disco D.

Other DJs supported by DC include AK1200, Andy C, A-Trak, Bailey, Calibre, Carl Cox, Doc Scott, Ed Rush, Future Cut, MC Justiyc, Hive, Marcus Intelex, Paul Oakenfold, Rabbit in the Moon, MC Rage, Randall, Sandra Collins, Sasha and Digweed, South, Storm, Timo Maas, Triple Threat, and X-Ecutioners.

and DC took this category hands down. *Big Brother* also performed a reader survey, and DC won the distinction of being the "most pop-ular skateboarding shoe."

It was during this time that employee benefit plans were imple-mented to include 401(k) profit sharing and retirement in addition to the full medical, dental, and optical care that had been in place since 1996. The owners also transferred 10 percent of their owner-ship in the company to an employee share trust, a thank-you for loy-alty and hard work. As Blehm puts it, "They earn every penny. If it weren't for the expertise of our management team and their fine staffs, we wouldn't be where we are." Block adds, "Our team and our products represent us to the public, but most kids who like our stuff have no idea what it takes to get those shoes on their feet."

BMX ENTERS THE DC EQUATION

By 2000, BMX racers and freestylers had been wearing DC shoes for years, and there wasn't even a question that they deserved DC's wholeheart-ed support. The first DC BMX advertisement intro-duced a formidable team of proven riders: Jerry Bagley, Robbie Morales, Robbie

This ad, which debuted DC's first BMX power-house team, appeared in the May 2000 issue of Ride BMX.

Miranda, Neal Wood, Chris Doyle, Chad Kagy, and Colin Winkelmann. Winkelmann was destined to join Danny Way as the second DC athlete to break a world record, for longest jump on a BMX bike (see page 134).

At the end of 2000, BMX's wonderboy, Dave Mirra, joined the DC team, asserting that "the support and credibility of DC is a great asset for the BMX community." Mirra designed the first DC pro-model BMX shoe in 2001, which led to DC being voted the number one and number two favorite brand of shoes by reader surveys in two of the sport's largest magazines, *TransWorld BMX* and *Ride BMX*.

DC VOTED NUMBER ONE SKATEBOARDING SHOE

Board-Trac announced the results of its 2000 survey, and DC became the "coolest brand of shoes" and "next year's hottest brand." Add this to various magazine reader surveys (including *TransWorld SKATEboarding* and *Big Brother*) and it was official: by most accounts DC was considered the most popular skateboarding shoe in the world.

It was a massive realization, and something Block, in particular, heard with bittersweet emotions. Since his father's death, he had set out to become number one, because "losing my father when he was fairly young made me realize how short life can be. It made me want to work harder than ever to be successful."

"When it comes down to it, we pretty much owe everything to skateboarding."

— Damon Way

Still, there was no rest for the weary. Block, Way, Blehm, and the entire DC team, both athletes and in-house, saw the recognition as a challenge to better themselves and the sports and lifestyles they represented.

BUILDING THE FOUNTAIN OF YOUTH

It's 2002 and DC once again has been voted the number one coolest brand of shoes for 2001 and "next year's" hottest brand for 2002. Nearly 150 young and young-at-heart employees have a difficult time finding parking space at the DC headquarters, which have expanded from part of a single building near the end of a dead-end road into four buildings, nearly the entire block, and 150,000 square feet of warehouses and offices. Jokingly referred to as "the building that makes the money," the original building (Building One) houses departments for accounting, information technologies (aka computer), legal, cut and sew (pattern making), administration, and domestic and international sales. Marketing, public relations, and team managers have their own wing downstairs.

Building Two is "the building that spends the money": shoe production and apparel design, advertising, and Web site design, as well as big, bright, ultramodern "creative" offices with glass walls, polished concrete floors, and DC logos built into ironwork, a stainless-steel video-conference room, an executive kitchen, and showers in the bathrooms. This is also where Jai Baek and Jeff McCall work. Baek is a multimillion-mile flier as DC's international director of footwear manufacturing. His first visit to South Korea, in 1994, yielded 20,000 Danny Way and Colin McKay pro models. In 2001, more than two million pairs of shoes came out of DC's factories. Jeff McCall has also grown with the company since his consulting days and is the domestic director of footwear manufacturing. Both buildings have computerized shipping and receiving departments with employees who know more about international geography and zip codes than your average postal worker. And let's not forget the product, the foundation of all this madness: boxes of shoes and DC's clothing line are piled to the ceiling in the warehouses attached to Buildings One and Two.

Tacked to a bulletin board in the sales department is a handwritten note that reads "this is DC" with an arrow pointing to a quote by Stewart B. Johnson: "Our business in life is not to get ahead of others, but to get ahead of our-selves—to break our own records, to outstrip our yesterday by our today." No one knows that better than DC's owners.

"We have a saying in Korea: if you surround yourself with youth, you will remain young beyond your years."

— Hwang Young Sun, owner, DC shoe factory

The company's chief financial officer (CFO), Clay Blehm, just shy of seventy and going on thirty-five, sits in his leather chair overlooking the warehouse in Building Two. A wall-to-wall Turkish rug he bought in Istanbul accentuates the worldly souvenirs that surround him, all of which he's collected in the past few years. "Making up for lost time," he says, "but really, things evolve as they should. Evolution takes its own course, you can't rush it. DC is the perfect example of that. It seems fast, but we took our time."

Blehm remains the company's hardball decision maker, continuing to use "the bottom line" as the basis for most decisions—a black-and-white, sometimes gruff affair that can frustrate the right-brained reasoning of his younger associates. But both Block and Way respect Blehm's set ways and are more than happy with his watchdog attitude about DC: attacking bottom-feeders who try to pirate logos, steal shoe designs, sell product to unauthorized dealers, and move into DC's territory.

"I won't stand for any dishonest or hostile business practice," says Blehm. "If someone, or some corporation, screws with DC, I don't care how big they are, on principle alone I'll see to it that they go down." He's proven his steadfast determination on numerous occasions. "Trust me, you don't want to be on the receiving end," says one close friend.

"I'm the asshole, Damon is the angel, and Ken falls somewhere in between."

— Clay Blehm

His position makes perfect sense. After all, "DC gave him back his life," says Rudy Candito, one of DC's warehouse managers who had originally worked for Blehm at his child-care business during the mid-eighties. "Every

A far cry from the folding table that served as his first desk: Clay Blehm in his plush office overlooking one of DC's four warehouses.

Damon Way with a classic 8mm video camera. His office is decorated with, among other things, a Thomas Campbell painting and a Kartell modular shelving system holding various action figures.

time I see Clay roll up in his shiny car, it puts a smile on my face, because I saw him hit rock bottom. Not too many people his age bounce back up like he did."

Blehm keeps it in perspective by tirelessly thanking all the company's employees—including his right hand and DC's controller, Donna Kokinelis, and Jack Gentle, the "computer wizard"—who, in Blehm's words, "make my life easy" (he adds with a wink) "or at least easier." But in particular, he's at once grateful to and respectful of Block and Way: "Ken and Damon, well, they're geniuses. I want that to be clear if it isn't already. They pioneered the whole show. Without the opportunities they opened up, I really don't know where I'd be."

IMPACT OF A CHILDHOOD TOY

"My life has been fulfilled," says Damon Way, DC's vice president. He's sitting in his spacious modern office, where model helicopters hang above his desk on thin wires and a tiny Bose stereo plays, at mid-volume, Spacemen 3, one of dozens of CDs that fill a long slender rack. A Kartell modular shelving system behind his desk showcases action figures by Michael Lau, Kaws, Futura and Nigo, Gundam, and G.I. Joe. There is a large Thomas Campbell painting above the action figures and a Kaws painting to the left. Low Barcelona leather chairs are grouped around a B&B table holding books on art, Asian architecture, the history of camouflage, and a photo album documenting early skateboarding days and some of Way's own grassroots marketing campaigns, like "wheat pasting" thousands of Stevie Williams posters all over the streets of San Francisco.

The intercom on his desk comes to life. It's Duke Johnson, DC's director of apparel, who is "so on it" that Way doesn't know what he'd do without her. She sounds rushed, maybe a little frazzled. "I sense stress in your voice," says Way. "What's going on?" A few minutes later, Johnson and an entourage enter the office, one of whom is wearing a new T-shirt style that

Way examines, pulls on its sleeves, feels the fit, and confirms: "Yeah, the sleeves are kind of funky. Wash it again, and then let's check it out."

The kid who stole wood from construction sites to build a halfpipe in his backyard has come a long way since that serious injury in high school put an end to his pro skateboarding aspirations. Those painful memories have all but been swallowed up by the fortunate life he's worked so hard to achieve. Another unfortunate chapter in his life, however, is much fresher in his mind.

On December 31, 2000, Tim O'Dea, the man responsible for assembling Damon and Danny Way's first skateboard, was out for a morning surf at Torrey Pines in Southern California. (He was remarried with two young children, but maintained his father figure status with the Ways and was well aware of the success born from a scrap of wood and a set of wheels.)

Still an avid surfer at fifty-one, O'Dea had decided to take a wave in after battling the current for a long time. "As he was walking in with his board in knee-high water, he suffered a major heart attack," says Way. "He died on the spot. For him, I cannot think of a better way to go: doing what he loved most, surfing."

Way saw the death as a tragedy for his stepfather's family, but as a fairly spiritual person, he was personally consoled by the full life O'Dea had led. "My stepdad had an incredibly happy life, and he had an incredible influence on me and my brother," says Way. "He showed us skateboarding and surfing, among many other things. I'm not sure if he ever knew how much influence he had in shaping my and my brother's lives. Without him, we would be somewhere entirely different from where we are now."

> **"Ken and Damon's current offices are about the size of their entire first warehouse. They've both advanced their lives so much, but they try really hard to advance other people's lives as well. They're very generous with what they have."**
> – Mario Rubalcaba, former Droors pro skateboarder; current drummer, Rocket from the Crypt

Reflecting back on his own young life, Way can't help but notice how his current success has been built upon so many tragedies. Perhaps that's the reason for his utterly optimistic attitude about life and a positive and gentle nature that would be part of his personality regardless of whether or not he and his associates were self-made multimillionaires. But if Way, in particular, could take back the pain and depression he suffered as a result of his injury, would he?

"I'm not sure if I would. Sure, I've had to deal with my share of frustration and emotional pain, but all of that has helped to build the person I am today." He explains that he's had so many incredible experiences since he was fifteen, and shared his life with so many amazing people, that "to roll the dice and go back and hope that my life would turn out as well as it has would be a serious gamble. We're only here for a short time anyway, so it is up to us to make the best with the circumstances we are dealt. I'm often thankful that I am not in a wheelchair and that I can enjoy life as I always have, with maybe just a little less athletic prowess than I once had."

Not one to dwell on the negative, Way focuses on the positives in his life: he's engaged to his longtime girlfriend, Suzy Jazdzewski, and heading to his second residence in the heart of San Francisco for the weekend to explore other creative outlets in art and music.

For now, he remains focused on the job at hand, patiently waiting for whatever is around the next corner.

AND IT ALL
STARTED WITH . . .

Within the span of a fifteen-minute meeting, Ken Block has been interrupted by six people who step into his office and say, "This will just take a second." The interruptions range from questions like "Do you like this photo of Anthony?" and "Did you get a chance to look at that press release yet?" to Jai Baek showing off a new sample: an almost robotic-looking snowboard boot. Block switches gears seamlessly. There's a shoe box with new graphics waiting for approval on a brushed-steel conference table that has a giant pad of paper, custom-made to fit the tabletop and that's "great for brainstorming during meetings." His desk is organized into prioritized piles and he has seventy-one unanswered e-mails. "This is what my life has become," says Block.

Then he chuckles, the trademark Ken Block laugh that is slow, deliberate, and happy. You can tell by the fire in his eyes that he truly loves what he does, even though he has a cold and hasn't slept much lately because he's super excited about a new idea he's been working out in his head. When probed for details, he at first defers with a "you'll see," but then he cracks and "confidentially" spills the beans. (Sorry, you'll just have to wait and see.)

The wood floors of Block's office jut up against DC-stamped concrete walls, one of which is covered with framed artwork by legendary skateboarder Lance Mountain and co-creator of MTV's *Jackass,* Jeff Tremaine, old *Blunt* covers, advertisements, and a Droors branding iron that was once an ad prop. The magnetized board behind his desk has photos of the "modern mountain home" he's building near Park City, Utah, snapshots of him with celebrities like Adam Sandler and Goldie, and behind-the-scenes team party photos from various road trips. Some eBay-purchased collector's snowboards that he intends to hang in the stairwell of his new home stand in a corner.

> *"DC was the first skate shoe company to really fire on all cylinders. Products, marketing, riders, distribution, each one strong enough to support your average mediocre skate shoe company, all combined into an unbeatable entity. I don't think anyone out there has a chance in hell to beat them."*
> – Steve Rocco, owner, World Industries

A friend walks in and sees the snowboards, classic Sims, Avalanche, Look, and a Burton. "No way, a red and black Elite 140—that was my first board," he says.

The board cost Block $300, but he doesn't even hesitate before saying, "Do you want it?"

"Serious?" the friend responds.

Block replies, "It's yours. I'll find another one." One of his favorite things is to hook people up whenever he can.

The friend leaves, and in file the three team managers, Brian Botts (snow/BMX), Blair Marlin (surf/motocross), and Brian Dvorak (skate), who are excellent athletes in their own right and can "hang with the team," no problem. They plop down on low couches for a meeting during which Block brainstorms avenues for athlete involvement and okays some requests while nixing others, decisions he makes within his loosely drawn job description of president of DC Shoes.

"I can guarantee you Ken Block is the most involved president of any $100 million company," says Colin McKay. "He can go and ride with Jeff Emig on his bike or Todd Richards on his snowboard, and he can keep up."

It's difficult to fathom that DC was poised to make nearly $100 million a year in gross sales less than a decade after the founder of the company was staying late after class, screen-printing T-shirts at the local community college. Says Block, "It's really pretty scary when you look at all the ingredients it took to make this company—meeting Damon, Danny, Clay—and then all the stories behind the stories that eventually made the DC story. I could never thank enough all the people who have helped out along the way."

The "DC" stenciled walls of Ken Block's think-tank office were the backdrop for Stevie Williams's "the Reason" commercial, which aired in the fall of 2001.

CLOCKER FIRST RELEASED: SPRING 1996

Originally designed by Ken Block, the Clocker was the first DC shoe to have a visible arch in the sole, which increased arch support and gave the shoe a dramatic appearance. The Clocker also had a fatter tongue than other skate shoes, which provided superior cushioning for extended comfort, and thermoplastic rubber (TPR) lace loops that helped protect laces from griptape friction.

The Clocker ad campaign was equally dramatic. Featuring a long lens black-and-white skate shot of DC's newest rider at the time, Carl Shipman, doing a huge frontside transfer at an undisclosed indoor skate park, the layout earned an "ad style of the year" award from *Thrasher* magazine.

In order to accommodate new shoes in the following season's catalog, the popular Clocker went out of production in winter 1996. In spring 1997, DC released the Clocker2, and in fall 1997, the Clocker3, both of which featured the same design but incorporated different materials—heavy canvas, synthetic leather, and durable Cordura. Despite their popularity, the Clocker2 and Clocker3 were dropped in winter 1998 to make room for the next season's line.

LYNX FIRST RELEASED: SPRING 1998

In 1998, DC's newest team member, Josh Kalis, and shoe, the Lynx, were announced to the public simultaneously, via an ad that featured a black-and-white photo of Kalis clearing a large walkway with a 360 flip. It read "Grip Tape Has Finally Met Its Match."

The Lynx was the first skate shoe ever to incorporate the revolutionary abrasion-resistant material known as PAL AB2000—more durable than leather but flexible like rubber—on the heel and toe cap, contact points that notoriously wear out from repeated contact with a skateboard's abrasive griptape. Subsequently, the Lynx became one of the most resilient and versatile skate shoes on the market, as well as one of DC's best sellers at skateboard shops around the world.

Despite its popularity, the Lynx was phased out in fall 1999 to make room for the following season's line. After being out of production for only six months, it was brought back by popular demand: DC reintroduced the shoe in the holiday 2000 catalog with three new colorways and an updated design of 100 percent synthetic materials. Since its original release, the Lynx's reputation of quality and performance have rendered it a shoe to which other skate shoes are compared.

BOXER FIRST RELEASED: SPRING 1996

Highly durable elements such as rubber lace loops and an extra layer of suede in the ollie area made the Boxer a technical skate shoe that was "distinctly different from most skate shoes on the market at the time," says Boxer designer, Ken Block. The sidewall on the Boxer was one millimeter thicker in the ollie area, a detail that not only made the shoe more durable but also gave it a unique look.

The Boxer became such a popular product in the months following its release that DC reintroduced it in November 1998 with five colorways. The shoe's popularity continued until it was removed from production in fall 1999 to make room for the following season's line.

DANNY WAY FIRST RELEASED: WINTER 1994

Designed by Danny Way and Ken Block in late 1993, the Danny Way was DC's very first skate shoe. Block used his growing computer skills to develop a three-dimensional shoe design that was then printed on paper and colored in with pens and pencils. After months of designing, samples were made in Etnie's production facilities, while DC's in-house sales reps began selling the Danny Way to shops around the world. So popular was Danny Way that the shops put in orders for his shoe sight unseen. Final pro-duction for 20,000 pairs of the Danny Way was carried over into the new DC facilities in Korea.

The Danny Way, which was available in three different colorways (black, white, and blue) and featured Danny Way's signature across the tongue, became the catalyst for everything DC has become and is known for. Although the original shoe went out of production in April 1995, hun-dreds of thousands of updated Danny Way pro model shoes are produced and distributed yearly.

In the eyes of some, skateboarding is a nuisance. It is often misunderstood. And, oh yeah, it's against the law in most public venues. But for the skateboarder, skateboarding is not just a form of civil disobedience, it's a way of life and form of self-expression and most definitely not a team sport, at least not in the traditional sense. Skateboarding has an established, albeit brief, history documented through the actions of the famous and almost famous who spent the best times of their lives in the streets nursing their wounds and urging their bodies to recover quickly so they might progress the sport they loved.

"Sidewalk surfing," as skateboarding was first called, sprung up during the late fifties as a method of transportation for California surfers headed for the beach and their quick fix when the surf went flat. What these surfers didn't know was that the concrete would replace the beach for many of them once the popularity of skateboarding grew an industry all its own.

Skateboarding has seen highs and lows: early legal problems resulting from equipment failure (clay wheels disintegrated, sometimes causing fatal wipeouts and prompting cities to ban the use of skateboards) in the sixties. A boom in the seventies when urethane wheels were created and hundreds of skateboard parks opened across North America. And a decline in the late eighties and early nineties when escalating insurance premiums as a result of injuries at the parks forced them to close their doors. Skateboarders took to developing skills on backyard halfpipes, vert ramps, and the streets. Soon enough, the streets, too, became off-limits—an unfathomable scenario for those fifties-era skateboarders who might have thought banning the use of public cement as futile an effort as closing the ocean.

History repeated itself with another boom in the late nineties that's been holding strong ever since, thanks to a new generation of open minds and a captivated worldwide audience. But despite the notoriety skateboarding has acquired and the media frenzy of late, public streets are still closed to skateboarders. Yes, skateboarding in America is illegal except in designated venues (just try it and see), a confirmation that few people really understand its intricacies.

One reason for this is that the "sport" doesn't fall into the same category as our other national pastimes. It doesn't really fall into a category at all. Sure, there are board sports that have borrowed from, if not imitated, skateboarding, but none embody its progressiveness or are as raw, defiant, bodily taxing, and severe. Grand-slam home runs and touchdowns made on kickoff returns are appreciated as some of the finer moments in sports. Hopefully, it won't be long before a frontside bluntslide down a flight of ten stairs on a handrail is given the same applause as an alley-oop slam dunk.

Fueled by an underdeveloped marketplace and the goal to improve and progress the design and performance of skateboard shoes, the DC

Mike Blabac

Brian Wenning worked his way up from DC's amateur squad into the pro ranks with clean, stylish skateboarding, as seen in this switch heelflip at Love Park. Philadelphia, Pennsylvania, 2000.

SKATEBOARDING
AN AUDIENCE OF ONE
BY NANCY CARLSON

Canadian amateur Ryan Smith was recruited by Colin McKay because of his mastery of street skills. A noseblunt slide in Toronto, Canada, 2001.

Mike Blabac

Melbourne, Australia, pro Jason Ellis crossed the Pacific to join DC's American-based team of pros. Though his titles range from actor to pro skateboarder to TV personality, Ellis's comedic demeanor is most at home on vert ramps worldwide. Here, he performs a frontside heelflip ape hanger while Danny Way talks on his cell phone. DC's indoor training facility, Vista, California, 2002.

shoe brand was founded in 1994, a time when the skate industry was at its lowest. In addition to setting new standards in manufacturing, the company sponsored some of the most progressive pros in the industry. Although DC's team is a group of eccentric and diverse personalities, it is united by astonishing abilities in both vert and street skating and a common drive to push skateboarding into a new era—while having as much fun as possible along the way.

DC founding pro Danny Way, one of skateboarding's rawest veterans, has been setting his own skateboarding standards since he picked up his first deck at the ripe old age of five. His credits include the Guinness world record for highest air on a skateboard as well as two different famed helicopter drops. Known primarily for his vert prowess, Way is also recognized and respected for his street skating ability that rounds him out and indubitably makes him a legendary figure in skateboarding. DC's other founding pro, Colin McKay, is a legend in his own right. He tackles complex and elaborate lines on vert and has an equally elaborate sense of humor: you could say that McKay's presence on DC's team is somewhat like a jester in a king's court. Charisma and style: enter Rob Dyrdek, whose unique trick combinations and legendary storytelling ability have made him one of skateboarding's most recognized personalities. Josh Kalis with his uncanny technical ability and Stevie Williams with his smooth, fluid lines continually push themselves, along with Anthony Van Engelen (soft-spoken, technically explosive) and Brian Wenning (New Jersey's finest).

The team's positive media attention hasn't come without personal sacrifice. All its members have fallen down hard (countless times) while training for mentally draining competitions or on-demand photo and film sessions. They've maintained their focus on the job at hand, often alone and late at night and despite an army of persistent rent-a-cops. It's those unseen moments of preparation that have fueled skateboarding since the beginning.

After all, the driving force behind success is an audience of one.

Brian Wenning, switch backside lipslide, Philadelphia, Pennsylvania, 2001.

Brian Wenning, switch ollie in Philadelphia, 2001.

Ryan Smith, 5-0 grind in San Diego, 2002.

Brian Wenning, switch heelflip, Barcelona, Spain, 2001.

Mike Blabac

Mike Blabac

Mike Blabac

DANNY WAY

WITHOUT REGARD

BY JOEL PATTERSON

Greatness is not a genetic gift; the price of admission is usually pretty steep. It demands that one experience physical and emotional pain, it requires dedication and hunger, it doesn't wait for injuries to heal or personal problems to be solved, and its downs are often as tremendous as its ups. Danny Way has run the gamut of the human experience—an unstable childhood, the death of a mentor, the birth of a son, years of rehabilitating from injuries, setting world records—and emerged as one of skateboarding's all-time greats.

The challenges began even before Danny knew what was going on. The Way household was more California hippie than *Leave It to Beaver* when he was born on April 15, 1974. When Danny was just six months old, his father died and his twenty-four-year-old mother, Mary, became the sole provider for her young family. A couple of years later Mary married Tim O'Dea, the man responsible for building a skateboard out of scrap wood and wheels for Danny's older brother, Damon. The toy mesmerized Danny.

There was eventually a divorce, but O'Dea maintained his father-figure presence in the brothers' lives, encouraging them to excel in team sports like baseball and football, as well as surfing and skateboarding near O'Dea's Pacific Beach home.

With vert and street skating still in their infancies during the late seventies and early eighties, skate parks reigned supreme. Nearly every California megalopolis had its share of concrete parks frequented by talented young skateboarders. Parks in Winchester, Milpitas, Marina del Rey, Upland, Lakewood, Orange, Colton, and Whittier produced legendary skateboarders like Steve Caballero, Ray "Bones" Rodriguez, Keith Meek, Duane Peters, Christian Hosoi, Chris Miller, John Lucero, Neil Blender, Jeff Grosso, Lester Kasai, and the Albas.

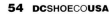

Danny Way, the most stylish and composed bailer in skateboarding, is fully prepared to beat himself into the ground while learning a new trick. San Diego Super Ramp, 2001.

Mike Blabac

Dan Sturt

Danny Way winning the
1999 MTV Sports and
Music Festival high-air
contest (fourteen-foot
backside air), two days
after his shoulder injury.
Las Vegas.

San Diego County's most popular skate venue was the Del Mar Skate Ranch, and it, too, was turning out its fair share of incredible talent. Along with a preteen Tony Hawk, Billy Ruff, Kevin Staab, and Steve Steadham, six-year-old Danny and eight-year-old Damon began frequenting the Ranch, and by the time Damon was twelve he seemed on the road to becoming a professional skateboarder. Danny—inspired and challenged by local and visiting pros—was hot on his tail, albeit with a collection of nagging injuries that included chronic patella bursitis (when the bursa, or sac, in the knee leaks, causing it to swell up like a water balloon), probably the result of bailing head-high airs wearing only children's knee pads.

Though he loved the vertical world of the Ranch, Danny wasn't always able to get there for logistical reasons. This made street skating his main source of entertainment. In 1985, he became a member of the Vista Skate Locals (VSL), a group of older skateboarders that included Damon. This crew, many of whom would become pros down the road, provided a kind of family that the Ways didn't find at home. It also pushed the tagalong little brother to perform—not only did Danny want to fit in, he also had a fiercely competitive personality. "Danny would do just about anything to earn approval from my friends," says Damon. "I mean, he was trying gay twists [on vert] when he was twelve years old, before he could even do decent airs or inverts. I think after years of that, he figured out how to eliminate fear from his mind."

The relentless VSL guys (and especially Damon) goaded, if not bullied, Danny into skating everything from street to mini ramps to vert to pools. Unknowingly, they were helping "High Voice," as he was nicknamed for prepubescent reasons, to mature into a multiterrain genius. "My biggest revenge was trying to be better than all of them at skating," says Danny. "That was a big motivational reason to learn a lot of stuff, to get better than my brother. I couldn't beat him up, but at least I could say, 'I can do airs better than you.'"

At only a decade old, Danny was already being sponsored as an amateur by such highly respected companies as

Mike Blabac

D.W., backside 5-0 grind on a crane basket, eight and a half feet above the outdoor DC Super Ramp in downtown San Diego, 2001.

Skateboards and Vision. By 1986, he was quickly emerging as one of the first skateboarders to tackle both street and vert, combining elements of both in either discipline. Grant Brittain, *TransWorld SKATEboarding* photo editor since the early eighties, remembers the first time he saw Danny skating at a 1986 demo in Oceanside, California: "He was really small for his age, but he was really good. I had heard a lot about him, and from the first time I watched him skate, I could tell he had it. He was super innovative, just one of those natural-born skaters. You could tell he was going to go places."

A new skateboard company named H-Street also recognized the young skater's talent and encouraged him to turn pro when he was still twelve. He shrugged off the monumental opportunity and joined H-Street's team as an amateur. At the same time, his older brother had developed a long-standing sponsorship with Alexander's (which would become Pacific Drive), a skateboard shop in Pacific Beach.

Just when it looked like the Way family had produced two future pros, the unexpected happened. Early on November 17, 1986, Danny woke up to find Damon in the throes of an unexplained seizure. Danny didn't know what to do, didn't even know what was going on—and he was faced with the possibility that his brother might die in front of him.

The night before, Damon had been hit in the head at a high school football game. An artery in his brain had ruptured, causing a resulting condition described as a kind of stroke. Just like that, Damon's dreams

Dave Swift

Danny Way, frontside 50-50, Seaside Reef parking lot. Cardiff-by-the-Sea, California, 1998.

of becoming a professional skateboarder were seriously altered, if not gone forever.

Danny was horrified by his brother's condition and looked to the one thing he could always count on to pull him through: skateboarding. But Damon's absence at the skate sessions weighed heavily. Danny remembered how, if he could make a certain trick and Damon couldn't, he'd be one up on his brother. "He was always a little better than me, and that drove me to try to learn more," says Danny. "When he got hurt, I didn't have that extra edge." Suddenly, Danny was wishing his brother was there to one-up him.

As Damon's recovery allowed, Danny brought his skateboard with him to the hospital. According to their mother, Danny would be in Damon's hospital room every day, helping him with therapy and showing him the new tricks he was learning. He wanted to see his big brother skateboard again, and he made a pact with himself to go pro when the time was right, not only for himself, but for Damon as well.

And eventually Damon did skate again, though never at the same caliber as before. It was almost fitting that the Del Mar Skate Ranch closed in July 1987, only eight months after the accident.

It was the end of an era in which vert skating had reigned supreme and professional skateboarders were extremely faithful to their sponsors, often spending an entire career with only one

Frontside lipslide. D.W. in Carlsbad, California, 1999.

Dave Swift

Danny Way, frontside tail-grab at the Eiffel Tower. Paris, France, 1989.

Spike Jonze

D.W., tuck knee Indy at McGill's Skate Park in Carlsbad, California, 1989.

Grant Brittain

D.W., eggplant in Paris in 1988.

Grant Brittain

D.W., one-foot 540 in 1988, in Lansing, Michigan.

Michael Ballard

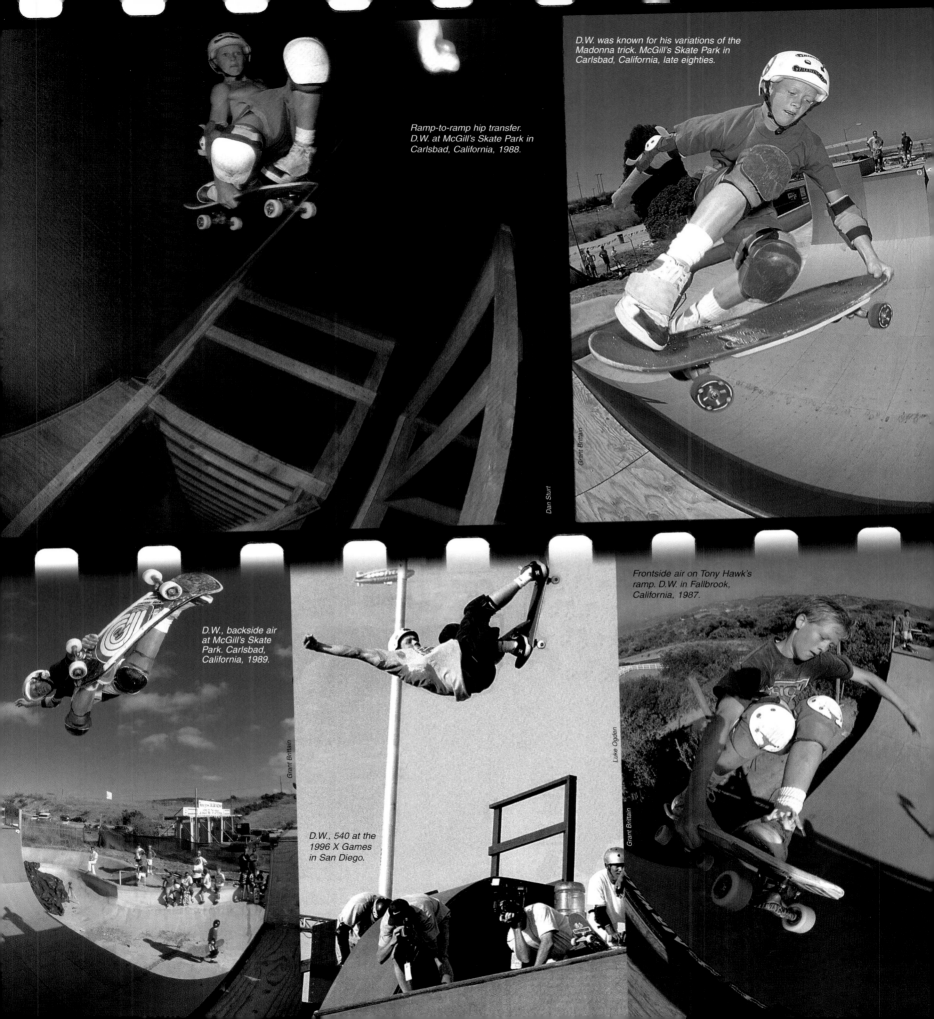

Ramp-to-ramp hip transfer. D.W. at McGill's Skate Park in Carlsbad, California, 1988.

D.W. was known for his variations of the Madonna trick. McGill's Skate Park in Carlsbad, California, late eighties.

D.W., backside air at McGill's Skate Park. Carlsbad, California, 1989.

Frontside air on Tony Hawk's ramp. D.W. in Fallbrook, California, 1987.

D.W., 540 at the 1996 X Games in San Diego.

Dan Sturt

Grant Brittain

Grant Brittain

Luke Ogden

Grant Brittain

company. Danny, however, had been going against the norm, having already jumped from two major companies. He was firmly entrenched as a young prodigy with H-Street, which had been founded by ex–pro skateboarder/vert legend Tony Magnussen and Mike Ternasky, a skateboarding veteran who had gained invaluable industry knowledge by running camps.

Danny Way on television presenting the "skater of the year" award to Eric Koston at the 2001 ESPN Action Sports Awards. Universal Amphitheatre, Los Angeles.

Mike Blabac

It was with H-Street that Danny, now thirteen, and Ternasky became close. Ternasky approached the job of team manager much the same way that Stacy Peralta had run the tight-knit Powell Peralta Bones Brigade team, taking an interest in the lives of the skaters, not just acting as a glorified travel agent. Eventually he and Danny seemed more like father/son than team captain/team rider.

At fourteen, Danny began filming for a much-anticipated video production by H-Street. He had been in videos in the past with other sponsors, but always as the amazing kid who could pull a lot of the pros' tricks. The production, *Shackle Me Not,* helped kick off the newly emerging video generation in skateboarding, and document the era when Danny Way stopped looking like a kid on a skateboard and started looking like a pro-level skateboarder. His airs had evolved from "big for someone his age" to just plain huge, previewing his actual pro debut less than a year later, in 1989.

H-Street's next production, *Hokus Pokus,* focused on the progression of the technical side of street, mini-ramp, and vert skating, not scripted scenes and contest footage, and had an amazing roster of talent that included Mike Carroll, Alphonzo Rawls, and Danny and Damon's pals from the VSL days: Matt Hensley and Steve Ortega. Both *Shackle* and *Hokus Pokus* established the company as a favorite among the growing number of street skaters who, since the death of the skate park, were emerging as the dominant group in the skate community. While the videos' lack of overly slick finish and high-quality film stock disappointed some, most young skateboarders couldn't get enough. Danny's paychecks reflected this; $20,000 for one month of board royalties was huge money for a kid who had grown up on an annual family income that rarely, if ever, topped that amount.

The skate industry was hit by economic hardship just as Danny was beginning to enjoy the monetary success of his endorsements, so in 1990, he discussed his options with Ternasky. Ternasky agreed there were greener pastures flourishing on the other side of the fence at Blind Skateboards, and he supported Danny's decision to join that team. Danny rode for Mark Gonzales and Steve Rocco, industry icons with deep roots in skateboarding via World Industries, one of the most successful skateboard distributors in the world.

> "DANNY'S MOST VALUABLE ASSET, IN RELATION TO HIS ATHLETIC PROWESS, IS HIS ABILITY TO DISREGARD FEAR AND CONSEQUENCE AS THOUGH IT WERE NOTHING MORE THAN THE SUBTLE DISTRACTION OF SWEAT RUNNING DOWN HIS FACE."
> – Damon Way

Meanwhile, Ternasky left H-Street to launch Plan B in late 1990. It was essentially skateboarding's Dream Team, with a superstar lineup that featured Danny, Colin McKay, Ryan Fabry, Sal Barbier, Matt Hensley, Rick Howard, and others. This electic mix of different styles, approaches, and personalities was an enormous source of strength—at least in the beginning. Without a doubt, Plan B's first film, *Questionable Video,* transformed skateboarding forever. And, though the video lacked a weak link, Danny's part was undeniably the strongest. At only seventeen years of age he did sequences of tricks that skateboarders who'd dominated vert skating for ten years hadn't even conceived. His street skating was equally unbelievable, complete with every flip trick imaginable, triple-set ollies, and twenty-plus-stair handrails.

D.W.'s fourteen-foot tribute to Christian Hosoi.
Christ air at the DC Super Ramp, downtown
San Diego, 2001.

Mike Blabac

Danny Way took the seventeen-foot roll-in
for this switch kickflip off the lower hip—after
seven hours of skateboarding at the indoor
DC training facility in Vista, California, 2001.

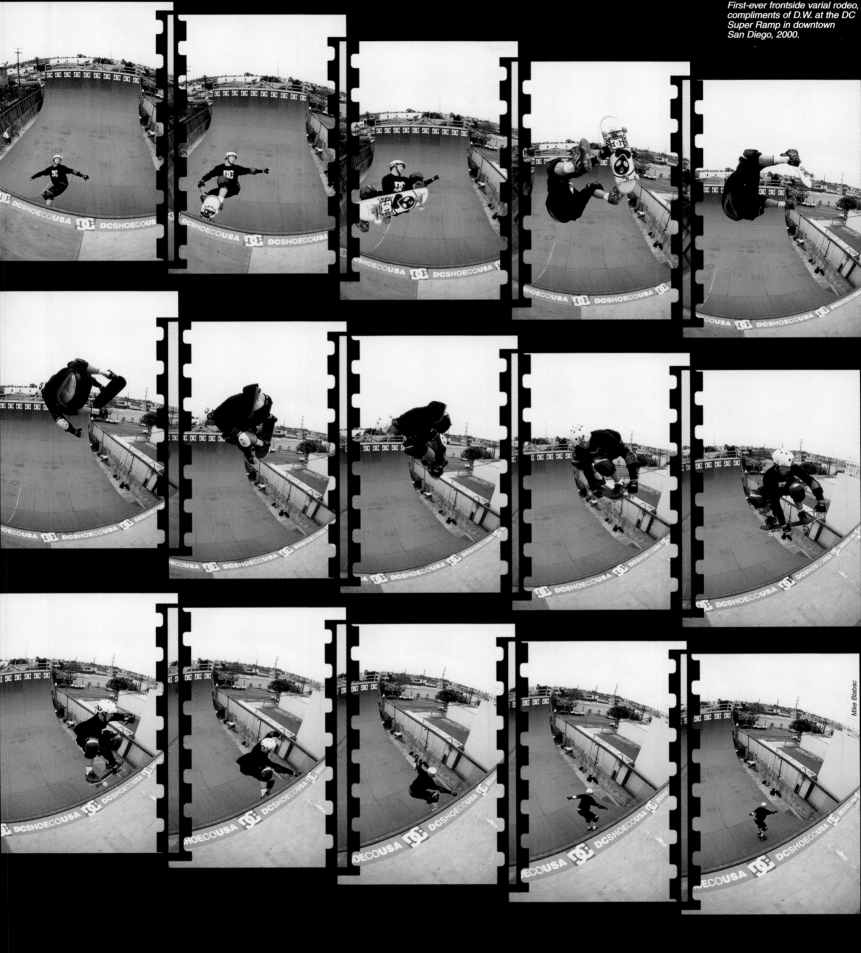

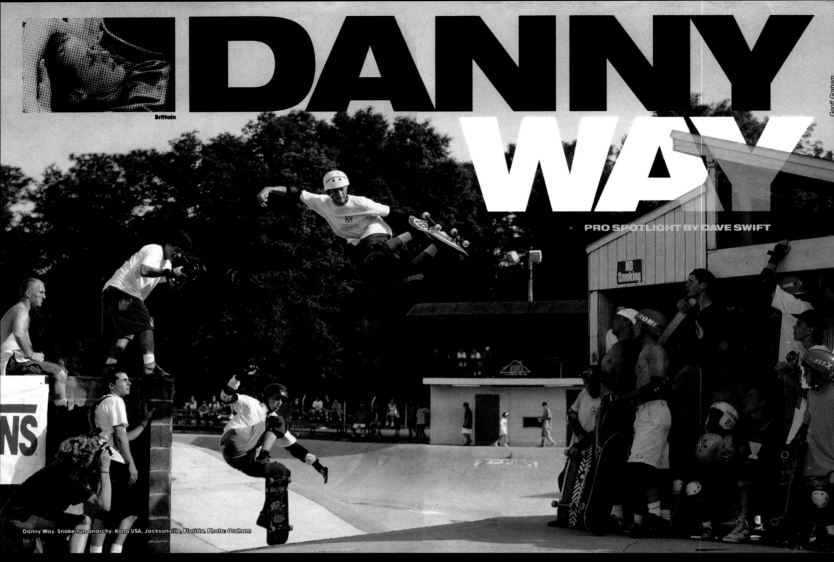

DANNY WAY

Brittain

Geoff Graham

WAY

PRO SPOTLIGHT BY DAVE SWIFT

Danny Way. Snake-run anarchy. Kona USA, Jacksonville, Florida. Photo: Graham
56
57

ABOVE: *Danny Way sessioning with Tony Hawk at Kona Skate Park USA in Jacksonville, Florida.*
This was the opening spread of Danny's first pro spotlight in the October 1991 issue of TransWorld SKATEboarding.

BELOW (LEFT TO RIGHT): *Just a sample of Danny Way's cover presence in the annals of skateboarding history:* Big Brother, *February 2000 (photo by Dan Sturt);* Slap, *May 1995 (photo by Lance Daws);* Thrasher, *December 1991 (photo by Luke Ogden);* TransWorld SKATEboarding, *April 1993 (photo by Grant Brittain); and* Thrasher, *September 1997 (photo by Luke Ogden).*

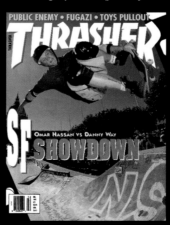
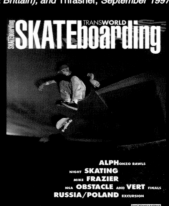

Combine all that with the mystique and salability of Steve Rocco's World Industries—the newly named distributor of Plan B.

The truth is, anyone paying attention to skateboarding in 1992 would have expected this über company to do big things, but no one could have anticipated *Questionable Video*. It essentially redefined what street skating was, ushering in the handrail generation. Kids around the world rewound the tape until it broke. And Danny was unofficially established as skateboarding's reigning king.

Damon, who had mostly recovered from his stroke but was unable to pursue his dreams of turning pro, had started the clothing company Eightball along with Ken Block. Skateboarding was at an all-time low, and finding a paying clothing sponsor was essentially impossible, so fellow Plan B pros were into it when Danny hooked them up with free Eightball gear, even though it was just T-shirts and sweatshirts. This grassroots form of promotion soon paid off. The company's designs appeared on the chests and backs of a new generation of amazing skateboarders.

Had it not been for *Questionable Video, Virtual Reality* (1993) would have been considered equally revolutionary. Danny got the coveted final part, and projected an aura of greatness beyond the huge rails and vert lines featuring back-to-back flip tricks. His posture, attitude, and intensity sent the message that there wasn't anyone he couldn't beat or any trick he couldn't master in an afternoon.

Unfortunately, by 1993, tension within Plan B had divided the company: a random assortment of disgruntled World Industries and Blind pros and amateurs on one side, and Mike Ternasky, Colin McKay, and Danny heading up the other side. Danny believes the rift occurred when certain riders became impatient with Ternasky's vision for the company: "Mike was basically going to set everyone up in the long run, but those guys couldn't wait," says Danny. "They just didn't have the faith. And when they left, they left in such a disrespectful manner. They destroyed Mike's van on purpose, I mean really destroyed it. They poured sugar in the gas tank, ripped up the interior, keyed the side. He [Mike] had done so much for every one of those guys, and they couldn't comprehend that. They really forgot where they'd come from."

Ternasky, Danny, and McKay scrambled to replace the amazing talent they'd lost, and while they would never rebuild Plan B to its original strength, they succeeded in pulling together a strong team. For a while, it was business as usual.

Then tragedy struck. In May 1994, Ternasky was killed in an automobile accident while on his way to work. The news left the skateboard industry shocked and Danny devastated. "My real dad died when I was a baby," he says. "My stepdad was there for my whole life, but my parents got divorced when I was really young, and my mom had a lot of different boyfriends. My stepdad was amazing; he did as much as he could, but I always felt that Mike was like a second dad. It was a really hard loss."

The day before Ternasky died, he and Danny had flown home together from British Columbia's Slam City Jam contest. Ternasky was excited because he had sat down with most of the ex–Plan B pros who'd left to start Girl. The conversation had

D.W.'s first pro contest win at age fourteen: the 1989 Modern Skate Contest at the Lansing Civic Center, Michigan. ABOVE: 360 varial. BELOW: Cab, Indy nosepick.

Mike Blabac

gone well and a huge weight had been lifted off his shoulders. He was excited about skateboarding again and invited Danny to come over the following morning so he could check out some new board graphics. That was the last time Danny saw him alive.

Ternasky left Danny a legacy of business smarts, which he used to run the company along with Colin McKay and Ternasky's widow, Mary, as best he could. Meanwhile, Damon Way and Ken Block's company had scored mass appeal and was starting to get a little too trendy for Danny's taste. He suggested marketing another brand. Enter Droors clothing. Damon and Block began making jeans and using Danny as a front man to parody mainstream companies like Calvin Klein and the GOT MILK? campaign in advertisements. Danny also used his reputation to bring in talented skateboarders and maintained his presence as a behind-the-scenes sounding board for ideas, one of which was Droors Clothing shoes, or DC shoes.

As Droors and then DC grew and prospered, team riders of the highest caliber were added to the company's skate roster—

guys like Rob Dyrdek, Colin McKay, Rudy Johnson, Mike Carroll, and Rick Howard.

Then Danny's life was violently interrupted again.

On a warm June day in 1994, while surfing a south swell in north San Diego County, the twenty-year-old dived off his board and crashed headfirst into a sandbar. The impact forced Danny's chin to his chest, tearing the muscles and ligaments that hold the top two vertebrae in the neck in place. This pinched his spinal cord, which resulted in temporary neurological damage, scrambled brain messages, and some strange side effects. Without warning, his arm would become intensely hot or his eyeballs would twitch in their sockets.

Conventional doctors didn't have the answers. They just told him that there weren't any broken bones, put him in a neck brace, and said he'd have to wait and see what happened. For about a year, the once-limber athlete was "completely rock-solid stiff" from his waist up.

Danny was unable to skate when the time came to create the first DC ad, so Block searched for an alternate way to showcase the

Mike Blabac

Danny Way's method 540, just shy of midnight on the scary, wet DC Super Ramp in downtown San Diego, 2001.

Danny Way pro-model shoe. He decided to focus on the product—a picture of the shoe plastered on a wall—with Danny standing, stiff and in pain, alongside. Outside his close circle of friends and family, few people knew how seriously injured Danny was in this advertisement.

For nearly a year, Danny searched for someone who understood his injury and could help him not only heal properly but also regain his place in skateboarding. After a multitude of bogus exercises and cures, he landed in the office of physical therapist Paul Chek, who is renowned for working with people normal doctors have given up on and who had dealt with cases similar. to Danny's.

Danny's rehabilitation was long and tedious, involving strengthening his neck muscles, regaining mobility, and hundreds of hours of weight lifting, balance work, and chiropractic care. It was ultimately successful. Danny recovered almost completely and learned the importance of fitness to a professional athlete's longevity.

To demonstrate the success of his rehab, Danny showed up at the 1996 Tampa Pro contest and won the vert competition amid the frenzied cheering of spectators and fellow pros alike. The next year, he broke the world's highest air on a skateboard record on DC's Super Ramp (see page 246), and his wife, Keri, gave birth to the couple's son, Ryden.

In 1998, with the pressures of being a father, a professional skateboarder, and a businessman wearing on him, Danny, along with Colin McKay and Mary Ternasky, decided that Plan B should close its doors forever. While closing up shop caused both nostalgia and some questioning about the salability of an older, "injured" skateboarder, the move opened up a world of opportunities that he didn't know were ready to knock on his door.

Danny focused on Alien Workshop, an Ohio-based skateboarding company that had been building its reputation steadily for eight years and had established its most powerful roster ever. Alien's strengths had been built on a strict democratic process in inducting new team members, a process that usually took much deliberation. "In Danny's case," says Alien co-owner Chris Carter, "the decision was made instantaneously and unanimously without question."

The year 1999 saw Danny enter and win the MTV Sports and Music Festival in Las Vegas with a massive fourteen-foot air, even though he'd severely separated his shoulder two days before when dropping into a vert ramp from a hovering helicopter. The win was huge, but just days after the event he underwent surgery to reattach a tendon in his shoulder. The shoulder surgery was

"The first time I saw Danny skate was at the Avalon Gale Webb Skate Demo in Vista in 1987. People had been talking about how rad he was for a little kid, and he was. He skated really hard and slammed super bad one time and started crying, but don't print that because he'll find me and beat me up. He knows where I live."
– Grant Brittain

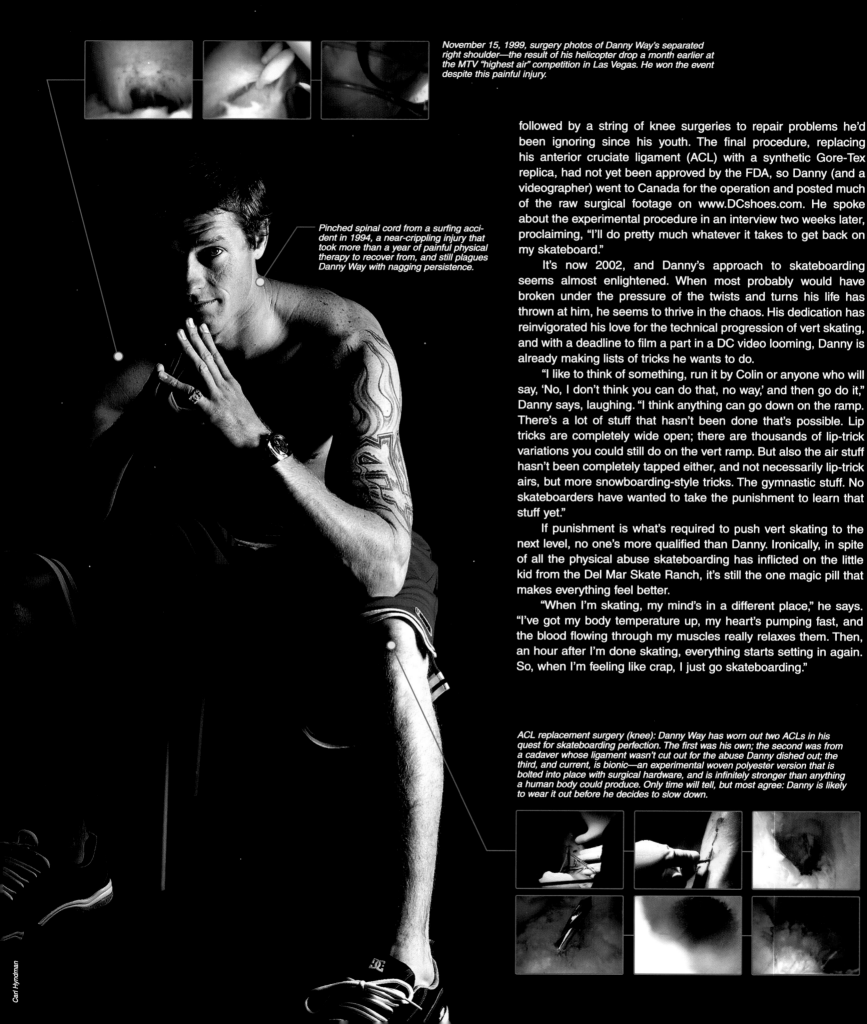

November 15, 1999, surgery photos of Danny Way's separated right shoulder—the result of his helicopter drop a month earlier at the MTV "highest air" competition in Las Vegas. He won the event despite this painful injury.

Pinched spinal cord from a surfing accident in 1994, a near-crippling injury that took more than a year of painful physical therapy to recover from, and still plagues Danny Way with nagging persistence.

followed by a string of knee surgeries to repair problems he'd been ignoring since his youth. The final procedure, replacing his anterior cruciate ligament (ACL) with a synthetic Gore-Tex replica, had not yet been approved by the FDA, so Danny (and a videographer) went to Canada for the operation and posted much of the raw surgical footage on www.DCshoes.com. He spoke about the experimental procedure in an interview two weeks later, proclaiming, "I'll do pretty much whatever it takes to get back on my skateboard."

It's now 2002, and Danny's approach to skateboarding seems almost enlightened. When most probably would have broken under the pressure of the twists and turns his life has thrown at him, he seems to thrive in the chaos. His dedication has reinvigorated his love for the technical progression of vert skating, and with a deadline to film a part in a DC video looming, Danny is already making lists of tricks he wants to do.

"I like to think of something, run it by Colin or anyone who will say, 'No, I don't think you can do that, no way,' and then go do it," Danny says, laughing. "I think anything can go down on the ramp. There's a lot of stuff that hasn't been done that's possible. Lip tricks are completely wide open; there are thousands of lip-trick variations you could still do on the vert ramp. But also the air stuff hasn't been completely tapped either, and not necessarily lip-trick airs, but more snowboarding-style tricks. The gymnastic stuff. No skateboarders have wanted to take the punishment to learn that stuff yet."

If punishment is what's required to push vert skating to the next level, no one's more qualified than Danny. Ironically, in spite of all the physical abuse skateboarding has inflicted on the little kid from the Del Mar Skate Ranch, it's still the one magic pill that makes everything feel better.

"When I'm skating, my mind's in a different place," he says. "I've got my body temperature up, my heart's pumping fast, and the blood flowing through my muscles really relaxes them. Then, an hour after I'm done skating, everything starts setting in again. So, when I'm feeling like crap, I just go skateboarding."

ACL replacement surgery (knee): Danny Way has worn out two ACLs in his quest for skateboarding perfection. The first was his own; the second was from a cadaver whose ligament wasn't cut out for the abuse Danny dished out; the third, and current, is bionic—an experimental woven polyester version that is bolted into place with surgical hardware, and is infinitely stronger than anything a human body could produce. Only time will tell, but most agree: Danny is likely to wear it out before he decides to slow down.

Danny Way, backside noseblunt slide,
using a Ramp Logic funbox for reentry
on the DC indoor training facility in Vista,
California, 2001.

SPECIAL**PROJECTS**

Since skateboarding's inception, footwear has played a role in the self-expression and individuality of the sport. Skateboarders have always found a way to personalize and customize their shoes, whether changing the laces, spray-painting them, or drawing on them with permanent markers.

Using shoes as an outlet for artistic expression took a leap forward with DC's recent development of the Artist and Double Label projects, which honor the creative subcultures that mesh with both skateboarding's lineage and DC's progressive philosophy. The projects allow skateboarding and street artists, musicians, record labels, and retail stores, among others, to express themselves on special-edition DC shoes. Ultimately, they are a way to cross-brand DC shoes with the creative influences surrounding the action sports industry.

The Artist Projects, which began in 2001, includes the work of Shepard Fairey, Thomas Campbell, Kaws, Dave Kinsey, and Phil Frost. The Double Label Projects features collaborations with streetwear boutiques such as Kbond and Supreme and underground record labels like Metalheadz, founded by drum 'n' bass mogul Goldie.

Whether worn or collected, these shoes will no doubt become an integral part of skateboard history.

METALHEADZ

Known the world over as one of drum 'n' bass music's premier producers and DJs, Goldie reworked DC's Manteca using the same eye-catching style that he and the Metalheadz crew embody. This Double Label Projects shoe features timeless skateboarding style, a low-key Metalheadz logo, and a Goldie-endorsed color scheme of contrast and flash.

SHEPARD FAIREY

With DC's running shoe–influenced Swift model as its canvas, the Swift-Obey became the first Artist Projects shoe to be released. The guerrilla-style "sticker" marketing of Shepard Fairey's iconic Obey (Giant) artwork has been seen the world over in subways and on street signs and other urban billboards. For the Artist Projects, Fairey coupled his unique Obey character with a color scheme he handpicked for the sole, insole, and shoe upper. Fairey's artwork is also on the accompanying poster and shoe box.

KAWS

Street artist Kaws emerged from the world of graffiti art to become an internationally known fine artist with a subversive bent. He got his start by borrowing fashion advertisements from New York City bus shelters and phone booths, and "enhancing" them with his own characters and tags in his studio before returning the posters to their rightful places. He has moved on from throw-up tags and posters to canvas painting, sculpture, action figures, and, in 2002, DC's second Artist Projects shoe. Kaws refined his "Companion" character to graphics that fit nicely on the sole, insole, and uppers of the popular Gauge model, rendering this casual shoe a collectible from the guy who got his start, and still finds his inspiration, on the street.

THOMAS CAMPBELL

Painter, illustrator, photographer, filmmaker, and partner of the Galaxia record label, Thomas Campbell is an artist whose work has risen with the skateboard culture. His recognizable style has become a skateboarding subculture mainstay and has filtered into urban artwork collections around the world. Campbell's work set the stage for the third Artist Projects shoe, released in 2002. Using the same Swift model as Shepard Fairey's Swift-Obey, Campbell contrasted his distinct characters and colors with a more subdued shoe upper. The result was a skateable and casual shoe with an innate sense of style.

Right now, today, there's a story to relate about professional skateboarder Colin McKay—this winner of contests, bender of minds, blender of disciplines, this influential man, this Canadi-an.

McKay has landed himself on another cover of another magazine (*TransWorld SKATEboarding,* May 2001) by kickflipping into the roll-in of the uncomfortably tall DC Super Ramp, which is slyly situated near downtown San Diego. After suffering through the longest vertical skating drought his native Vancouver, British Columbia, had ever known, McKay imported himself to the land of eleven-month summers and fully extended über ramps to take care of both the business of skateboarding and skateboarding business.

The relocation to the sunshine state, the photo shoots, the magazine coverage, and the exclusive skate spots are just part of endless todays filled with freeway driving, surfboards hanging from the ceilings of eating establishments, and multiple kickflips off the top of a twenty-six-foot-high wooden platform. No big deal.

Tomorrow he'll okay the design of his ninth signature shoe with DC, whose team he's been on since 1994. The day after tomorrow, he'll shoot yet another television spot, skateboarding for the cameras of Mountain Dew or 1-800-COLLECT. Later in the week he'll push the bounds of technical vert skating in a casual session with vertical front-runners Danny Way, Bob Burnquist, Tony Hawk, or somebody like that. Seriously. For McKay, it's no big deal.

It's been that way since 1986, the year ten-year-old McKay was first introduced to skateboarding by his big brother, Casey. For a while, his BMX bike and skateboard shared equal ground until one day he couldn't remember the last time he'd ridden his bike. Skateboarding had become a way of life, one that exposed him to Canada's first great skateboarding oases in an era that ushered a ton of Canadian talent into the pro ranks.

McKay's talents allowed him to comfortably Tetris into the world of high-profile skateboarding, where he picked his own lines and created tricks for the prolific lens work of Stacy Peralta and his Powell Peralta video productions. Peralta's work of the late eighties and early nineties, which included *The Bones Brigade Video Show, Future Primitive,* and *The Search for Animal Chin,* pioneered the now-common visual medium of hyperreleased skate videos— the skateboard-moviemaking standard required to keep up with the sport's constant progression. Throughout skateboarding's definitive days it was Peralta's mixture of marketing cynicism, humor, and a do-it-yourself aesthetic that outlined skateboarding for a world of scattered but diehard outposts.

In 1988, in the middle of post–*Animal Chin* frenzy, the Richmond Skate Ranch was born in the industrial outskirts of Vancouver. Every one of its hips, spines, and transfers became the backdrop for McKay's boundless talents as well as Peralta's fourth skate production, *Public Domain.* Veteran professional skateboarder and fellow Powell Peralta rider Lance Mountain was one of the many

COLIN**McKAY**
THE REAL DEAL
BY KEVIN WILKINS

hammer swingers responsible for constructing those first Canadian ramp mazes, and he has vivid memories of McKay as a youth brightening up the Skate Ranch warehouse. "This was during a real dry spell in skating and there was a big gap between good and not good," he says. "There were a few guys who were standouts, but there weren't too many little kids that were good. [Colin] definitely stood out."

Other Skate Ranch names like Rob "Sluggo" Boyce, Rick Howard, and Moses Itkonen stood out as well. Says Mountain, "Just having a place accessible to you is what usually does it. You can really see it today. There are so many good kids because there's so much stuff to skate now."

Of course, having a "place" to skate was pivotal to McKay's development. His drive to skate every place he could—British Columbia's weathered bowls and snakeruns, any vertical structure he could get his hands on, and, most notably,

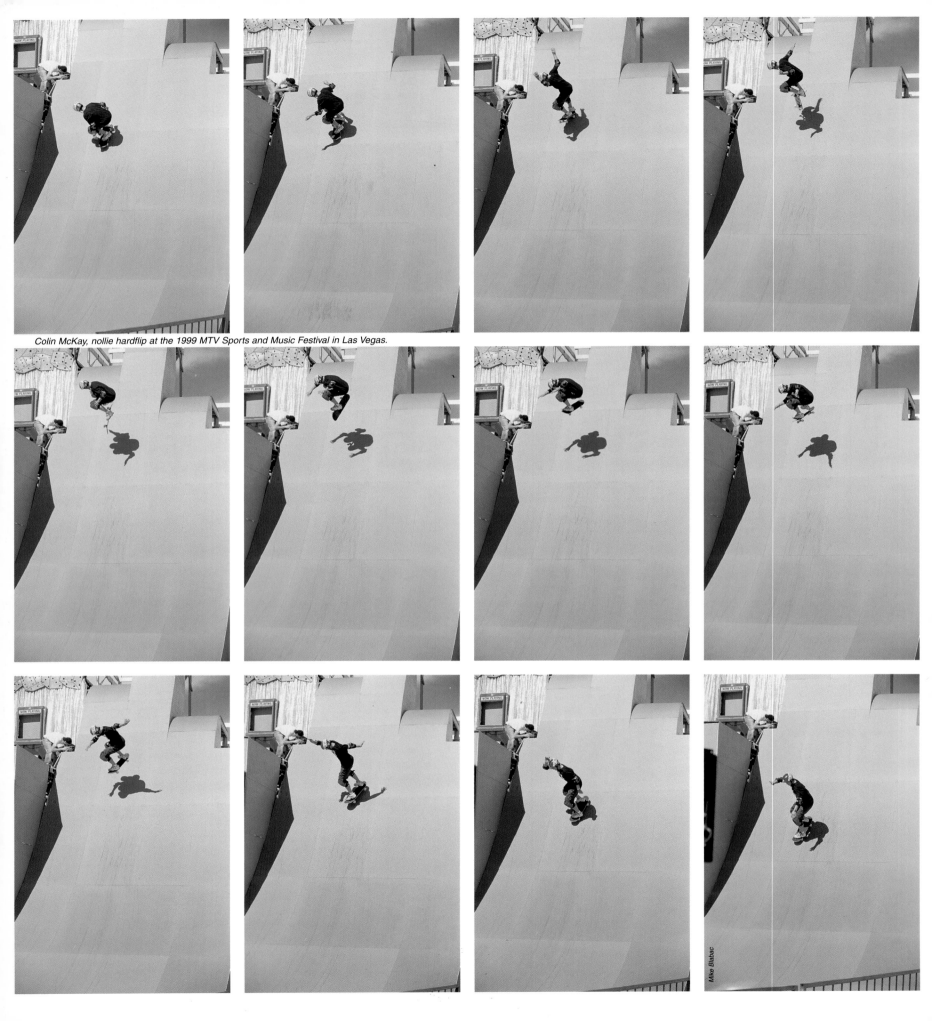

Colin McKay, nollie hardflip at the 1999 MTV Sports and Music Festival in Las Vegas.

Mike Blabac

aggressive attacks on the streets of Vancouver's downtown arena and its unsuspecting security guards—has meant the most to McKay's well-rounded prowess. "I had a purpose as a young guy," says McKay. "Having some activity gives you purpose. It doesn't have to be skateboard-ing; it can be snowboarding, basketball, math. But if you're not doing something, you'll find yourself getting into trouble."

Almost fifty years since that first beautiful union of skate and board, the activity still meets deep institutional and social resistance. The early nineties found McKay and his Canadian peers mastering the good fight, fending off security guards who banned them from certain skate spots and watching angrily as skate parks closed and sponsorship support waned. McKay and his generation of underappreciated and underpaid skaters learned that in order to make anything happen for skateboarding, they were going to have to rely on themselves. So in 1991, after teaching each other and the rest of the world how to change the course of skateboarding (both on the then-uncool transitions of vert and in the street), McKay and his friend Danny Way became teammates on the now-legendary Plan B team, an ensemble of equally talented young guns.

Plan B presented its followers with two of skateboarding's most trailblazing videos: *Questionable Video* and its companion, *Virtual Reality.* Both films are still held in the highest regard for their technical innovations, their no-nonsense documentation, and the sheer volume of new tricks they introduced. "These days, if you mention skate videos, people are going to bring up the Plan B videos," McKay says. "I didn't know they were going to have that kind of impact at the time, but I definitely knew that what the guys on the team were doing was groundbreaking."

Produced during one of skateboarding's erratic growth spurts, the Plan B videos' portrayal of the sport was contrasted sharply by a depressed economy that eventually yanked the rug out from under the entire country, taking the skateboard industry with it. In 1993, Colin McKay and profes-sional skateboarders everywhere found themselves in a tug-of-war between personal growth and skate-boarding's decline.

Times were tough and stakes were high, but in the midst of the boarded-up windows and bankrupt-cies appeared a new kind of company, seemingly oblivious to the carnage around it. This confident assemblage was DC Shoes, a survivor like McKay,

C.M., switch kickflip Indy over the setting sun. Encinitas YMCA, California, 2000.

who immediately said yes when he was asked to help design a signature shoe in his honor.

DC was one of the first companies to create a shoe that skateboarders could use to invest in themselves and the future of skateboarding, which helped inspire McKay to do what he'd wanted to do for years. He dived into a slew of business dealings. Partnerships with friends and family have yielded Center Distribution, a Canadian distributor of skateboards and related accoutrements, and two skate shops, one in Vancouver and one in Encinitas, California (named RDS after McKay and his buddies' Red Dragons, a semigag gang spawned during the tumultuous nineties to protect the kids from the perils they encountered during skate explorations of urban environments). Under McKay's skater-steered business idealism, the ventures have flourished.

But without professional skateboarding, McKay wouldn't have these types of businesses to run, a fact to which the vertical vet is very attuned. The main reason he transferred to north San Diego County—otherwise known as Vert City, USA—in 1997 was to stay on top of his game. On any given night or day, McKay is able to choose among a handful of slow-transitioned Masonite structures: it's the kind of all-access skating that has yielded a string of career highlights, including exposure to pro skateboarders like Tommy Guerrero, Steve Caballero, Tony Hawk, Lance Mountain, and Kevin Harris, whom he credits as some of his early influences.

Nowadays, McKay is in the rare position to return a favor to the world of skateboarding. "It's the same as when Lance [Mountain] came to Richmond," he says, remembering the effect world-class skateboarding had on him. "That had a huge impact on me as a kid and really pushed me to want to go further with skateboarding."

The long trip from being influenced by skateboarding to influencing it back has been a good one for McKay. With his animation of imaginative tricks, his technical advancements, and his natural style, McKay has consistently brought a different approach to the sometimes compulsory feel of the vertical discipline. Admittedly, his main focus is inventing and learning new tricks for documentation in his sponsors' video productions, but even if these are tricks "you wouldn't necessarily be able to do in a contest," McKay says, each one can and does move the sport in ways it's never gone before.

In June 1999 in San Francisco, ESPN hosted its fifth incarnation of the X Games. For McKay, for skateboarding, and for the entire world of sport, this weekend would be forever marked as a turning point, played over and over on the highlight reel of the world's collective memory. Part of the X Games' roster of made-for-television skateboard competition was the "best trick" event: in essence, the world's best skaters attempting the world's most difficult tricks, with the winner determined by a panel of peers.

On this particular weekend, the call was an easy one. In the ultimate showing of control and focus (witnessed by a television audience numbering in the millions), Tony Hawk spun and landed skateboarding's Holy Grail—not just the first-ever televised, not just the first-ever in competition, but the first-*ever* 900. It was this singular event that many have since proclaimed skateboarding's climax, raising the trick meter to a level equal to more established statistic-chasing team sports.

Colin McKay, noseblunt slide.
Encinitas YMCA, California, 2000.

Mike Blabac

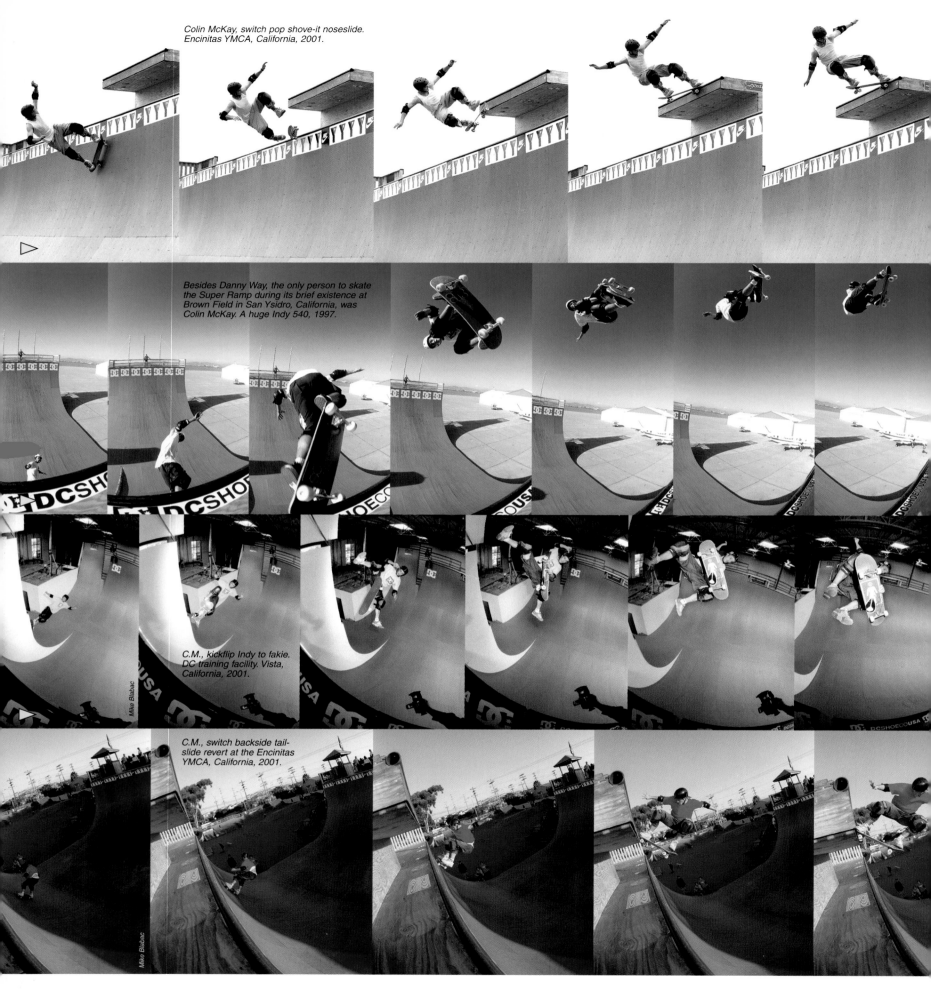

Colin McKay, switch pop shove-it noseslide.
Encinitas YMCA, California, 2001.

Besides Danny Way, the only person to skate
the Super Ramp during its brief existence at
Brown Field in San Ysidro, California, was
Colin McKay. A huge Indy 540, 1997.

Mike Blabac

C.M., kickflip Indy to fakie.
DC training facility. Vista,
California, 2001.

C.M., switch backside tailslide revert at the Encinitas
YMCA, California, 2001.

Mike Blabac

Mike Blabac

Grant Brittain

skateboarding

Jamie Mosberg

December 1993 U.S. $3.50 Canada $4.00

12

0 71486 01548 2

northwest on fire

**jason adams speaks, rodney mullen, too.
vegas, greece, and some other poo.**

*The caption for this December 1993 TransWorld SKATEboarding cover
read: "On the cover this month we have Colin McKay doing a switch-stance
crooked grind while a building goes up in smoke behind him." It doesn't
mention the two speeding tickets photographer Mosberg got en route.*

TRANSWORLD

Skateboarding

Colin McKay
kickflip in
San Diego, CA

Jody Morris

Brian Wenning
East Coast Thunder

7-Day War
Bring Your Skills To The Battle

FDR Soldiers
Skate Free Or Die

May 2001
U.S. $3.99 CANADA $4.99

0 5>

0 09281 01548 2

skateboarding.com

*The May 2001 TransWorld SKATEboarding
cover. C.M. kickflips into the massive roll-in of
the DC Super Ramp in downtown San Diego.*

Colin McKay, Cab one-foot at Tony Hawk's
Fallbrook, California, ramp in 1989.

That history-making day was also important for many other skaters in the X Games "best trick" event, one of whom was McKay. "That's probably one of the best sessions I've ever had in my life," he says, going over a list of street-influenced combinations that on any other day would easily have yielded him a first-place check. "I did a backside nollie-flip revert. I did a frontside Caballerial kickflip. I did a switch pop shove-it tailslide to switch shove-it out. And then I did a backside tailslide to big spin out." But aside from his in-the-zone performance, it was his involvement with somebody else's moment of glory that he found truly special.

And ironically, it's McKay's ability to recognize and appreciate the achievements of others while looking upon his own as "no big deal" that Tony Hawk himself admires. In his book, *Hawk: Occupation: Skateboarder,* Hawk breaks it down:

"In skateboarding, people are almost uniformly indifferent about their accomplishments and contest records. But somebody like Colin McKay, who could easily walk away with the winner's trophy (and has many times), doesn't care too much if he doesn't even make the cut to the finals. Contests are not a measuring tool for a skater's abilities. His sponsors don't care about his contest placings (they're happy if he does well, but if he doesn't, you won't ever see them bawling him out) because skaters respect the guy . . ."

Respect. At the end of the day, that's the one thing many skateboarders cherish more than a paycheck. It's a hard-won reward that goes hand in hand with skaters who have influenced others while on their own journeys to perfection. These roads are filled with humbling lessons that eventually reveal a game plan not only for skateboarding, but also for life.

"Don't get too down when things are bad, and when things are going great, try to keep it in perspective," says McKay about his own lessons learned. "An example of that is the first Slam City Jam [1993]. I won the contest in my hometown. It was one of my first contests. I won the thing in front of my parents, with my brother there, you know, my whole family. Skated great—second in street, first in vert. Probably, to that point, the best day I'd ever had in my entire life, and the next day, one of my best friends dies in a car accident.

"I just try to live each day, try to be a good person, and try to treat others how I'd like to be treated. Just enjoy yourself and don't take yourself too seriously."

This is an attitude that lends itself perfectly to McKay's sense of humor. During Tony Hawk's Super Tour, McKay was the motivator, getting the show on the road every morning by blasting what became the tour's unofficial theme song, Daft Punk's "One More Time." "Every morning, Colin was up, cranking that song and dancing," says Matt Goodman, the show's director. "Serious boy band moves, and let me tell you, he can dance."

The joke escalated in North Carolina during a rainstorm, when those in the tour bus were trying to figure out what they should do so they wouldn't disappoint the 2,000 fans who'd shown up. "That's when Colin stood up and said, 'I know what I'm gonna do,'" says Goodman. McKay went out on stage in front of the skateboarders, put on "One More Time" at high volume and started dancing. In a few minutes he had everybody dancing. "That's Colin. He just doesn't care."

His is a philosophy that highlights tomorrow's goals, remembers yesterday's struggles, but lives for today, and all with a sense of humor. Above all, McKay is a professional, both an ambassador of and a true believer in the sport of skateboarding.

Thirteen-year-old Colin McKay, frontside ollie stalefish at the Richmond Skate Ranch. Vancouver, Canada, 1989.

Grant Brittain

A young C.M. saw Chris Miller on a TransWorld cover doing this same trick, so he couldn't help but emulate the master with his own frontside version at the Selynn Bowl. North Vancouver, Canada, 1988.

Grant Brittain

ABOVE: Colin McKay, fakie 540 one-foot tailgrab. DC indoor training facility in Vista, California, 2001.

ABOVE: C.M., switchflip, downtown Vancouver, Canada, 1995.

ABOVE: C.M., 540 out of the Griffin Bowl. North Vancouver, Canada, 1995.

ABOVE: C.M., kickflip, downtown Vancouver, Canada, 1994.

ABOVE: C.M., superlong backside 50-50 at the indoor DC training facility. Vista, California, 2001.

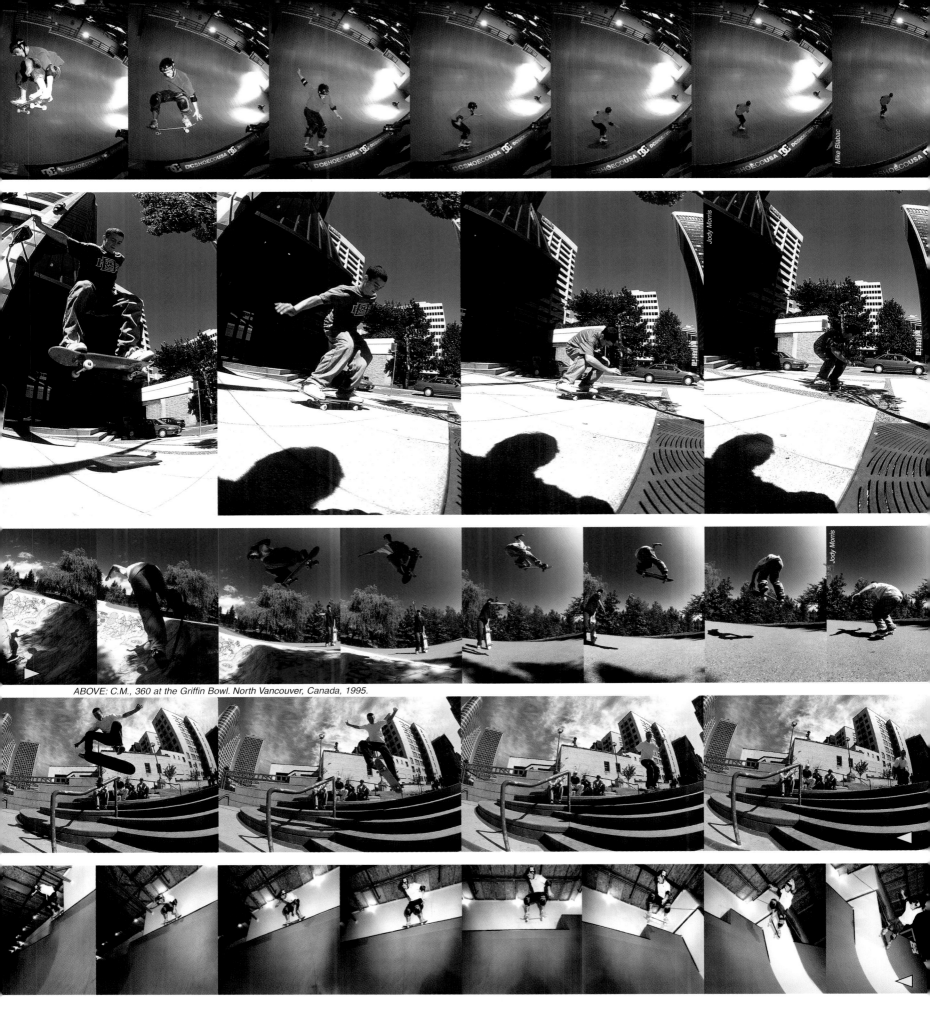

ABOVE: C.M., 360 at the Griffin Bowl. North Vancouver, Canada, 1995.

CELEBRITY SIGHTINGS

Continuing in the footsteps of Eightball grassroots marketing via Cypress Hill and Droors sightings on the Beastie Boys, Green Day, Foo Fighters, and Sonic Youth, DC has gathered its own eclectic following.

DC has been seen on or flowed to (among others): Jennifer Aniston, Courteney Cox Arquette, David Arquette, Beck, Eric Clapton, Deftones, Philly's Dieselboy, Dub Pistols, Goldie, Greyboy, Helmet, Fenix TX, Incubus, Jurassic 5, Korn, Limp Bizkit, Linkin Park, Alyssa Milano, Brad Pitt, P.O.D., Primus, Rage Against the Machine, Red Hot Chili Peppers, Rocket From the Crypt, Adam Sandler, Sum 41, System of a Down, Tha Liks, and The Chemical Brothers.

During the Beastie Boys' Hello Nasty Tour, the band donned DC shoes as part of their one-piece work suit "stage outfits." Fred Durst of Limp Bizkit wore a DCSHOECOUSA tee while crowd-surfing at Woodstock 2000; Adam Sandler had on a DCSHOECO sweatshirt for an appearance on Jay Leno and another at the June 2000 MTV Movie Awards when accepting his "best comedic performance" award for *Big Daddy;* Staind singer Aaron Lewis was in a DC T-shirt during MTV's *Rock and Roll Hall of Fame,* August 2001. DC has also shown up in various prime-time television shows and feature films.

These appearances in the public eye are important elements to success. Without the media, DC wouldn't be close to the icon it has become. Above all, however, DC's owners consider the most important people wearing their shoes and clothing to be the kids on the street, on the dirt, in the mountains, or in the water, perfecting their own game.

(1) J-Ro of Tha Liks during a studio session. Los Angeles, 2001. (2) Brain of Guns N Roses during a recording session. Los Angeles, 2001. (3) Actor Paul Walker at the DC warehouse, 2001. (4) Danny Way, Colin McKay, and fellow skateboarder Jason Ellis with Phoenix and Mike Shinoda of Linkin Park at House of Blues. Los Angeles, 2002. (5) Goldie, 2000. (6) The X-ecutioners (Roc Raida, Rob Swift, Mista Sinista, Total Eclipse). Salt Lake City, 2001. (7) Travis Barker of Blink 182 during a DC photo shoot, 2002. (8) Adam Sandler at the MTV Movie Awards in Los Angeles, 2001. (9) Sonny and Wuv of P.O.D. during their video shoot for "Alive." Huntington Beach, California, 2001. (10) Adam Sandler at his Happy Madison Productions office in Los Angeles, 2001. (11) Danny Way, Rob Dyrdek, and Trainwreck with Fred Durst of Limp Bizkit. During the "Break Stuff" video shoot in 2000.

1	2	3	7	8	9	10
4	5	6		11		

SNOWBOARDING
JUST ADD WINTER

BY ERIC BLEHM AND LEE CRANE

Nineteen sixty-five was a big year. In March, Soviet cosmonaut Aleksei Leonov became the first man to walk in space. By fall, the Beach Boys had sold 12 million albums, miniskirts had seduced America, and Watts, California, threw a block party that wouldn't be surpassed until the 1992 Los Angeles riots. On the other side of the Pacific, the United States had officially entered the Vietnam War.

On December 25, two weeks before *Time* magazine named General William Childs Westmoreland its "Person of the Year" for being "the sinewy personification of the American fighting man," a quiet, thin, industrial gases engineer, Sherman Poppen, built something in his Muskegon, Michigan, garage that would change the face of winter forever.

Josh Dirksen eyes the landing of this cool and composed frontside underflip at the world-famous Mount Baker road gap. Washington, 2000.

Kevin Zacker

ABOVE: This skier-built monster gap would have been difficult to clear with a straight jump. Josh Dirksen's lofty 100-foot backside 900 looks effortless. Grizzly Gulch, Utah, 2001.
BELOW: Long and scary switch frontside boardslide. Jason Murphy in Salt Lake City, Utah, 2001.

BELOW: Eddie Wall (nominated as TransWorld SNOWboarding's 2002 "rookie of the year"), gap to frontside boardslide. A Mammoth, California, secret spot, 2001.

Torey Piro

▶

Ethan Stone

Poppen, a landlocked surfing wanna-be, looked at his neighborhood sledding hill and saw a wave, so he went into his garage, picked out a pair of his kids' snow skis, and screwed them together with some dowling "to act as foot stops." He gave the invention to his daughter, Wendy, and she took it up to said hill. The hill was already crowded with all manner of snow-sliding devices, but when the other kids saw Wendy snurfing on the Snurfer (snow + surfer), they all wanted one of their own. The idea was patented and sold to mega sporting goods manufacturer Brunswick, which in turn sold millions to the forefathers of those who would become today's snowboarders.

While it could be argued that the Snurfer was not technically a snowboard because it had no bindings, it was what got Jake Burton Carpenter hooked on "snurfboarding." Winterstick's founder, Dimitrije Milovich, was reportedly inspired by surfing, but used ski engineering to further advance the "wintersticking" technology that enabled him to ride big-mountain terrain. Tom Sims mass-produced a skateboard deck on top of a molded plastic base and called his version "skiboarding."

Regardless of the name, Poppen got the idea rolling at a mass-market level, and Jake "Burton" followed through to become the largest manufacturer of "snowboards" after Poppen told him he couldn't use the name "Snurfboard."

So, modern-day snowboarding can be fairly accurately traced as a bastard son to surfing and, ultimately, skateboarding. In 1979, Mark Anolik discovered the Tahoe City Halfpipe while looking for new terrain behind the Tahoe City, California, dump. The glorified gully with one hit became known as the world's first snow halfpipe. It attracted the likes of the father of freestyle snowboarding himself, Terry Kidwell, his friend Keith Kimmel, and photographers from skateboard magazines, who related to snowboarding the second they witnessed Kidwell's tweaked-out backside airs. In fact, much of the skate community related to snowboarding both because of the tricks and because of its early ban at nearly all ski areas worldwide (supposedly due to safety concerns regarding unsatisfactory equipment).

In time, however, equipment improved, but it was the almighty dollar that won out as more and more kids chose snowboarding over skiing. Still, many resorts persisted, claiming their "no snowboarding" policies were warranted because of "unsafe equipment." Most snowboarders saw this as blatant prejudice, and chuckled inside when nearly all these resorts backpeddled and built snowboard terrain parks and halfpipes to attract a new generation of

Carl Hyndman

Travis Parker stepped it up with a frontside 180 to switch 50-50 to frontside Cab off for a $1,000 "best trick" contest during DC's Decadence Tour. Alta, Utah, 2001.

(1) Josh Dirksen, Todd Richards, Jason Murphy, and Travis Parker—DC's 2001 Decadence Tour in Utah.

(2) Kim Bohnsack, DC's first sponsored female, headed to Australia and found that this Mount Hotham boardslide was perfect rehab for a blown knee, 2001.

(3) Travis Parker, clean and serene switch backside 720. Mount Baker, Washington, 2001.

(4) Nice big quarterpipes are perfect for extra-large underflips. Josh Dirksen concurs. Mount Hood, Oregon, 2000.

(5) One of Josh Dirksen's favorite tricks: a nice, mellow method at Mount Hood, Oregon, 2000.

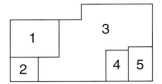

Carl Hyndman

Scott Serfas

Nate Christiansen

Cory Grove

Cory Grove

SNOWBOARD CAMPS
USSTC.NET
SNOWBOARD CAMPS

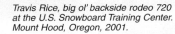

Travis Rice, big ol' backside rodeo 720 at the U.S. Snowboard Training Center. Mount Hood, Oregon, 2001.

snowsliders, who subsequently pulled dozens of resorts out of an economic gutter.

DC's owners were snowboarding well before the company's inception. During the Eightball and Droors era, Ken Block and Damon Way translated their skateboarding style of clothing to the mountain by sewing together the first baggy water-resistant nylon jeans—and making the mistake of wearing them to a TransWorld Snowboarding Industry Conference where competitors took note. Then they constructed ultratechnical outerwear via Dub, published progressive freestyle documentation within the slick and nasty pages of *Blunt* snowboard magazine, and formed close ties with Type A snowboards—all of which led up to designing snowboard boots that would further the scope and reputation of DC's skateboard shoes.

The resulting boots attracted more skate-influenced snowboarders, some of whom became DC's first snowboard team in 1997. Today, team rid-

ers like Olympian Todd Richards and freestyle film star Scotty Wittlake are equally at home on a skateboard, along with Josh Dirksen and others who translate their freestyle skateboarding abilities to big mountains and freeride terrain or, depending on their mood, halfpipe and jib parks. The key link among all DC riders, like all DC sports, is progression and creativity.

Fittingly, no other board sport born in America, or the world for that matter, offers a wider range of unique settings to push the envelope of fun, be it a crowded New York City street after a midwinter dump; a desolate, steep, and hairy Alaskan peak; a finely groomed halfpipe in SoCal; a kicker built in the back of a trailer park in Minnesota; or, oh yeah, that sledding hill in Muskegon, Michigan, where fate met desire back in 1965.

The sport itself hasn't stopped evolving since then. In fact, its only constant ingredient has been snow.

And even that's optional.

SNOWBOARD BOOTS
ANATOMY OF A REVOLUTION

DC's snowboard boot campaign began in 1998 with the creation of its first high-performance boot, the Serum, by Ken Block. The following year DC introduced its first women's snowboard boot, the Petra, which expanded upon a new generation of snowboard footwear specifically designed to fit a woman's foot.

From conceptualization to production, DC boots incorporate skate-style aesthetics and functionality that make them some of the most durable and versatile boots in the industry. DC took this a step further in 2000 with the development of a patented air bladder system, available in the Revolution—built to be the lightest, most formfitting boot on the market. This air bladder technology evenly distributes air around the ankle and heel, eliminating heel lift and ensuring proper comfort and a custom fit while riding.

So popular was the Revolution that in winter 2001 the air bladder was incorporated into the Revolution2 and the men's Phantom and women's Eris, which had evolved from the Serum and Petra. DC's snowboard boot line continues to revolutionize the industry by consistently producing technically progressive, high-performance, quality products that set the curve in freestyle fashion but maintain the support necessary for freeriding the most demanding terrain.

Though DC prides itself as a skateboard shoe manufacturer, its snowboard boots are found cut open and dissected in the research and development labs of its competitors—veteran boot company designers who continue to look to DC as an innovator in all aspects of footwear.

SERUM
FIRST RELEASED: 1998

PREMIER
FIRST RELEASED: 1999

REVOLUTION
FIRST RELEASED: 2000

STRATUS
FIRST RELEASED: 2002

PHANTOM
FIRST RELEASED: 2001

THE INSIDE OUT

Underneath the skateboard shoe aesthetics of DC's snowboard boot line is a highly technical snowboard boot designed for snowboarders' various needs. The refined DC look never interferes with function: comfort, warmth, traction, and support.

CIRRUS
AEROGEL LINER

Like a cloud custom-fitted to the foot, the Cirrus Aerogel Liner's technology is the pinnacle of DC's liner program. A patented inflatable air bladder molds itself to the foot, and a silicone gel pad in the toe cushions impact.

HEATED INSOLE

Using licensed technology from Heat Factory, Inc., DC has taken comfort a step further with a removable heat pack, which sits in the insole of the boot and provides warmth in even the most treacherous weather conditions.

JOULE GEL LINER

A big, spongy pillow, the Joule liner has patent-pending silicone gel pads in the heel and toe to absorb the shock of impact, and rubber patches on the heel and calf to minimize slippage in the boot.

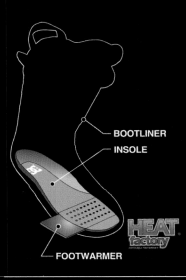

- BOOTLINER
- INSOLE
- FOOTWARMER

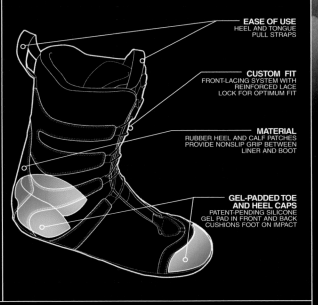

EASE OF USE
HEEL AND TONGUE
PULL STRAPS

CUSTOM FIT
FRONT-LACING SYSTEM WITH
REINFORCED LACE
LOCK FOR OPTIMUM FIT

MATERIAL
RUBBER HEEL AND CALF PATCHES
PROVIDE NONSLIP GRIP BETWEEN
LINER AND BOOT

**GEL-PADDED TOE
AND HEEL CAPS**
PATENT-PENDING SILICONE
GEL PAD IN FRONT AND BACK
CUSHIONS FOOT ON IMPACT

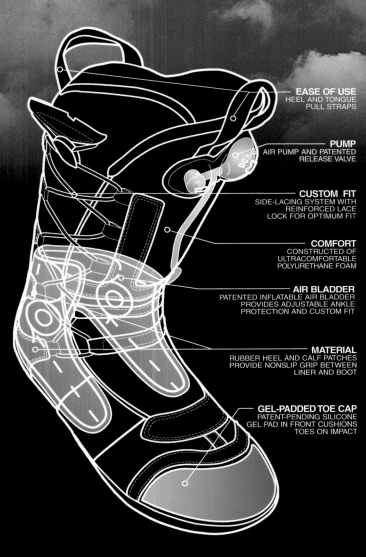

EASE OF USE
HEEL AND TONGUE
PULL STRAPS

PUMP
AIR PUMP AND PATENTED
RELEASE VALVE

CUSTOM FIT
SIDE-LACING SYSTEM WITH
REINFORCED LACE
LOCK FOR OPTIMUM FIT

COMFORT
CONSTRUCTED OF
ULTRACOMFORTABLE
POLYURETHANE FOAM

AIR BLADDER
PATENTED INFLATABLE AIR BLADDER
PROVIDES ADJUSTABLE ANKLE
PROTECTION AND CUSTOM FIT

MATERIAL
RUBBER HEEL AND CALF PATCHES
PROVIDE NONSLIP GRIP BETWEEN
LINER AND BOOT

GEL-PADDED TOE CAP
PATENT-PENDING SILICONE
GEL PAD IN FRONT CUSHIONS
TOES ON IMPACT

BOA LACING SYSTEM

The licensed BOA system allows for precise and effortless fit adjustments. To tighten, simply push in the knob and rotate clockwise. To loosen, pull out the knob and push tongue forward.

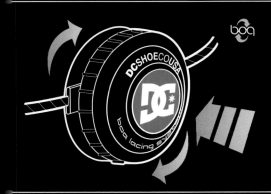

TIGHTEN   LOOSEN

OTHER FEATURES

**IMPROVED
LACE LOCKS**
KEEP LACES IN PLACE AND ADD
SECURITY FOR A BETTER FIT

**SHOCK-ABSORBING GEL
HEEL SYSTEM**
ADDS AN EXTRA BARRIER TO HELP
DISSIPATE THE EFFECTS OF IMPACT.

**IMPROVED
LACE ROLLERS**
ENABLE QUICK TIGHTENING OF
THE CORD LACES AND RESIST
RUST AND CORROSION

AIR BAG
PROVIDES PROTECTION FOR HEEL BY
ABSORBING IMPACT

TODD
RICHARDS
REINVENTING HIMSELF

BY JOEL MUZZEY

All the leaves have fallen from the trees. An autumn breeze carries a chill, and the light of day is fading. Youth Brigade cranks from a battered radio while Wachusett High sophomore Todd Richards, alone on a backyard skateboard ramp of plywood and pool coping, gives himself three more tries to make the trick, and then he's heading home.

Richards's wheels sing as he sets up with a backside air. He goes frontside on the next wall, floats, and drops his tail on the coping with a smack like a home-run hit. Made it. Finger-flip lien to tail . . . finally. But one make doesn't make it clean, so Richards catches his breath, now visible in the cold, and takes another run. Always another run.

In Massachusetts, where winters are long and brutal, the warm—i.e., skate—season is always too short for someone like Richards. But in 1987, at the age of seventeen, he discovered in the back-of-the-book advertising section of *Thrasher* magazine a way to stay sane: a new pastime called snowboarding. That winter he took his skating to the ski slopes—strapped into a snowboard and began making the same solitary promises he'd made to himself while skating. Get the tricks down, one by one.

"When I tried it, I seriously hated it, because it was really wet, and I couldn't do a damn thing on the snowboard," Richards says. "I thought I was going to be able to do all the tricks I could do on my skateboard, straight off. I was wrong. I fell on my head. I ended up cold and miserable."

But a few less-than-epic days spent struggling with the mechanics of riding an all-wood board at a snow-covered local golf course weren't enough to deter him. After two trips to ski areas in New Hampshire and Vermont with his folks (both avid skiers), it was all skateboarding—minus the wheels.

Rich Van Every

Todd Richards during the post-Morrow era, fishing for a new sponsor. This space wasn't vacant for long. Rossignol picked him up a few days after this photo was taken in 2001.

Todd Richards, alley-oop backside
air at the first Grand Prix Olympic
qualifier. Mammoth, California, 2001.

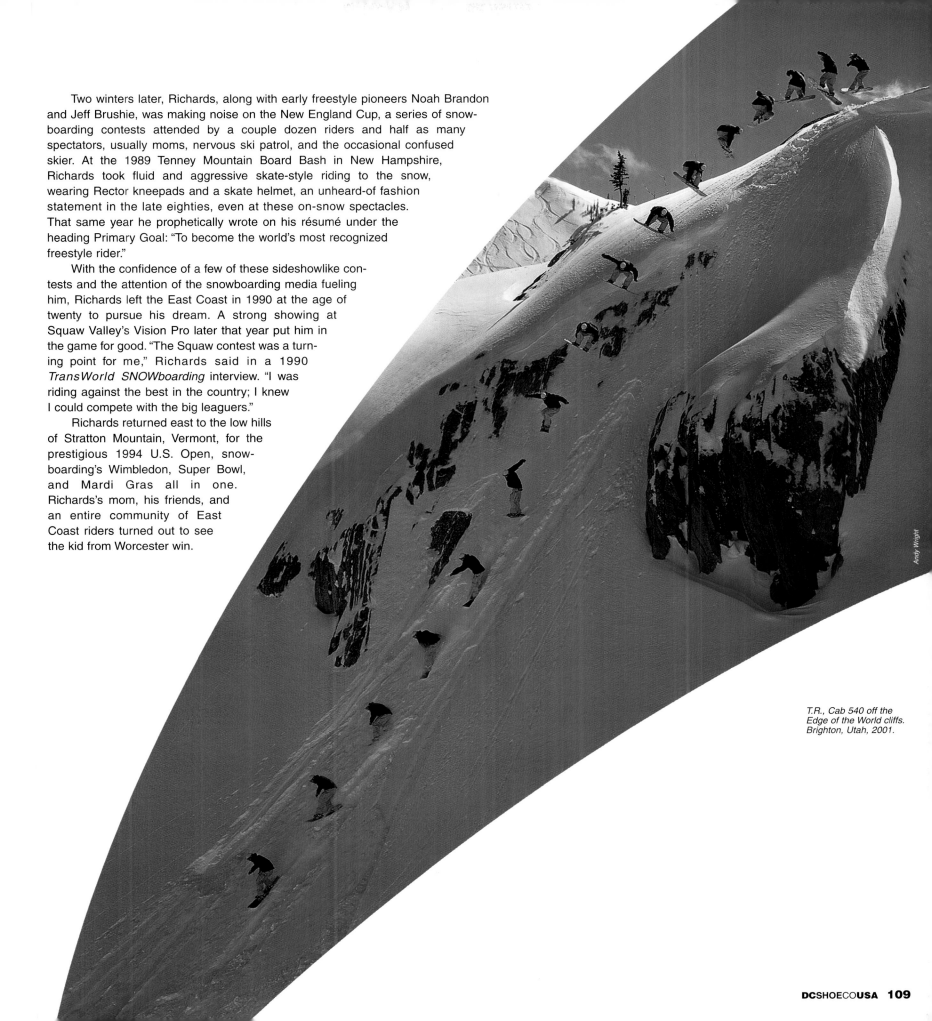

Two winters later, Richards, along with early freestyle pioneers Noah Brandon and Jeff Brushie, was making noise on the New England Cup, a series of snowboarding contests attended by a couple dozen riders and half as many spectators, usually moms, nervous ski patrol, and the occasional confused skier. At the 1989 Tenney Mountain Board Bash in New Hampshire, Richards took fluid and aggressive skate-style riding to the snow, wearing Rector kneepads and a skate helmet, an unheard-of fashion statement in the late eighties, even at these on-snow spectacles. That same year he prophetically wrote on his résumé under the heading Primary Goal: "To become the world's most recognized freestyle rider."

With the confidence of a few of these sideshowlike contests and the attention of the snowboarding media fueling him, Richards left the East Coast in 1990 at the age of twenty to pursue his dream. A strong showing at Squaw Valley's Vision Pro later that year put him in the game for good. "The Squaw contest was a turning point for me," Richards said in a 1990 *TransWorld SNOWboarding* interview. "I was riding against the best in the country; I knew I could compete with the big leaguers."

Richards returned east to the low hills of Stratton Mountain, Vermont, for the prestigious 1994 U.S. Open, snowboarding's Wimbledon, Super Bowl, and Mardi Gras all in one. Richards's mom, his friends, and an entire community of East Coast riders turned out to see the kid from Worcester win.

Andy Wright

T.R., Cab 540 off the Edge of the World cliffs. Brighton, Utah, 2001.

Trevor Graves

(1) *Todd Richards McTwists his way through practice day at the 1998 Olympic Games in Nagano, Japan.*

(2) *T.R., tuck-knee invert, zero gravity. Nashua, New Hampshire, 1991.*

(3) *T.R. exhibiting the epitome of mute-air style at Stratton Mountain, Vermont, in 1989. Check those massive pipe walls.*

(4) *T.R., lofty backside 540. Breckenridge, Colorado, 1999.*

(5) *T.R. took fourth in his specialty, the "two-foot-high pipe." 1990 Op Pro at Mont Avila, Quebec, Canada.*

(6) *Another fourth for T.R. at the 1990 U.S. Open, Stratton Mountain, Vermont. Behind the who's who of veteran freestylers (right to left)—Craig Kelly, Shaun Palmer, Jeff Brushie, T.R., and that's Jimmy Scott with the smooth Ugg boots.*

1	2	3	4	7	8	
					9	
6		5		11		10

Trevor Graves

Jeff Potto

Trevor Graves

Shem Roose

Chris Owen

(7) T.R., method at the 2000 Vans Triple Crown of Snowboarding,
Breckenridge, Colorado.

(8) T.R. got hooked up by New Deal Skateboards in 1991. Backside tweaker at Jamaica
Jim's skate park in Denver, Colorado.

(9) Melon grab in New Zealand, 1994: T.R.'s best trip ever with his first pro model board, a
Morrow with dinosaur graphics.

(10) Method at the 1999 Mount Snow, Vermont, X Games. Best-ever contest for T.R., who
took first place with his mom watching pipeside.

(11) T.R., frontside air in Marseille, France. On a fun European road trip from Münich,
Germany, to Valencia, Spain, in 1998.

Carl Hyndman

Carl Hyndman

"This rail was massive. I was nervous until I took one to the dome, and it knocked the butterflies out of me." – Todd Richards, half-Cab boardslide near Alta, Utah, 2000.

Carl Hyndman

FUJI RVP

The pipe was glazed and choppy from all-day eliminations during which competitors vied for glory and cash in front of a fired-up Vermont crowd. Richards nailed back-to-back 720s, a feat no snowboarder had pulled off in a competitive format, and instantly became the East Coast champion. This victory, one of two he would earn at the internationally respected U.S. Open, was a hallmark in an unbelievable laundry list of competitive successes. It was one of his best-ever days of riding and a lifetime goal that cemented his name and signature style in the hearts and minds of snowboarding fans worldwide. Still, Richards wanted to go bigger and higher, with a secret goal of an Olympic medal.

While pipes of old allowed for a few hard-earned overhead airs near the top, modern competition halfpipes have evolved to over four hundred feet long and roughly fifteen feet deep with perfectly sculpted transitions and several feet of vertical. Ever-improving construction techniques allow riders to go bigger, faster, consistently overhead, with inverted rotations, all of which have caught the attention of MTV, ESPN, and major television networks. Richards had risen to the top of the snowboard media food chain. He was, and still is, featured annually in top snowboard films, on dozens of magazine covers and signature model snowboards, and in video games and as action figures. His life consisted of nonstop global travel for photo shoots and films, rigorous competition schedules, the physical punishment of riding over two hundred days a year—and the spoils. His home outside Boulder, Colorado, housed his almost fetishistic toy collection, an outdoor Jacuzzi, and a sporty 1998 Porsche 911 Carrera 2S.

When rumor turned to reality and the snowboard halfpipe became part of the 1998 Winter Olympics in Nagano, Japan, Richards had another chance to take it further. But although he was the odds-on favorite going into Nagano, his Olympic debut fell victim to the "bad day" factor, and a random fall in the pipe took him out of the running.

Richards's frustration with his finish in Japan was short-lived. He came back the next season with a plan: to ride harder and better but slow down his competition schedule. It was a time for re-evaluation, a time for shutting out the hype and getting back to riding just for fun. Since then, he's logged dozens of victories and thousands of vertical feet, reinventing his game plan over and over again, with no sign of letting up.

The ongoing relationship between Richards and DC has been another natural step in his progression. "DC knows what they are doing," he says. "So well, in fact, that I don't even have to think about it. They transfer their skate influence into snowboard boots, which is exactly where I'm coming from. That makes it easy for me to concentrate on riding."

From pass-the-hat cash purses to six-figure payoffs, from waist-high banks of ice to the modern, perfectly sculpted Superpipe, from duct tape and dungarees to bona fide product advancements, Richards has seen it all. But while many top pros of his generation have taken their game out of competition and into the backcountry, Richards has stood by his sport with a good attitude and an ever-expanding bag of tricks, matching its exponential growth with his own progression. The same mind-set that kept him on the ramp until dark keeps him hiking to the top of unforgiving icy halfpipes, season after season. Says veteran snowboard photographer Jon Foster, "Todd Richards is the hardest-working man in the business. He started out as a shy kid, but has become one of the most consistent and confident riders the sport has ever seen."

On June 17, 2001 (Father's Day), Richards's wife, Linsey, gave birth to Camden Thorne Richards, heir to a legend. Camden's father is one of the—if not the—most defining and recognized figures in freestyle snowboarding.

INSET PHOTOS (LEFT TO RIGHT):
Super-icy backside lipslide. T.R. at The Canyons, Utah, 2001.

T.R. indulges: the Decadence Tour at its finest. Heli-boarding in Utah, 2001.

The world's worst frontside hit was discovered in the Utah backcountry during DC's 2001 Decadence Tour. T.R. makes it look way better than it was—the mark of a true professional.

T.R. portrait, Utah backcountry, 2001.

This long, splintered rail was rickety and in front of some-one's house near Lake Tahoe, California, so Scotty Wittlake figured he only had a few chances to nail it. The result: a clean boardslide and the poster boy for Kingpin Productions' 2001 movie, Brainstorm.

Andy Wright

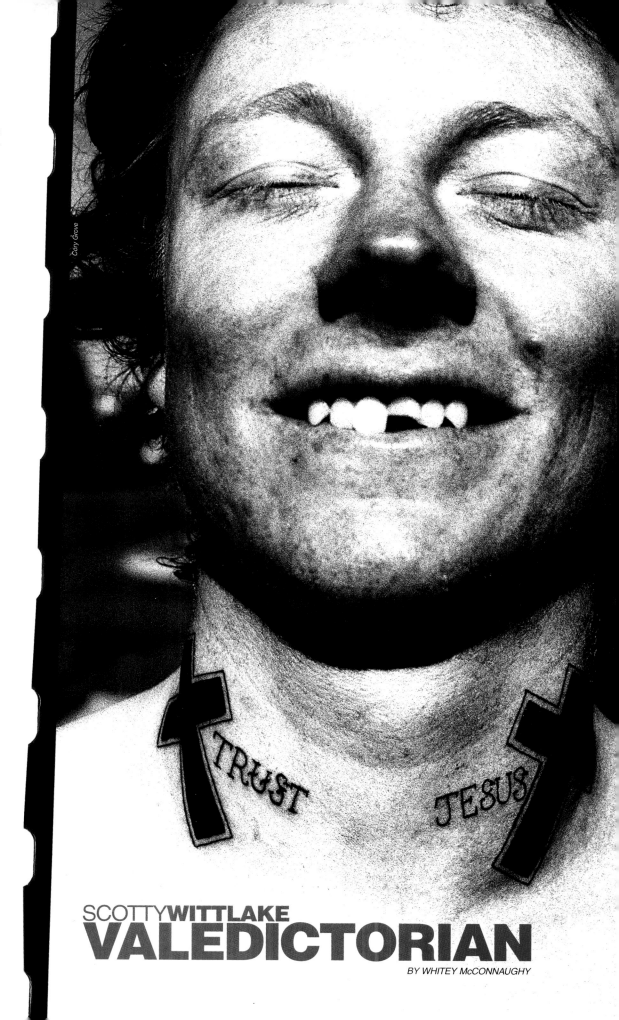

When snowboarding first hit ski resorts in the mid-eighties, it was considered an outlaw sport, the young snowboarder being the Antichrist to middle-aged skiers everywhere.

Many of these snowboarders didn't give a damn about how they looked or acted, and they rode with an attitude that spawned new thinking. They continually innovated snow sports by pulling such antics as riding backward on nonsnow surfaces and grabbing their boards like skateboarders—unheard-of actions for skiers. Their gangster flannels, over-the-eyes beanies, lock-your-car-doors-when-you-see-'em-lurking looks prompted vacationing families of skiers to give them a wide berth on the slopes and in town.

But over the span of a decade, snowboarding has changed dramatically, from a renegade alternative to skiing to a multimillion-dollar industrial monster. Today, the term "extreme sports" is milked by the corporate advertising world, which uses the snowboard and skateboard lifestyle to market everything from ketchup to cell phones.

Pro snowboarders, too, have changed. Many have adopted a role-model look complete with crisp $500 outfits and baseball caps that fit perfectly over well-groomed hairstyles. Like it or not, snowboarding has become mainstream, and with that comes normalcy, and *that* spells boring.

Then there's Scotty Wittlake, a new breed with an against-the-grain attitude that hails back to snowboarding's birth.

Wittlake is "punk" in all aspects of the word. He rides with a determination to take snowboarding to a not-yet-defined level, with complete disregard to what the snowboarding world is doing, and with no thought to what pain and abuse his body goes through. He searches out terrain that others steer clear of: wood rails with kinks and splinters; jumps with nightmare take-offs and punishing landings; cement ledges with chains blocking the run-outs. Not obstacles, but challenges to Wittlake, who has broken teeth, ribs, both ankles, his nose, collapsed a lung, cracked a femur, and crushed the bones in his

Cory Grove

SCOTTY**WITTLAKE**
VALEDICTORIAN

BY WHITEY McCONNAUGHY

Scotty Wittlake is always looking to slide some
sketchy wood rail. This 50-50 to gap to boardslide
in Lake Tahoe, California, is a prime example, 2001.

Andy Wright

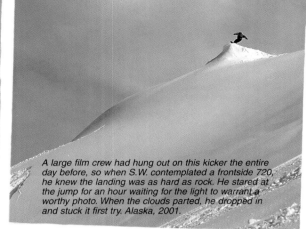

A large film crew had hung out on this kicker the entire day before, so when S.W. contemplated a frontside 720, he knew the landing was as hard as rock. He stared at the jump for an hour waiting for the light to warrant a worthy photo. When the clouds parted, he dropped in and stuck it first try. Alaska, 2001.

Andy Wright

cheek resulting in the loss of sight in his right eye during his quest to stick the scariest of landings.

In 1999, snowboard cinematographer Brad Kremer, who'd been filming Wittlake in Lake Tahoe off and on for about a year, told a snowboard movie producer about this crazy new kid whose riding was burly as hell. At the time, Wittlake didn't have any sponsors, just some boards borrowed from friend and M3 rider Blaise Rosenthal. Halfway through the winter, the producer viewed Kremer's sample footage of Wittlake sticking more tricks than most of the "big time" pros. The producer was blown away.

One trick that particularly stood out was Wittlake landing a ridiculously huge backside 180 off a cornice into three feet of powder on an extremely steep slope. After seeing this, the producer called Kremer and said, "Whatever you do, keep filming Scotty. That kid is gnarly."

It wasn't long before the producer gave the nineteen-year-old Wittlake a shot to be in his snowboarding movie. Eventually he met Wittlake in person and was able to see, firsthand, what a unique individual he is. Wittlake comes across as not having an ego; in fact, what he has is more of an antiego. After doing an insane line for the camera, truly a remarkable move, he'd ask the filmer in a quiet, apprehensive voice, "Was that okay?" with a modesty the producer at first took to be sarcasm (it wasn't).

The producer also found that in addition to being sincere, Wittlake is smart. Really smart. With some digging, he discovered that Wittlake, who was born on January 29, 1979, had failed ninth grade some four years earlier and had been forced to attend summer school to catch up. From that year forward, Wittlake earned straight A's and was class valedictorian for his Lake Tahoe high school. He refused, however, to give the speech at his graduation, and he ignored various offers of

Scotty Wittlake landed this death-defying 40-stair boardslide off a cliff clean, really clean, into the cold mountain water of Lake Tahoe, California, 2002.

higher education, instead following his heart to continue his snowboarding education, which had begun in 1990 at age eleven.

Back—or is it forward?—to winter 1999: Wittlake continued to surprise film crews with a go-for-broke style on and off the mountain, and at season's end he had earned what I saw early on in the editing room—one of the best video parts in the movie. I know, because I'm the producer, and it was my movie, *The Revival,* which coincidentally was voted the best snowboard movie of the year by almost every snowboarding magazine out there. I can't think of a more fitting movie title for Wittlake to call his debut. He was a revival for me, and, more importantly, for snowboarding.

Soon after *The Revival* premiere, the rest of the snowboarding community began to recognize Wittlake's talents and quickly set him up from head to toe with sponsors that included the film's title sponsor: DC. The following season, Wittlake won "rookie of the year" at *TransWorld SNOWboarding*'s Riders' Poll Awards.

Despite his fame and all the "free" gear, Wittlake has never given in to the pressure to dress like the rest of the snowboard community. To this day, whether it's a three-day trip to Colorado or a twelve-day mission to Japan, he packs the same small backpack of bare essentials: one pair of black shoes, one pair of black jeans, a T-shirt, and a sweatshirt. He straps his DC boots to his snowboard and checks the ensemble through. Who needs a snowboard bag?

Wittlake thrives on struggle; it's what pushes him to look for new obstacles to overcome, new tricks to learn on new terrain, to nail on film. In 2000, he came back with another stellar video part in Kingpin Productions' *Destroyer.* As soon as that movie was released, he began work on the 2001 KP film, *Brainstorm,* vowing to have the best segment he could possibly deliver. His on-snow brilliance delivered once again, scoring him the movie's video-box cover. In the photo, as in the film, he's boardsliding a crooked forty-four-stair-long splintered-up wood handrail that no one else wanted to touch.

To Wittlake, it was heaven.

ANTHONY VAN ENGELEN
SLIPPING THROUGH THE CRACKS
BY AARON MEZA

Greg Hunt

There could never be a skateboarding version of *Hoop Dreams,* the documentary that follows two youngsters on their way to professional basketball status. Theirs was a cutthroat yet predictable world of high school athletics, scouts, scholarships, tryouts, and draft picks. Skateboarders, hypothetically speaking, would face an entirely less predictable list that includes geographical location, chance encounters, knowing the right people, and word of mouth. These variables bear as much weight on a skateboarder's success as talent does.

Nonetheless, in a sport with no standardized method of turning pro, Anthony Van Engelen was as "Hoop Dreams" as it got. He grew up in Southern California amid a heavy skate population and the bulk of skateboarding's industry; he skated schoolyards with the ultimate endorsement, skateboarding living legend Mark Gonzales; and he got sponsored as a young teen by local board company Channel One. It seemed that all the building blocks to success were in motion.

Then he started partying too much and his mother sent him to Russia.

Born on November 20, 1978, in San Diego, California, Van Engelen was the only child of his unwed parents, who separated soon after his second birthday. Although his father came into and out of his life periodically, he was raised by his mother, Celynnda Ingrande, who took young Anthony with her as she moved around Orange County and Los Angeles—a lifestyle that made it difficult for him to find and keep friends. He lost himself in a world of video games and comic books until skateboarding, notorious for attracting loners and misfits, made Van Engelen its next inductee.

Van Engelen was only seven when he first experienced skateboarding, in the form of standing on a board and being pulled by his mother's boyfriend's dog. He would not ride, or be towed, again for another three years, though not from a lack of trying. When he was eight, his father bought him the quintessential board of the eighties, the Hosoi Hammerhead. Just the board. No wheels, no trucks, no bearings, not even griptape, and before Van Engelen had the chance to pull his allowance together for the accessories, his board did a disappearing act: a teenage neighbor, who had promised to put griptape on the board, never returned it. Being a fairly quiet kid, Van Engelen didn't push the subject.

A couple of years later, an older and wiser Van Engelen informed his mother and her boyfriend at the time, Rudy Mosqueda, that all he wanted for his upcoming tenth birthday was a skateboard—an entire skateboard this time. Mosqueda, who was a sort of father figure for Van Engelen, gave the birthday boy a hundred-dollar bill and told him to "bring back fifty." That was on top of the eighty dollars Van Engelen had won the night before. "Rudy and his friends were always playing cards at my house," says Van Engelen. "Rudy would be like, 'Son, come up here and play some poker!'" Not only lucky, but fateful, considering the eventual good fortune that would arise from a late-night poker game when most kids his age were in bed.

The following morning, Van Engelen headed straight to a local skate shop and put together a board that incorporated almost every color in the spectrum: a red and yellow Vision Lee Ralph with mismatched blue and red trucks and black wheels. It was a purchase "based off of colors rather than shape or size."

For its first two years the rainbowlike Lee Ralph was more of a toy than a way of life. Van Engelen admits that he wasn't a die-hard skateboarder in the beginning; he'd occasionally cruise around on his board, and in between these random sessions it collected dust in the closet. In time, Van Engelen

Anthony Van Engelen, switch 50-50 in Los Angeles, 2000.

Mike Blabac

noticed other kids doing tricks, and he started picking up skateboarding magazines. Slowly, ollies and other tricks became part of his growing repertoire. Soon he was taking tech tricks to bigger and gnarlier obstacles, doing things—like switch frontside crooks—that got him noticed.

In 1993, while he was sessioning a schoolyard in Orange County, none other than legendary skater Mark Gonzales rolled up. "He told me that my backside flips looked weird but he liked them," remembers Van Engelen. At the end of the session, Gonzales asked for Van Engelen's phone number and told him he would send him some boards. In skateboarding you couldn't ask for a greater accolade then Gonzales wanting to hook you up, but the impressionable Van Engelen cracked under the pressure and sputtered out the wrong phone number.

Even though the Gonzales deal never went through, fifteen-year-old Van Engelen was sponsored the very next day by Channel One when a friend of his on the Channel One team hooked him up. Channel One, a Huntington Beach company better known for its old-school skaters,

was happy to acquire Van Engelen, who was creative and fresh and represented the new guard in technical street skating.

Although Van Engelen respected the Channel One team, he was the low man on the totem pole—getting little more than free boards—and didn't feel the company was taking him on the career path he deserved. His attention span waned and his priorities shifted to partying and chasing girls.

By the time Van Engelen was seventeen, he had quit his sole sponsor, dropped out of school, and didn't have a job. "I was on the brink of becoming a total burnout," he says.

And his mom wasn't having it.

Van Engelen's mother had been separated from Mosqueda for nearly a decade, but her ex remained a major part of Van Engelen's life, dispensing advice and looking out for his best interests. When Ingrande expressed her concerns about her teenage son's future to Mosqueda, he offered to take Van Engelen in. "I plan on opening a restaurant," Mosqueda told her over the phone. "He can come live with me." There was only one hitch: Mosqueda was calling from Saint Petersburg, Russia, where he'd been for two years.

Surprisingly, Van Engelen was willing to go. "I was smoking weed all day, I didn't go to school, I didn't skate, I didn't do anything," he says. "So it seemed like there might be something over there for me. My mom was like, 'You're going to school or you're going to live in Russia with Rudy!' I hated school so much that I decided to go to Russia. Plus I thought it was a way to see the world."

In June 1995, a culture-shocked Van Engelen found himself living with Mosqueda in a one-bedroom apartment, keeping himself fed on grilled cheese sandwiches and fried eggs. Mosqueda was still working out the details for his restaurant, so he got Van Engelen a full-time job at a friend's bar. It soon became obvious that this wasn't your common neighborhood pub. Says Van Engelen, "Making drinks for Russian Mafia and Chechnyan soldiers at a bar that was basically a whorehouse was pretty bizarre. I didn't get paid, because I was just supposed to be training for my job at the restaurant they were going to open, and it's not customary to tip in Russia."

In addition to his financial woes, Van Engelen couldn't speak Russian, which made it next to impossible to form friendships—a throwback to his

Mike Blabac

A.V.E., backside big-spin flip off an
electrical grate and over a picnic table
in a Los Angeles school yard, 2001.

Mike Blabac

early years as a loner. When he wasn't working, he found himself alone, contemplating life and his reason for living. He thought a lot about God, not in a traditional religious sense, but more like "there's got to be more than this out there." In his words, "There was a heavy weight on my shoulders." These soul-searchings occupied his thoughts more often than not, but skateboarding still crept into his dreams. Although Van Engelen had brought along a board, wheels, and bearings, he had no trucks or griptape. A Russian skateboarder offered to grip his board for him and give him some trucks, but he soon discovered that this meant strips of red sandpaper glued to the top and some old Tracker trucks, a ghetto setup that especially didn't work on cobblestone skate spots.

After six months, Van Engelen had had enough. He wanted to go home. There was a fire burning inside him, something he couldn't understand, much less explain. He realizes, in retrospect, that his time in Russia was a period of self-development that wasn't clouded by drugs or partying. It was within this environment, where survival really was an issue, that he realized how absolutely amazing it is to be alive. "It blew me away how insane life is," he says, "and I started thinking about really obscure things, like how the human body works so perfectly. It was like God was coming to me."

Van Engelen says that Russia was exactly what he needed: he got away from his chaotic home life, and it made him think hard about school and a desk job, two things he knew weren't right for him, because one, he's dyslexic, and two, a day-in, day-out workweek in a suit and tie would drive him to more partying, not success. "So I prayed to God, but it was a god I couldn't even define. It wasn't religion, it was just figuring things out and asking for help."

He found his direction through skateboarding, in the form of a premonition in which he'd seen himself rising to the top of his game. Suddenly it became all that he wanted to do. Nevertheless, his mother didn't see his focus on skateboarding as much of an improvement. Says Van Engelen, "I'd be like, 'You don't understand, Mom. I'm skating really well.' She'd be like, 'So what. Get a job. Show me that you are doing something with yourself.'"

But Van Engelen knew what he wanted to be and he could see where he wanted to go, and although he fears that his premonitions of success may sound cocky, they're anything but. "I just had

Anthony Van Engelen, switch 360 flip in South Gate, California, 2001.

Switch backside nosegrind across two picnic tables. A.V.E. in the San Fernando Valley, California, 2000.

Mike Blabac

this new hunger after being in Russia, a hunger for self-improvement, and skateboarding was kind of my way to slide through the cracks and keep me from being a burnout," he says.

Whatever support Van Engelen was missing at home was made up for by friend and already established professional skateboarder Jason Dill. Dill, among other pros, recognized Van Engelen's ability to bring raw power and aggression to difficult tricks centered on precision and finesse. Dill ultimately led the way for Van Engelen into the world of professional skateboarding, helping him to get sponsored by 23 Skateboards and, in 1997, Alien Workshop. "I was just boasting to everybody that Van Engelen was the best," says Dill. "He sets his own pace. He takes the road less traveled, and it reflects in his skateboarding."

At nineteen, Van Engelen had his board sponsor, Alien Workshop, in place. It was only logical that he would start shopping for a shoe sponsor, although he really had only one in mind. "DC was the elite shoe company and it had all the skaters that I respected: Danny Way, Rob Dyrdek, Rick Howard, and Mike Carroll," he says. "I wanted to skate for DC and be associated with those guys."

Having garnered the respect of his Alien Workshop comrades, Van Engelen was making a good impression with DC skaters, some of whom—Way, Dyrdek, and Josh Kalis—were also on the Alien team. By his twentieth birthday, Van Engelen had scored DC.

The next two years were a whirlwind for Van Engelen. He filmed an acclaimed video part for Alien Workshop's *Photosynthesis,* traveled to Canada and Japan and on U.S. tours that stopped in virtually every state, and found himself the center of an ever-increasing popularity, all of which led to his own DC signature shoe, something that both stoked and freaked him out.

The A.V.E., released in 2001, was tangible evidence that Van Engelen had figuratively and literally walked the road less traveled after diverting off a sure-fire pathway to professional success. His story is a rare documentary that tracks his life from SoCal skateboarding résumé heaven to the unlikely cobbled streets of Saint Petersburg and back to the California dream. But he's the first to admit that he had rough periods even after he was on the Alien and DC teams. "I strayed off the path more than once and still have my struggles today. Sure, I've worked them out through skateboarding, but that's just a tool. I can tell you, I wouldn't have skateboarding without my faith. That's what kept me out of a deep, dark crack in the sidewalk."

Anthony Van Engelen, nollie backside 180 flip off a loading dock in
South Gate, California, 2000.

Mike Blabac

DEUCE FIRST RELEASED: **FALL 2001**

Durability is a crucial feature for any skateboarding shoe. The Deuce, Danny Way and Colin McKay's second combo signature shoe, is one of the most durable and dramatic shoes DC has ever produced. Its sidewalls are highlighted with injected thermoplastic rubber (TPR) detailing to guard the upper against ollie damage, which makes the Deuce both long-lasting and distinctive. Its design also features a synthetic leather and mesh upper, protective leather lace loops, and a high-abrasion, sticky gum rubber bottom for excellent traction and board control.

HOWARD1 FIRST RELEASED: **SPRING 1997**

The street-skating ability and unique style of Rick Howard inspired the design of his debut signature shoe, the Howard1. It was both the first DC shoe to feature a clear rubber sole and the first skate shoe to have a sole made of injected thermoplastic rubber (TPR) instead of the commonly used gum rubber.

The TPR sole allowed for excellent tackiness and exceptional grip on the board and was thought to be one of the most high-performance soles in the skate industry at the time. DC implemented the TPR sole on several other models following the Howard1's release, including the Howard2 in spring 1999. Although the original Howard was discontinued in 1998, it remains a classic in the history of DC Shoes.

DYRDEK2 FIRST RELEASED: **FALL 1996**

Rob Dyrdek's second signature shoe, the technical and versatile Dyrdek2, complemented the street skater's aggressive style, yet encompassed a look that was more sports-oriented. Because it integrated several high-performance features that were new to the industry—including an angle-edged sole that added further sole longevity and an extra middle heel cushion in the midsole that helped absorb additional impact shock—the Dyrdek2 became one of the most popular skate shoes of 1996.

The Dyrdek2 was also the first DC shoe to use a strong adhesive rather than sole stitching to fasten the sole to the suede upper. This adhesive ensured that the shoe wouldn't come apart as its sole was worn down by griptape friction, a detail that DC would incorporate into many future shoe designs. The Dyrdek2 was available for over five seasons and was recognized as one of the most durable and versatile skate shoes of its time.

ESSENCE FIRST RELEASED: **SPRING 1999**

Since its release, the Essence has maintained a reputation as a skate shoe that outperforms and outlasts most other skate shoes on the market. Its bold design evolved from the Syntax, another popular DC shoe that was available from 1996 to 1999. The Essence's upper was constructed from several highly durable materials, such as action nubuck and heavy-duty suede, and came equipped with a high-abrasion V1 Buck 5000 toe cap that helped guard against ollie damage.

In spring 2000, a kids' version of the Essence was developed, followed by a women's version the following season. All three models were worldwide top-sellers on the DC line. The original Essence went out of production in winter 2000 to make room for 2001 shoes.

BMX DIRT, VERT, AND STREET

BY HAROLD McGRUTHER

During the early seventies, SoCal teens too broke to buy a respectable minibike hopped up their spindly Schwinn Sting-Rays with motorcycle parts and sprinted around dirt tracks in jackboots and deck shoes. The fathers of these early BMX pioneers—mostly a bunch of pipe fitters, fab shop operators, and even a couple of beauticians—cobbled together BMX bikes for their kids using sections of chromoly steel tubing salvaged from old airplane fuselages. It was from these bootstrap beginnings that the BMX industry was born.

Technically speaking, the sport's earliest machines didn't differ greatly from the state-of-the-art bikes that top BMX athletes currently ride. Although the high-strength alloy wheelsets and high-performance tires and brake systems found on modern machines are culled from the mountain bike scene, many of today's best-built frames, forks, and cranks are manufactured by the same companies that grew out of the California dust three decades ago.

The bikes may have stayed virtually the same as the sport progressed, but many of the kids who rode BMX grew tired of cruising around unchallenging dirt tracks. They upped the ante with jumps and berms, and it wasn't long before speed took a back seat to air and style. Introducing the twenty-inch bike to man-made skate environments like halfpipes and skate parks during the early eighties expanded the sport's dirt-born horizons even further. Not all skateboarders welcomed the migration of BMX riders to their sacred gardens, but fresh attitudes between open-minded athletes ultimately prevailed. Nowadays, skateboarders and BMXers are bonded by a similar lifestyle and the never-ending quest for new terrain options.

DC recognized this brotherhood, and in 1999 began supporting riders and designing the future in BMX footwear. Four months after DC assembled its first team of world-class dirt-, vert-, and street-riding professionals, DC pro Colin Winkelmann shocked daredevils everywhere by sailing over twelve cars on a BMX bike. He repeated the feat in fall 2000 with a jump over thirteen SUVs that set a new distance-jumping world record. That same year, DC's Robbie Miranda won the first round of the richest downhill BMX series in the sport's history, the Triple Crown of BMX at Woodward Camp in western Pennsylvania. Chris Doyle, another founding member of the DC team, beat out the world's greatest jumpers for the 2000 and 2001 Dirt Circuit championship title. Starting 2001 off with a bang, DC pro Dave Mirra—action sports' all-time leading gold medal winner and current king of bicycle stunt riding—obliterated the high-air world record with a nineteen-foot flight above that vert behemoth known as the DC Super Ramp.

And the progressive onslaught continues.

Ronny Chalk graced the covers of three different BMX magazines in 2001, taking dirt and street freestyle into a fresh direction, like this fully extended Superman seat grab at the Real Ride Skate Park in Perris, California.

中華文化中心

There's a huge ledge, with hardly any run-in and with severe consequences, tucked away in Chinatown, San Francisco. That's where Chad Kagy nailed this feeble grind on DC's West Coast road trip, 2000.

RIGHT TO PASS BY PERMISSION AND SUBJECT TO CONTROL OF OWNER SECTION 1008 CIVIL CODE

Mark Losey

Robbie Miranda, turn-down over a very difficult set of doubles in Pennsylvania on DC's East Coast road trip, 2000.

Steve Buddendeck

Neal Wood tabled up at 91 Trails. Riverside County, California, 2000.

Keith Mulligan

Carl Hyndman

Rob Darden whipping some tail at the Real Ride Skate Park in Perris, California, on the 2001 Dave Mirra Super Tour.

Robbie Miranda sucks it up at high speed on the way to winning a $15,000 first-place finish at the Vans Triple Crown of BMX. Woodward, Pennsylvania, 2000.

Steve Buddendeck

"In February 1999, The Offspring contacted a few jumpers to compete in a long-distance car jump for a thirty-minute video they were producing that showcased all sorts of crazy stunts. Colin [Winkelmann] and I showed up at the location, a dry lake bed in El Mirage, California, where it was a $10,000 first prize. Flush Fernandez was our main competitor because he was there to win no matter what. It was super windy and scary drifting through the air at sixty miles per hour. On nine cars, I got blasted by a strong wind and overshot the landing, so I asked the motorcycle driver who was towing us in to slow down on the next one. It was too slow, and I came up about six inches too short, cased my back tire on the ramp, and my bike exploded into several pieces. My helmet hit the handlebars so hard I bit through my upper lip and knocked a tooth loose. Then it was Colin's turn, and soon enough it was him and Fernandez on twelve cars and almost dark. He cleared it, and called it quits. Then Fernandez did twelve, and then thirteen, and won the cash. A week later, the photos came back, and everybody realized that Fernandez had only cleared twelve, too. So they tied. The whole operation was pretty shady; if there would have been more light I bet somebody might have gotten killed. Colin said he wanted to do it right some other time." – Robbie Miranda

Steve Buddendeck

BELOW: "After the dry-lake shoot, this 'shooting ranch' [a Hollywood-frequented ranch in Agoura Hills, California, where the Fonz jumped a bunch of trash cans for a *Happy Days* episode] was almost too professional. There were stunt coordinators, caterers, and RVs. Colin [Winkelmann] was so smooth and relaxed that the producers asked him if he could pass up the jump once and say 'It didn't feel right' to build up the drama, but Colin told them to forget it. He could have jumped more cars, but I'm glad he didn't—thirteen vehicles and a new world record was enough." – Mark Losey, December 20, 2000

Mark Losey

Steve Buddendeck

Chris Doyle lives in fear of forgetting how to do his tricks, so he's constantly practicing—making sure he doesn't lose any of his favorites, like this flat 360 at 401 Trails. Raleigh, North Carolina, 2000.

Steve Buddendeck

Chris Doyle does these turn-down 360s better than anybody, so they're always showing up in print. This one, in 2000 at Buck's Trails in Erie, Pennsylvania, was destined to end up somewhere.

Steve Buddendeck

It was fall in Raleigh, North Carolina, and if you look closely, you might see blood on the leaves from an unfortunate "practice" run by another rider just a few minutes before Chris Doyle slid this superfast rail in 2000.

DAVE MIRRA

SECOND BEST IS **NOT** AN OPTION

According to the big-haired blonde on The Weather Channel, the torrential downpours that accompanied winter 2001 vaulted usually sunny SoCal ahead of soaking-wet Seattle for total rainfall. Not the news Dave Mirra wanted to hear. The twenty-seven-year-old BMX megastar had just become DC's newest team member, and was planning to seal his deal by setting a world record on a replica of Danny Way's eighteen-foot-high Super Ramp—a feat only possible if the plywood is dry. So on January 5, Mirra traded in the icy climes of his Greenville, North Carolina, home for what he hoped would be clear San Diego skies.

Mirra had already missed the opportunity to sample this ramp's potential at the 1999 MTV Sports and Music Festival in Las Vegas, where his vert-superstar peer Kevin Robinson had set the then–world record at fifteen feet three inches. After the festival, MTV donated the Super Ramp to the DC cause. That ramp now at his disposal, Mirra didn't think a sixteen-foot air was out of the question, at least not with plenty of practice. But he was facing a week full of meetings, phone calls, and interviews, with only a one-day window of opportunity on the ramp.

That day arrived with dead-calm air and crystal-clear skies, and Mirra's aerial attack went off with only one hitch. Roughly thirty minutes into his warm-up, he augured his back wheel into the steel coping on the edge of the massive transition and slid to the bottom of the ramp, his mangled bike tumbling in high-speed pursuit. Cell phones erupted in a flurry of damage-control calls. In under an hour, Ken Block delivered a new back wheel, and Mirra made the long climb to the thirty-eight-foot-high roll-in, bombed the transition, and catapulted seventeen, eighteen, and finally nineteen feet into the air. The all-time X Games vert and street king had effectively joined the ranks of Danny Way and others in the coveted world-records club: highest halfpipe air on a bicycle.

His California press junket complete, Mirra rushed home to check on the progress of his custom-built house, which included plans for an enormous backyard halfpipe with a soft resin landing. Since his reign of domination began in the mid-nineties, competition among the sport's elite athletes had grown fierce, and Mirra considered this new ramp essential to raising his gold medal count

Just a handful of Dave Mirra's X Games medals. He's won more of these than any other athlete in X Games history.

Carl Hyndman

Two different views of one incredible world record: highest BMX air on a halfpipe—nineteen feet above the eighteen-foot-high DC Super Ramp in San Diego or twenty-seven feet off the ground. Dave Mirra likes to air to the left, but the Super Ramp's roll-in is on the far right, so he's actually doing an alley-oop. If the roll-in had been on the left, the air would have been even higher. 2001.

© Mike Blabac

above a baker's dozen by the end of the season. As it had been with him from the beginning, second best was not an option.

Like practically every young kid in America born after Schwinn introduced the twenty-inch wheel via the Sting-Ray in 1963, David Michael Mirra (born April 4, 1974) got a BMX bike as soon as he was big enough to straddle its frame. He was ten years old, and quickly felt at home cranking the pedals around his neighborhood. Two years later Mirra had progressed to the dirt trails and BMX tracks surrounding his home in Syracuse, New York. However, the structured format of BMX racing and Mirra's puny stature killed any long-term hopes he might have had for dominance on the race scene, so he began competing in local flatland and quarterpipe freestyle events.

When he was thirteen, Mirra took second-to-last place in his first American Freestyle Association (AFA) contest. Though by no means an incredible accomplishment, he was hooked on the competitive freestyle scene. He hung up his racing number plate, put front brakes and pegs on his bike, and a year or so after making his AFA debut, swept the quarterpipe and flatland divisions for his age group at the AFA Masters in Wayne, New Jersey. Mirra dominated the young amateur division at other events on the AFA circuit, but quickly grew tired of the old-school contest scene. In 1989, he entered an event at action sports' mecca: the famed Woodward Camp in western Pennsylvania.

Statistically speaking, Mirra's halfpipe vert debut at Woodward wasn't his best work—he placed eighth among thirty amateurs between the ages of fourteen and twenty. Still, his runs provided Woodward onlookers a glimpse into the future of the sport. Kim Boyle, a longtime friend of Mirra's and the team manager who gave the prodigy his first factory ride at age fifteen, remembers Mirra's early performances well:

"Dave wasn't strong enough to do spinning tricks like 540s. Instead, he went super-high and did incredible straight-air variations. What I remember best about Dave in the early days was his drive and determination. The kid was just so in love with the fun of riding. He would want to get up and ride so early, sometimes seven in the morning. I finally had to dump him on a bunch of old pros who lived in a different neighborhood. When Dave stayed at my place he wore me out."

Even today, youthful exuberance and brash determination personify Mirra's riding style and infuse him with a competitive nature that borders on the maniacal and can be—according to some of his peers—downright unnerving. Fellow DC teamster Colin Winkelmann, an innovative rider in his own right and another pro on the Greenville freestyle scene, hones his skills on many of the same backyard ramps and street spots Mirra uses. "Mirra, a couple of other guys in town, and I like to play B-M-X on our bikes," Winkelmann says. "You know, the way basketball

Carl Hyndman

players shoot H-O-R-S-E. Most games start out easy, but we always step it up toward the end. I've seen Dave lose a couple of times, but when he's in control of a game, it's a scary act to follow. He just won't lose."

How right Winkelmann is. Out of Mirra's eleven final-round vert and street appearances at ESPN's X Games since 1996, he's only failed to win gold twice. Add his 1999 and 2000 Gravity Games victories to this streak, and it's easy to see why so many game junkies and thirteen-year-old couch potatoes know the moves that Mirra made famous—tricks like the no-handed 540 to barspin, the carving flair, and the double backflip.

During his lifelong mission to pull the trick that made him a household name at the 1999 X Games, Tony Hawk captured the 900: skateboarding's Holy Grail. In BMX, the elusive double backflip has become as fabled as Hawk's nine. Since the early nineties, vert riders and dirt jumpers have practiced the death-defying move into foam pits and over soft dirt doubles, but no one had pulled one at a contest. No one, that is, until Mirra.

The date: May 7, 2000. The event: round-two preliminary qualifiers for the Crazy Freakin' Bikers Pro/Am contest at Utopia Skate Park in Raleigh, North Carolina. On the giant wallride facing an oversized box jump in the middle of the park, Mirra carved extra high and sprinted toward the six-foot lip. Arms and legs loaded, he pumped the transition, snapped his head back, and jerked violently on the handlebars. In a stunt nothing short of miraculous, Mirra rotated both spins perfectly and touched down on the wedge-shaped landing. He'd conquered the double backflip and immediately set his sights to do it again at the X Games.

That following August in San Francisco, Mirra unleashed another double backflip that both won him a gold and effectively raised the BMX bar to freak-show status. Every X Games fan in the world would hear about Mirra's feat. He could bank on it.

Dave Mirra's helmeted head is plastered on Slim Jim® meat stick boxes from San

Carl Hyndman

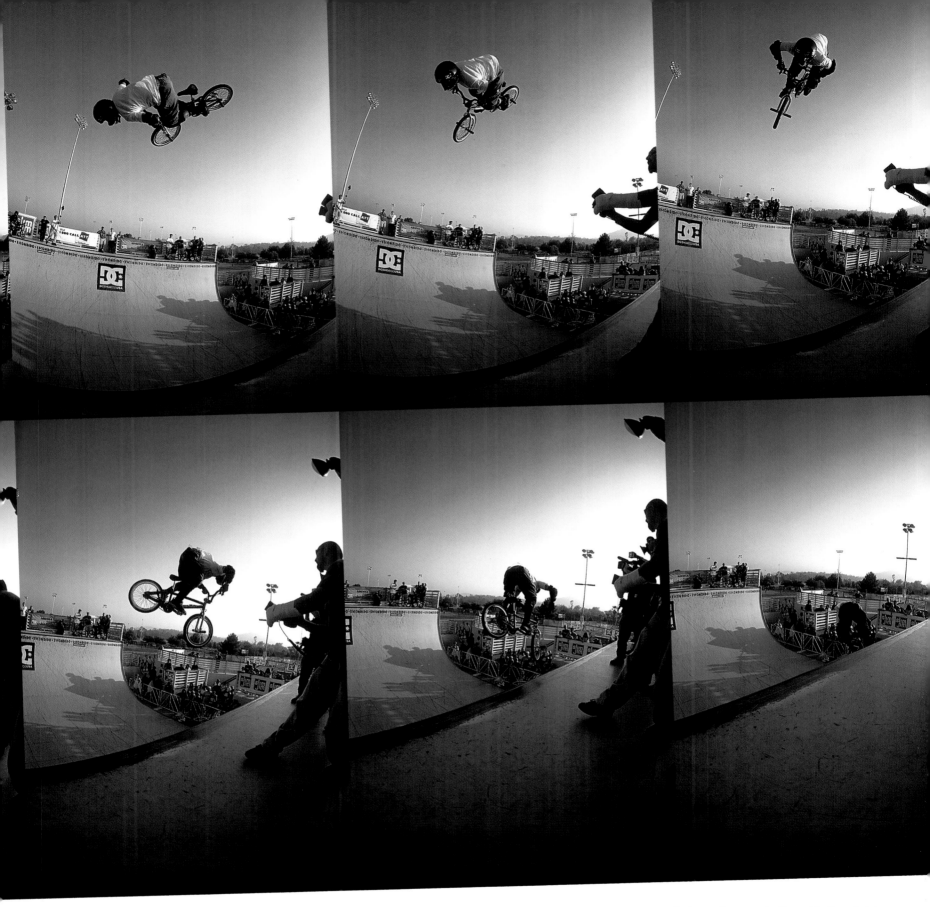

Dave Mirra executes a flawless corkscrew at the Escondido Skate Park in California during his 2001 Super Tour. This trick came alive just prior to the 2001 season when Kevin Robinson created it at the Woodward Camp in Pennsylvania. By the beginning of the season, Mirra, Robinson, and Jamie Bestwick had it dialed, taking vert BMX to a whole new level.

Dave Mirra makes this low cash X-up look absolutely effortless
while practicing at the Escondido Skate Park in California, 2000.

Carl Hyndman

Diego to Syracuse. Lucky Charms® might be magically delicious, but hungry BMXers start their day off right with a big bowl of Dave Mirra™ cereal. Little Leaguers chew Miracle Boy™ bubble gum, just like the life-size superstar whose mug graces the action figure that comes with Dave Mirra finger bikes. The enormous wheels of the Mirra media machine turn twenty-four/seven, and a sports marketing agency called The Familie adds grease to the whole thing. A close-knit team of bean counters, youth culture jacks-of-all-trade, X jocks, and media mavens led by Steve Astephen, The Familie (as well as other like-minded agencies) sees to it that action sports athletes like Mirra are well compensated for their daring, crowd-pleasing work ethic.

Take away Mirra's custom home, park his muscle car, tear down the resi ramp, and shut down the moneymaking machine, and what remains is a guy who loves to ride a bike. But Mirra has learned the hard way that legendary status and financial security can be a gilded cage—the bars make it easy for people on the outside to take shots at you. And when the BMX pundits and hard-core riders lurking in the shadows of the media spotlight ("player haters," according to Mirra) label him a sellout or question the purity of his motivations for riding, his blood boils. Mirra defends himself by reminding anyone who will listen that he couldn't do these tricks if his heart wasn't in it. "Riding a bike has always been my dream," he says. "More than anything, I love to have fun. If you can do what you love and have fun doing it, why would you do anything else?"

Mark Losey

"During the 2001 Dave Mirra Super Tour, we stayed in Atlanta for two nights. All the guys went out street-riding, and they found this kinked rail near the hotel. It took Mirra two tries to slide the whole thing. It was good seeing him do stuff on the street; he can do anything on a bike." – Mark Losey

During a 2001 X Games practice session in Philadelphia, Pennsylvania, Dave Mirra rode past photographer Adam Booth and said, "Hey Adam, shoot this." Booth scrambled for a good angle, and Mirra fired off a perfect double backflip—the trick that had sealed his win at the 2000 X Games in San Francisco and took him up yet another notch toward the untouchable status of BMX freestyle champion.

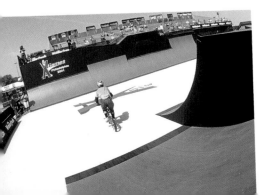

Adam Booth

In summer 2001, Mirra, fellow superstars Ryan Nyquist and Dennis McCoy, and a half dozen other BMX pros hit the highway on a DC-sponsored cross-country search for America's best riding spots. The Dave Mirra Super Tour was an opportunity for up-and-coming riders to make their mark and for more established pros to push the limits of their sport. When the Super Tour documentary aired on ESPN, viewers watched more than just Mirra and friends pulling crazy tricks; they saw mile-long lines of hungry fans waiting patiently for a chance to get autographs and stickers from their idols.

And somewhere in those throngs, no doubt, were young riders with fire in their eyes, studying the master, plotting to emulate and eventually surpass the stunts that Mirra made famous. Some day Dave Mirra might consider such an advance by a young gun as the ultimate compliment. For now, however, he intends to keep a stranglehold on his exceedingly difficult bag of tricks.

Look at Stevie Williams and what do you see? A gangsta kid, right? Got the sleepy eyes, the baggy jeans, the ice-dipped platinum, the Rollie, the bling-blinging Range with the fat beats flowing out the windows. Got the hip-hop walk and the crispy kicks to match. (DC, you know. Which pro model you want? He's got two.)

Listen to Williams and what do you hear? A gangsta kid, right? Voice is Philly born and raised with a touch of Cali, stringing ghetto phraseology together like fellow Illadelph head Beanie Sigel: incredible, illogical threads like "Let's do this, na mean, ya heard, holla!" Conversations are fat-laced with profanities, like Run-D.M.C. But the voice works for Williams—the flow is natural and unforced.

In a sport where tricks often make up for a skater's lack of personality, Williams has both. His section in TransWorld's 1999 video *The Reason* is as filled with his off-the-board flow as it is with his Rakim-complex skateboard combinations. Confidence pours out of him like sweat. "I was the best dude on the block in basketball, football, track," he says. "I was gonna be something."

He is.

By the ripe old age of twenty-one, Williams had already been all over the world: New Zealand, Australia, Sweden, Japan, Mexico, not to mention the United States—east to west—and Europe. Skateboarding has taken him there, but know this: even without skateboarding, Stevie Williams would almost definitely be worldwide.

"The thing about Stevie," says roommate and fellow pro skateboarder Lee Smith, "is that he's not only an amazing skater, but he has the pizzazz, the flavor that people like." That's not skating. That's reality. If Williams wasn't a skateboarder, he could have been anything he damn well pleased. You only have to talk to him for a minute to realize that.

Rewind. December 17, 1979. Williams is born in North Philly, in the hood. At ten he moves with his mom to West Philly, and things there aren't much better. "Niggas selling crack, people jumping rope," he says. Like most little kids, he finds a way to cope. "Basketball, running track, messing with

STEVIE**WILLIAMS** **THE GIFT**
BY RUSS BENGTSON

girls, lifting up skirts—almost got into selling drugs and shit. That's when I started skating. It worked like that. God blessed me."

God arrived in 1989 not long after Williams got used to the new neighborhood. He'd run into some older kids who made a bet on whether they could teach the little guy how to ollie. Little Stevie (as he would come to be known) picked it up quickly—before the end of the day he was ollieing up curbs and doing shove-its. Then he really started getting into it and a whole new reality opened up. Says Williams, "Landing new tricks, there's nothing like it in the whole wide world. I guess I got addicted to that. I keep feeling that. Feeling the same shit, even if it's an easy trick."

That was love. Then came Love.

Stevie Williams, switch backside nosegrind in the San Fernando Valley, California, 2000.

Little Stevie was skating around his neighborhood when a friend invited him all the way downtown to this place called Love Park. He couldn't even tell his mom he was going there, because "you ain't supposed to be ten downtown by yourself without no parents." He went anyway.

What he found was a wide-open mecca of rails, ledges, and other supremely skateable obstacles right smack in Center City. It would become his training ground and his home. Back then, skating was at least tolerated in Love Park, so Williams got his game tight and got real with things. "I created a new breed at Love," he says. "The tricks that I was learning are the ones everybody does today."

An older (by three years) skateboarder from another neighborhood, Josh Kalis, had also made Love Park his home, and around 1992 he started falling into the Stevie group. "Stevie was super small," remembers Kalis, who'd usually meet up with Williams around 11 A.M. and skate until it got dark. The two didn't even think about coming up, going pro, getting sponsored. They just skated. When she found out what her son was up to, "Moms" was just happy that Williams wasn't getting into trouble.

S.W., switch heelflip over a trash can at
Love Park, Philadelphia, 2000.

Mike Blabac

Stevie Williams, frontside 180 flip in Los Angeles, 2000.

Mike Blabac

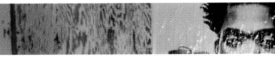

S.W., hardflip backside tailslide at Love Park, Philadelphia, 2000.

Mike Blabac

Guerrilla marketing: 2,500 Stevie Williams posters were "wheat pasted" all over San Francisco for the 2000 X Games; another 3,000 in Philadelphia for the 2001 X Games.

10 YEARS OF TEMPLETON 20 PAGE FEATURE & EXCLUSIVE INTERVIEW

THRASHER

Shelby Woods

BIG GUNS EL TORO 20 DESTROYED PAGE 2

STEVIE WILLIAMS
NO LUCK INVOLVED

AUSTRALIA
KANGAROO BOXING WITH
THE BUTCHER & PANCHO

HEADSHOTS
MELCHER · PULEO · LENOCE

SICK SOUNDS
ROCKET FROM THE CRYPT
BREAKESTRA · BLACK HALOS
RIVAL SCHOOLS · BELL RAYS

JULY 2001 · ISSUE 246
$3.99US $4.99CAN

07>
0 71486 03029 4
WWW.THRASHERMAGAZINE.COM

*Stevie Williams on the cover of the
July 2001* Thrasher *magazine.
Frontside noseslide in Los Angeles.*

Skating Love Park was still what got Williams hooked up with his first sponsor, Underground Element—"I was just skating in front of the right people. They loved me 'cause I was a little hood nigga."—and got him his first video part, for same. Little Stevie was getting large. TransWorld photographer Atiba Jefferson remembers Williams wearing the "ghettoest" clothes, but mainly he remembers his natural skating flow. Skateboard superstar Eric Koston remembers how small Williams was in the video, "but even for his size he had a lot of control. Back then who knows how long he had been skating for. It was just something he had. A gift."

Next step: West Coast. Yeah, you heard. At fourteen, Williams decided to step to Cali to check out the whole thing for real. He hitched with a friend who had a new ride and an even newer gas card, but decided not to tell "Moms" about his plans until he got where he was going. She—understandably—tripped when he called from San Francisco on a Friday. She demanded that he get home in time for school on Monday, but he knew that was impossible, which was why he had done it in the first place. So Williams defied his mom and stayed out there for a while, crashing wherever he could and hanging with others who were deep in the game.

But Williams had gone west first and foremost to figure out the skate thing, and that's just what he did, skating around Pier 7, learning about the skateboarding biz, and just surviving. He left Underworld Element to skate for Profile Skateboards (where he was flowed product but wasn't pro). Profile went under and F.I.T. Skateboards picked him up.

Mike Blabac

Eventually, Williams returned to Philly, bouncing back and forth between the two coasts—both of which were in his blood. When F.I.T. fizzled out, however, the seventeen-year-old lost patience with the unpredictable industry and began to consider alternatives. He was about ready to give up the gift. "I had the ill hustle scheme I was gonna do," he says. "I wasn't really trippin', I knew I was gonna get dough. I knew I could hustle my ass off, been hustling since I was little." Williams won't elaborate on what exactly he was hustling.

Before he could trash those seven years of hard work, trading one street life for another, his old friend Josh Kalis sat him down and laid it out in front of him, made him see the light, appreciate the gift. Williams credits Kalis with being "the angel on my shoulder" who kept him on the right track—skateboarding. "I put my mind to skateboarding and focused," says Williams, "and my hustle game was hustle skating, just wheelin' and dealin' and shit." Even without the sponsorship, he received plenty of support from his friends in Frisco and at Love Park, which by this time had become a skateboard battleground, complete with expensive citations and undercover police who rolled through in raids to confiscate boards. Skating continued, but with a new level of risk: you had to be ready to scatter at a moment's notice.

Through it all, Williams knew that he could make dough off skateboarding if somebody would cut him a break. "Nobody really wanted to give me a chance because I had a bad name," he says. "I was getting locked up, causing problems. So nobody wanted to put me on their team. I was like fuck it, fuck y'all."

This switch backside nosegrind became Stevie Williams's first DC ad. San Francisco, 1999.

The obvious question is: "What did you get locked up for?"

A pause. "Everything." A click as the phone disconnects. Buzz of a dial tone. It's just a coincidence, but a well-timed one. AT&T's way of saying "that discussion is over."

About nine years after he first learned to ollie, Williams put a demo tape together—just raw footage of him popping big tricks. His talent was undeniable, and he rolled back from a West Coast trip officially sponsored by Chocolate Skateboards and DC. For the first time his feet were on solid ground. He was part of a family.

But what transformed Stevie Williams into STEVIE WILLIAMS was Chocolate's 1999 video *The Chocolate Tour,* which dropped the same year he turned pro. Williams was so fresh to the Chocolate squad he didn't even appear in any of the Spike Jonze–directed skits that made up the video's loose "plot." His short skate section was

buried at the end, compiled mostly of footage from that infamous demo. It was his lines—original skate phrases like switch nose manual to fakie hardflip out, all performed with laid-back ease—that had street skaters around the world ready to bite his style.

Originality is, and always has been, his strong point. Asked to describe his style, Williams breaks it down like this: "Smooth. Flowing different. My style stands out from the rest. It's a style everyone would wish they had. Trying to stand out by being creative. Doing tricks that other people wouldn't thought of doing."

Don't mistake truth for arrogance. Williams twists tricks like Rahzel twists syllables—flips, manuals, and grinds every which way, either foot first or last. All with plenty of "tech, pop, and a lot of flavor," says Atiba Jefferson. "That's his shit. He can make a switch heelflip off flat ground look better than some average kid doing it off ten stairs. His style is

Mike Blabac

Mike Blabac

just off the charts, the way he can pop and do stuff. You hear pros saying 'yeah, I wanna pop it like Stevie,' because he's known for having that shit."

Williams calls it ghetto pop, and he doesn't mean Tropical Fantasy soda. Ghetto pop is what fuels his style, what lets him pull things that don't even exist in other people's minds yet. Even someone who's never stepped on a skateboard in his life—never seen a skateboarder before—would recognize that extra something in Williams.

His first DC signature shoe, the Williams (released in 2000, one year after his induction into the DC team), represents all that originality: it's pro-level skate shoe performance mixed with Air Jordan style. The Reason, his second signature model, hit the shelves the following year. Together they were the number two and three best-selling shoes on DC's line in 2001/2002.

So, fame and fortune? Whatever. He has those already. The Range and the Rolex, remember? Eating well isn't a problem. And this without contests or major coverage like the X Games, because Williams doesn't do ramps. Stevie Williams is no Tony Hawk; you won't find him spinning 900s on ESPN. That doesn't mean he's unmarketable. Anything but. He has a video game, an action figure, and a signature backpack to go with the kicks and deck. He was on the cover of the July 2001 *Thrasher* magazine, sliding a ludicrously high ledge, the sort of ledge mere mortals pass by.

Through it all, seen it all: Stevie Williams is still Stevie Williams. He's changed a lot, but really, he hasn't changed at all. The people who got him into skateboarding? He skates with them to this day. At the core, though, it's his originality—a ghetto kid making his mark. Stevie Williams knows that you don't just earn a rep, "you gotta keep earning it."

Even if it is a gift.

When Stevie Williams first started skating he could barely see over this wall. Switch frontside noseslide on a waist-high ledge, the highest in Love Park. Philadelphia, 2000.

S.W., nollie crooked grind on a long ledge in
the San Fernando Valley, California, 2001.

It's been almost a century since the ancient practice of riding waves migrated from its Hawaiian origins to mainland United States and Australia, where "surfing" spread like wildfire. Soon after, you could find surfers in South Africa, New Zealand, Japan, Great Britain, France, and South America. Within fifty years, surfing had swept around the globe and become, after swimming, the most popular water sport in the world.

With that popularity came a swift evolution—both the equipment and the act have undergone constant transition. Surfboards have been transformed from sixty-pound redwood logs into ultralight foam-and-fiberglass flying carpets. Surfers who trim two-foot Malibu are joined by masters who pull into twelve-foot, ten-million-pound barrels in Tahiti and those who launch rocket-fueled aerials at Florida beach breaks. There are sixty-foot waves being ridden, and six-foot airs being landed.

The diversity continues as bigger, faster, more powerful waves are discovered, feeding an undying hunger for exploration that has been joined by a powerful pulse of innovation. The mid-nineties saw an incredible leap in high-performance surfing made by the New School— Kelly Slater, Rob Machado, Shane Dorian, the Malloys, Ross Williams, Kalani Robb, Shane Beschen, and others—as well as the widespread emergence of aerial surfing pioneered by the likes of Christian Fletcher and other rebels.

The end of the twentieth century marked an intensely progressive new era of surfing, an era that fits DC's philosophy like . . . well, like a shoe. DC's exploration through the ranks of wave-chargers began when the company took on perennial top-five surfer Shane Dorian as its original surf team member. Dorian was joined, and then succeeded, by Andy and Bruce Irons, Hawaiian brothers who have had phenomenal impact on both the competitive and freesurfing realms.

DC's dynamic duo currently rate at the top of the list of the most publicized and influential surfers in the new millennium. They are a photographer's dream: if it's big and heavy, they're going for it; if it's small and ripable, they're pulling out more tricks than anyone else. Open a surf magazine anywhere in the world, and you'll most likely see a shot of one of the Ironses.

In essence, the brothers represent the spirit that DC reveres in surfing's cousins, skateboarding and snowboarding: raw progression in the face of severe consequences, with the added challenge of a watery stage. In skateboarding and snowboarding, surfaces are fixed and predictable; in the ocean, mountains and transitions are ever-moving. The shifting and unpredictable nature of waves is an unforgiving playground. Though softer than ice or concrete on the surface, a whole other world of respect in the form of razor-sharp coral and skull-crushing rock lies inches below.

That two kids from Kaua'i have grown up to have the surfing world's gaze fixed on their every move represents an evolution of sorts from the golden age of surfing, a spirit of riding waves that continually surpasses what was thought to be humanly possible. It's an energy that has traveled far and wide only to come full circle to the most special of places in surf lore, the spot where it all began: at home in the Hawaiian Islands.

All but the most disciplined and confident surfers would get as much speed as possible to outrun this Teahupo'o beast. Andy Irons, on the other hand, throws on the brakes right in its jaws. Tahiti, 2000.

SURFING
AN UNFORGIVING PLAYGROUND
BY SCOOTER LEONARD

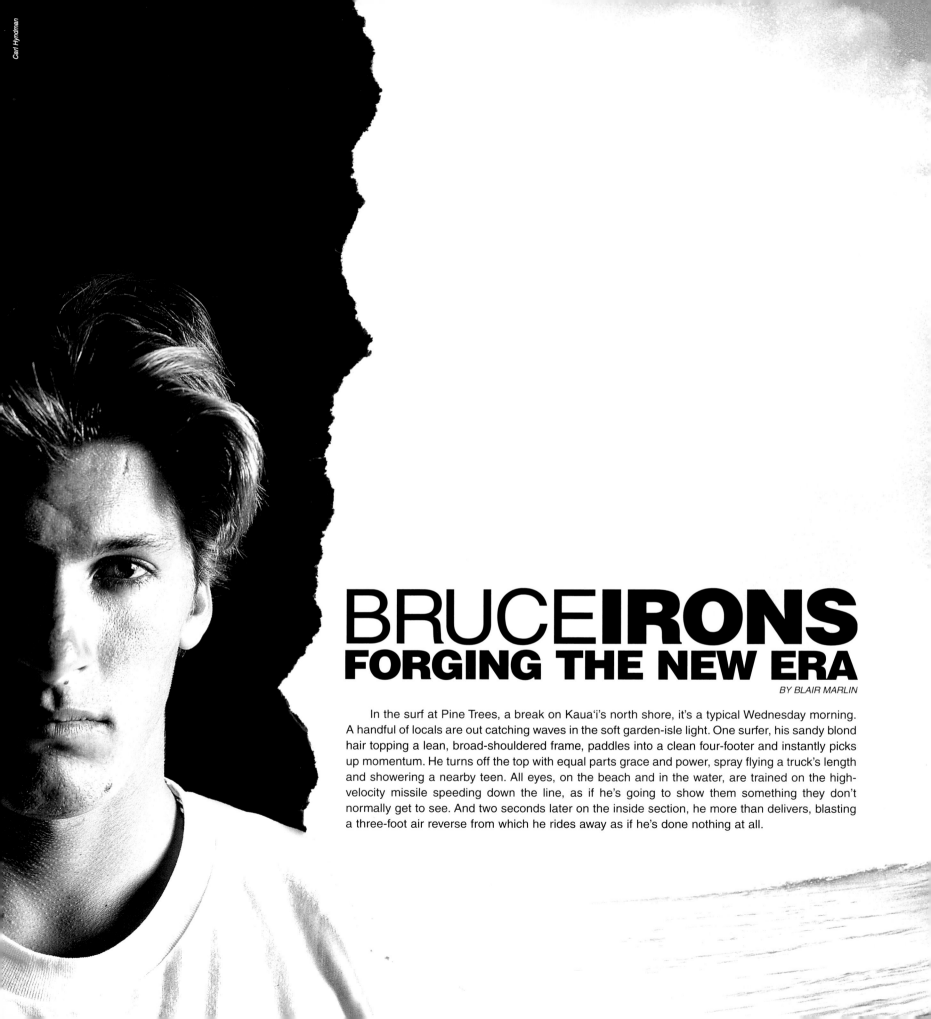

BRUCE**IRONS**
FORGING THE NEW ERA

BY BLAIR MARLIN

In the surf at Pine Trees, a break on Kaua'i's north shore, it's a typical Wednesday morning. A handful of locals are out catching waves in the soft garden-isle light. One surfer, his sandy blond hair topping a lean, broad-shouldered frame, paddles into a clean four-footer and instantly picks up momentum. He turns off the top with equal parts grace and power, spray flying a truck's length and showering a nearby teen. All eyes, on the beach and in the water, are trained on the high-velocity missile speeding down the line, as if he's going to show them something they don't normally get to see. And two seconds later on the inside section, he more than delivers, blasting a three-foot air reverse from which he rides away as if he's done nothing at all.

Bruce Irons defines confidence while standing tall in the pit of a Teahupo'o, Tahiti, barrel, 2000.

Everyone on the beach knows this young local. While he may be spending less and less time at home, Bruce Irons, the surfing world's "wonderkid" and younger brother of Andy (by a year and four months), has been a Pine Trees regular since birth.

Bruce makes his way up the sand, talks with some friends, and heads home, which just happens to be a small house that sits directly across the street from the beach—the same house he's been living in for as long as he can remember. A new magazine sits on the table (Bruce emblazoned in a heaving barrel on its cover) and two fresh white boards lie on the floor like magic carpets awaiting their master. He stuffs a couple of checks that have arrived from his sponsors into his backpack, loads up his board bag, says good-bye to his parents, and hits the road again. This time it's destination Australia for two contests, a photo trip, and whatever else the adventure gods may throw his way.

Grabbing what sleep he can on the flight, Bruce arrives in Sydney jet-lagged and still salty from the morning surf. Rather than sleep, however, he is energized by the rumor of a party and ends up rallying late into the night with friends and his childhood surfing heroes, whom he'll be facing in battle the following day.

You'd think that with this kind of program, a surfer might burn out. Not Bruce. He's a ball of fire who's been fueled by the desire to fight and succeed since birth.

On November 16, 1979, Bruce's mother, Danielle, was seven months pregnant when she began to get contractions while driving to the market. Bruce's first hours as a newborn were turbulent ones. As his father, Phil, puts it, "his lungs caved in right in front of me. Bruce almost died that day." The small hospital had only one electronic pump, which was being used by an elderly man, so the doctors had to pump Bruce with air by hand for the seven hours it took for the helicopter from Honolulu to arrive.

When he finally stabilized, the infant weighed in at a hefty 3.2 pounds. Bruce Pierre Irons had a whole lot of growing up to do.

Bruce has waterman genes that, judging from his brother, might have predetermined his destiny even before his rocky birth. He admits that he owes a majority of his surfing success to his surfer father for getting him started at such an early age, but it was his brother and his brother's circle of friends that really advanced his skills. He was that little punk kid who tagged along with the big kids, not so much in their shadow, but shadowing them, a relationship similar to that between Danny and Damon Way and the Vista Skate Locals. Bruce bore the brunt of their heckling in stride, and throughout his amateur career, strove to better Andy's performances and contest results. His is a fiercely competitive nature, whether it be the first to get tubed on a morning session or the first to win a World Qualifying Series (WQS) contest.

By 1998, eighteen-year-old Bruce had followed in his brother's footsteps to win each and every National

Bruce Irons's incredible ability to generate speed on any wave allows him to blast backside airs like this all day long, because even the Mentawai Islands in Indonesia aren't always overhead, 1999.

Tom Ruton

Use your imagination and try to figure out how Bruce Irons got his board in this position (and pulled it) at Lance's Rights, Mentawai Islands, Indonesia, 1999.

Tom Ruton

Bruce Irons, three fins out the back, yet still in utter control of another Mentawai situation. Indonesia, 1999.

Brian Bielmann

Scholastic Surfing Association (NSSA) amateur title. From there he wasted no time in moving up to the big leagues—getting filmed in massive surf and earning respectable results in professional contests on the island of O'ahu.

Among the young surfers of the world, Bruce is seen as a hero. Among his elders, he is the bold face of the new, the brash, the talented, full of energy and rebellion. He has engraved his presence on an international level with jaw-dropping performances at O'ahu's Pipeline and Tahiti's Teahupo'o, a monstrous beast of a barrel that slams onto a shallow, cheese-grater reef and is widely considered the world's heaviest wave. At the prestigious Hawaiian Island Creations (HIC) Pipeline Pro, the first contest of the 2001 WQS season, Bruce claimed his first-ever professional win. In December of that same year, he took the title of Pipeline Master at the Association of Surfing Professionals (ASP) Gerry Lopez Pipeline Masters. Among the riders in Bruce's final heat were Kelly Slater and world champion C.J. Hobgood.

Bruce has made a pact with himself, to give the 2002 season every ounce of energy he has in order to join his brother on the 2003 World Championship Tour (WCT). He had a good start at the beginning of the 2002 WQS season: another victory at the HIC Pipeline Pro on the North Shore of O'ahu. Those close to Bruce know it's only a matter of time before his natural freesurfing talent is honed into competitive domination. In a mysto crystal ball sense, the world of surfing has seen the future—and that future is Bruce Irons.

Rob Keith

Having returned to the Mentawai Islands for the 2001 Op Boat Challenge, Bruce Irons pulled out his arsenal of aerial tricks. It was borderline impossible to touch his zero-gravity approach to any section.

Be creative or go insane. Andy Irons plays with the lip while wasting away the days on a desert island in the middle of the Indian Ocean, 1998.

Jason Childs

ANDY IRONS
TOUGHER THAN STEEL

BY BLAIR MARLIN

In every sport, there are those athletes who succeed by following the past but work at being a little faster or a little stronger for an edge over their competition. More uncommon are those athletes who stand apart because they've broken from the mold. Surfer Andy Irons is such a mold breaker, and innovation is the fuel propelling him.

Andy Irons, who was born July 24, 1978, grew up at the ocean's edge on the lush, lava-encrusted island of Kaua'i, along with his mom, dad, and a little brother named Bruce. The boys' sandy, salty childhood was idyllic. "The beach and surfing were just part of my family's life back then," he says. "My dad got a house at Pine Trees [a beach break on Kaua'i] and we had everything we needed right there. We'd just hang out and surf, eat at the café, and then surf again."

In 1988, at the age of ten and with vast amounts of water time already under his belt, Andy entered his first amateur contest on the south side of Kaua'i, where he placed in the top five of the twelve-and-under division. This taste of victory sparked a competitive nature beyond his years. He began trying to imitate the older guys' tricks, but ended up falling more times than not.

This hotdogging nature eventually became the secret to Andy's success—once he settled down and learned instinctively when to pull out the right tricks at the right moments on the right waves. One by one, competitors fell victim to the grommet's persistent drive, and Andy continued to whoop the trunks off his peers throughout his amateur career. By the mid-nineties he'd won almost every amateur title possible and established a National Scholastic Surfing Association (NSSA) record by winning all forty-seven heats that he entered in the 1995/96 season. But even after Andy's prodigal abilities were noted on judges' score cards and magazine updates, nobody in the surf industry expected the young regular foot's next contest result, one that would win the attention of a grander audience than the amateur leagues.

The year was 1996, and the conditions at the Hawaiian Island Creations (HIC) Pipeline Pro at O'ahu's North Shore were perfect: ten-foot sets swept across the second reef, light offshore winds drifted through the palm trees, and a huge crowd lined the beach. In the water were Pipeline legend Derek Ho and World Championship Tour (WCT) standout Shane Beschen. Floating alongside them was seventeen-year-old Andy Irons, whose fateful semifinal heat win had put him in the unlikely, if not daunting, position of performing in front of a thousand spectators at one of the most challenging and life-threatening liquid stages on the planet.

Andy Irons boosting a backside air. O'ahu, 2000.

Tom Rulon

The teenager had already surpassed everyone's expectations (even his own). So, with nothing to lose and everything to gain, Andy put on a demonstration of backside barrel riding that rivaled anything the event's judges and the screaming crowd had ever seen. That afternoon he captured the HIC Pipeline Master title and the respect of the entire surfing world, a reminder that age and experience aren't always the best bets when raw courage and determination are in the lineup.

The following Monday, just another school day, Andy threw his half-finished homework in his backpack and headed for class. The first phone call to his house came at 8:30 in the morning, another a half hour later, and by the time he got home from school, there were almost twenty messages from surf companies wanting a piece of him. Life for Andy would never be the same; he had achieved fame literally overnight, and the only real option was to enjoy the ride. The Irons brothers' dad, Phil, remembers it well: "It

Mike Blabac

The heavy surf of Kaua'i schooled Andy Irons in the art of
no hesitation—a perfect curriculum for advanced education
at spots like O'ahu's Pipeline, 2000.

was weird. The boys were always being recruited as amateurs, free product and all, but after Andy won that contest the companies stepped it up to a whole new level." Phil took charge of handling these talent-hungry companies, enabling Andy to concentrate on his final year of high school and his surfing.

Anxious to join the professional contest circuit, Andy bolted the second he was handed his high school diploma. He began traveling the globe on the World Qualifying Series (WQS), and after a successful year, racked up enough points to qualify for one of forty-four spots on the WCT.

Despite bursts of sheer surfing brilliance, his first year as a rookie in the big leagues was tough. His results fluctuated like the peaks and valleys of his home island. His WCT rankings ultimately sank to a point that would kick him back down to the WQS for the following season. (Only the top twenty-eight of forty-four WCT surfers requalify each year, making room for the top sixteen WQS surfers to advance.) It was the equivalent of a pro baseball player returning to the minors. It was obvious that Andy was missing some pieces to the professional puzzle.

During the 2000 season, two-time world champion Damien Hardman retired after four events, leaving an open spot on the WCT. The points were tallied, and Andy moved back up to the "majors." Even with his late start on the tour, Andy went on to achieve his best WCT showings to date: a victory at Trestles, California, and an impressive performance at Pipeline, where he dominated and eliminated an in-form Kelly Slater to place fifth. Simultaneously, Andy continued surfing in every WQS event and took the runner-up spot on that tour as well, thus validating his top forty-four status.

Andy admits that he's stoked beyond belief to be in the company of the world's top surfers, but his professional goals spell out the future: "First, a top sixteen overall finish, and then a top five." As of April 2002, Andy holds the first-place position on the WCT, after winning at Bells Beach, Australia, that same month. Only time will tell if he has the focus and drive to keep heading in the direction everybody is anticipating: number one. Andy's dad has faith. "I knew Andy and Bruce were both going to take their lumps and bumps for a while on tour," he says, "but that's expected of all future champions, isn't it?"

That's not just fatherly pride talking, either. You'd be hard-pressed to find anyone who doesn't consider Andy a world-title contender, DC included. But scorecards and rankings aren't at the forefront of DC's decision to support this Hawaiian; it's his achievements in the water. Just as Andy credits younger brother Bruce as his greatest inspiration, DC credits Andy for keeping progressive surfing at the forefront of every decision, be it a split-second cutback in the pit of a heaving barrel (Andy scored a perfect ten on his first wave at the 2001 Gotcha Pro Invitational at Tahiti's Teahupo'o, reportedly the planet's heaviest hollow wave, on the shallowest of reefs) or Andy's specialty—giant floaters on scary sections normally reserved for quick exits, not massive reentries. Andy's personal drive in the water has proven his commitment to opening the sport's windows to innovation. Consistency and time will carry him all the way to the top. Stay tuned and see.

Daren Crawford

Andy Irons's confidence was hewn in the barrel and only sharpens as the consequences increase. Teahupo'o, Tahiti, 2000.

(A) **PLUG** FIRST RELEASED: **FALL 1996**
(B) **DASH** FIRST RELEASED: **SPRING 2001**
(C) **TEKRON** FIRST RELEASED: **SPRING 2001**
(D) **EXACTA** FIRST RELEASED: **FALL 2001**
(E) **RUDY2** FIRST RELEASED: **SPRING 1997**
(F) **IMPACT** FIRST RELEASED: **SPRING 2000**

(G) **BOXER2** FIRST RELEASED: **SPRING 1996**
(H) **AEROTECH** FIRST RELEASED: **SPRING 2002**
(I) **REASON** FIRST RELEASED: **HOLIDAY 2001**
(J) **DYRDEK2** FIRST RELEASED: **FALL 1996**
(K) **EXERO** FIRST RELEASED: **FALL 2000**
(L) **DYRDEK1** FIRST RELEASED: **FALL 1995**

theCHASE
THE MAKING OF A HOLLYWOOD COMMERCIAL WITH ROB DYRDEK
BY CARL HYNDMAN

Friday night, April 20, 2001. Raindrops batter the windshield of Ken Block's Mercedes as we drive north from Vista to Hell-Eh (L.A.) on Interstate 5. Tomorrow, theoretically, we'll be shooting a big-budget television commercial, a huge production. Lots of time, money, and energy have gone into planning the second major network commercial DC has produced (the first was with Josh Kalis in 1999). This time, the commercial will coordinate with print magazine advertising, point-of-purchase displays, posters, articles, and, most importantly, the release of Rob Dyrdek's new signature shoe model, the Exacta, another groundbreaking skateboard shoe packed with innovative features.

Hydroplaning in the fast lane, we try to be optimistic. The rain is forecast to continue all weekend.

We felt prepared for everything: insurance in case Dyrdek gets hurt, catering, hotel accommodations, spare custom T-shirts to replace dirt-smudged ones, tons of film, boxes of batteries, extra skateboard decks, water bottles, PowerBars, extra custom shoes, mobile generators, permits, props, actors, photographers, cinematographers, a full production crew, storyboards. We even hired a top-notch Hollywood director, Kevin Kerslake, to make sure it all comes together seamlessly, just like his work on national commercials for Quiksilver, Jobs.com, Sony, and Dickies, and big-name music videos for Green Day, Nirvana, and Cypress Hill. Now, with everything in place, Mother Nature threatens to scrap the entire budget.

Saturday. Two alarms and a wake-up call ring simultaneously. I'm absolutely not sleeping through skateboard history in the making. The weather has backed off and puddles in the streets are starting to dry. Notoriously brown smoggy skies have been washed clean and blue—optimal shooting conditions.

Base Camp looks like Super Bowl XXXV. People are everywhere. Eighteen-wheelers, VIP trailers, and E-Z Up canopies have taken over multiple parking lots. There are tables full of food and cups of Joe. Film and lighting crews are setting up across the street for the first scene; the LAPD is there for crowd control, doughnuts in hand. With all the big Hollywood budgets coming through this town, it's no wonder the cops sport the newest bikes loaded with the latest technologies. We'll forget about those shady characters breaking every other law in this part of town. This is more important.

I find Dyrdek at his "star" trailer with its satellite television hookup, special foods, assistants, built-in stereo, lounging area, and other luxuries. Dyrdek's nervous demeanor, however, seems very unstarlike. The day will require minor acting in addition to skating, and although Dyrdek is

Photos by Mike Blabac and Carl Hyndman

Rob Dyrdek and a cleanly executed 50-50 get-away from a mob of fans.

Carl Hyndman

loaded with natural charisma, he's not usually asked to cough it up on demand.

Ken Block's original idea was to have the script loosely based on the Beatles movie *A Hard Day's Night,* in which the superstars (in our case, superstar) are pursued by huge mobs of Beatlemania worshipers. Dyrdek's story mirrors the Beatles' narrow escapes, but instead of running or driving away, he out-skateboards a modern-day mob of starstruck fans through several urban obstacles. The climax is a huge, twenty-stair handrail with oversized rough-cut stone steps. No in-line skatin' Xtreme jumpin' stunt in Day-Glo colors followed by "Gnarly, dude!" This would be skateboarding, real and progressive with a lot on the line. Dyrdek won't be able to use the line "I'm not feeling it today."

The railing, which adorns a small amphitheater at the Omni Hotel, has never been done and is intimidating as hell. Security guards buzz the area like bees protecting their hive. Any unauthorized loitering in the area would be met with a swarm within seconds, but no matter: the rail's size and the consequences keep it devoid of skateboarders, of whom only the very best would even consider such a trick.

"I SURVIVED THAT DAY, BUT THAT'S HOW LIFE IS FOR ME. I'M JUST A SKATER TRYING TO LIVE THIS EVERYDAY STRUGGLE."
– Rob Dyrdek

Recommendations have been made to Dyrdek that he attempt something slightly less colossal, but he brushes them off. A frontside 50-50 on the "Holy (G)rail" will be his this weekend, thanks to guts, skill, a special permit obtained via Kerslake's production crew, and a promise to the hotel that not a single scratch or mark will be left on the rail or the tiled walkway after the shoot. To ensure this, the crew has painstakingly capped the railing with a flimsy metal "protector" that makes the already sketchy situation even more rickety. The precious run-in tiles have been covered with Masonite and painted to match. Nothing is left to chance in the damage control department. Still, hotel representatives are on standby to inspect their property after the shoot.

The first scenes, the "acting" scenes, are about to begin. Five-minute warning!

Initially, the closed-off street looks like chaos, but as the camera gets close to rolling, the experience of the crew becomes obvious. The first chase scene runs a little behind schedule, then clicks into synchronicity, with multiple angles and effects. Everyone from DC, including Dyrdek, critiques digital footage after each shot to make sure the filming is up to the critical standards of true skateboarding. After all, pro skateboarders tend to be perfectionists, who dissect things that would go undetected by the average shmo. It's a kind of catch-22: what seems pointless and trivial is what makes top-level skateboarding seem so effortless.

Action! Dyrdek crosses an intersection and casually looks back over his shoulder at the groupies chasing him. Again. And again. And again. The scenes continue: Dyrdek temporarily eludes the mob by ducking into a phone booth, then pauses just long enough to hit on a beautiful woman sitting on a park bench (a classic maneuver

Actor R.D. casually slips into a phone booth, thwarting, momentarily, his persistent fans.

Ending the commercial with an airborne climax, Rob Dyrdek kickflips off a semi-truck's trailer and casually skates away.

for Dyrdek, who rates picking up girls high on his list of real-life priorities). Unfortunately, the suave master's game is cut short by the fans, and the chase goes on.

Late in the day, a bicyclist—apparently a non–English-speaking bicyclist—inadvertently crashes the set. When shouting doesn't work, the crew motions wildly at the man, who, with his half-open eyes and potato-sack posture, also appears to be heavily intoxicated. He refuses to be deterred, making wobbly laps around the set until he eventually parks his bike in front of a seedy bar and disappears inside. A comedic, unplanned twist.

Day number two begins with heavy anticipation for the major skateboarding action shots to come. I blame my pissed-off stomach on last night's Mexican food and bottomless beers and tequila, but who am I kidding? Even I'm nervous for Dyrdek's fast-approaching moments of truth. There are a couple more minor acting scenes, then Dyrdek's semi-scattered demeanor melts away and is replaced by the focus I'm used to seeing in his eyes.

The Hollywood entourage gathers around the rail to scope out angles and lighting, and then huddles around Dyrdek to discuss and confirm last-minute concerns. Barricades are in place: no drunken bicyclists will be getting anywhere near these steps. It's a one-take deal for everyone—photographers, videographers, cinematographers, and even the extras have to be on it when the star lands his 50-50.

It seems that a good portion of Los Angeles has gathered to witness the event. Business suits, delivery drivers, tourists, skateboarders, and L.A.'s homeless jockey for position on the sidelines. Even one of the police officers on hand has brought his son along. The air is electric with anticipation.

Dyrdek puts his board on the less-than-solid capped rail to get the feel of the grind. He tries a few ollies on the approach to check the pop off the Masonite-covered tiles and to visualize the trick. After a few minutes of quiet contemplation, he's ready.

Action! Cameras rolling, fanatics in chase, Dyrdek stops inches from his ollie spot and yells in frustration. If it's not 100 percent feeling right, he isn't going to commit. Timing is everything, even when he's just out skating with buddies. With a shouting director and a watchful crowd, he's facing one hell of an added distraction.

Action! Dyrdek looks determined on the approach. He ollies. He's on! Sliding, sliding, mob in pursuit. He jumps off toward the bottom and rolls away past the bottom steps. This once-impossible rail is looking very probable. A quick dust-off, and Dyrdek's ready again. Having shaken hands with more than two-thirds of this monolithic rail, which is too big, really, to nail first go, Dyrdek's confidence is at an all-time high. Running back up the steps, he slides his hand intuitively across the rail's surface.

Action! With determination in his eyes, he approaches the rail at about a thirty-degree angle. The ollie: clean and accurate. The 50-50: locked-in, smooth, fast, and deliberate. The landing at the end: solid. The extras follow him down the stairs on cue. It's a wrap. Both the rail and the worst-case scenarios have been put to bed.

The script now calls for Dyrdek to escape the persistent extras by skating through a construction zone, past barricades, and up and off a flatbed truck, a straight and severe jump to freedom with a kickflip thrown in for good measure. Masonite is placed on the truck bed to smooth out the run-in. Some wood braces are added underneath to help give the wood some kick, a last-minute addition that Dyrdek eyes

R.D. after a hard day's work as actor, star, and skateboarding stuntman.

warily. He's ridden some shady terrain before, but this one—a Hollywood-ghetto construction, shaky at best—takes the cake.

The first two attempts are unsuccessful and Dyrdek's patience wears thin. He raises his board overhead, poised to hurl it in the direction of a cop who just happens to be standing in the line of fire. The officer jolts to attention. Almost as quickly as Dyrdek's temper flares, it subsides. The skateboard is lowered, and the cop relaxes.

Now calm and composed, Dyrdek pushes in for another go. Dialed speed, a nice pop, high catch, and a perfect landing. He skates away, looking back with a smile at the mob he's finally thwarted.

Weeks later, Dyrdek sits in one of DC's conference rooms watching edited footage on a widescreen television, a half-dozen boxes of his signature Exactas piled around him. Upon viewing the rail/kickflip climax, he deadpans a response while lacing up a new set of kicks: "I survived that day, but that's how life is for me. I'm just a skater trying to live this everyday struggle."

Enest Hemingway was the first writer to touch on the genesis of motocross. In his epic war novel *For Whom the Bell Tolls,* he wrote: "[The messenger] roared, bumping, down the shell-pocked mountain road between the double row of trees, the headlight of the motorcycle showing their whitewashed bases and the places on the trunks where the whitewash and the bark had been chipped and torn by shell fragments and bullets during the fighting . . ." It was these young messengers—soldiers riding military motorcycles over the singed, battle-ravaged landscape—who inadvertently brought to life a sport.

In autumn 1947, after the dark storm clouds of World War II had finally blown off the European continent, the first-ever world championship motocross race was held on the Netherlands' sandy, whooped-out Wassenaar circuit. Refined and organized by the French, this new form of professional motorsport, now known as motocross ("moto" meaning motorcycle, "cross" for cross-country), swept the continent. During the fifties and sixties, intrepid riders from Belgium, Finland, Sweden, East Germany, and the United Kingdom hustled their specially designed, British-made Matchless and BSA (British Small Arms) 500cc motorcycles around the majestic yet barbaric Grand Prix tracks of the low countries of Europe in an effort to become world champion. The fascinated youth of Europe came out in the tens of thousands to watch these wild-eyed iron men participate in a sport that was the ultimate synthesis of motorsport and athleticism.

By the seventies, the Belgians had taken control of the sport—two riders in particular, Roger DeCoster and Joel Robert, winning countless world championships for Suzuki, a powerhouse that had begun manufacturing motorcycles for Grand Prix motocross in the late sixties. Around the same time, motocross showed up in the United States.

Young Americans accustomed to dirt track racing, a sport consisting of rumbling Harley-Davidsons on county fair dirt ovals, were blown away by the high-flying, outlandish nature of the sport and the barnstorming Europeans who came across the Atlantic to compete in exhibition races. The Yankees soon adopted motocross, adding their own spin to it.

In summer 1974, a brazen West Coast rock 'n' roll promoter named Mike Goodwin took the rough-and-tumble sport and dropped it into clean, well-lit Major League baseball stadiums. Three decades of continuous growth later, this Americanized discipline of traditional motocross, known as supercross, is one of the most popular forms of motorsport in the world.

Rich Van Every

What price for glory? This celestial photo of Dustin Miller extending a cliffhanger into the setting sun kind of answers that question, doesn't it? At Mike Cinqmars's house in Apple Valley, California, 2002.

MOTOCROSS
WHAT PRICE FOR GLORY?
BY ERIC JOHNSON

Motocross began in World War II, when messengers were chased by bullets across the war-ravaged landscapes of Europe. It's highly unlikely the messengers ever had time to casually look back, as Ernesto Fonseca did at the Lake Street trails in Lake Elsinore, California, sixty years later.

Carl Hyndman

Rich Van Every

Kevin Windham whips it over the finish
line while practicing at the Anaheim,
California, 2002 Supercross Series,
Round Number One.

Ryan Hughes jumps
over a Glamis, California,
aqueduct in 1999.

Jimmy Button, high-speed over
some triples at the Yamaha test
track. Corona, California, 1999.

Michael Ballard

Derrick Swinfard

Although motocross in either format remains
a spectacular and graceful sport to both watch and
participate in, it also has a dark, unforgiving side. With
their legs and arms throbbing from the strain of holding on
to two-hundred-plus-pound motorcycles, sweat dripping into
their goggles and eyes, lungs crying for air, professional
motocross riders must traverse treacherous terrain that would like
nothing more than to reach up, grab hold, and violently throw them to
the ground. Every single world and national champion has, in fact, suffered
a major injury—broken back, ruptured spleen, fractured femur, and so on—
during his racing career.

The injuries in professional motocross are historically more severe than in any
other sport DC supports. For the sponsors, the fans, and ultimately the riders, this price
is not only an accepted hazard, but also an expected one. Determined to communicate a
"What price for glory?" message to all those who follow the sport (whether from a couch or the
seat of a motocross bike), DC produced a shocking, truth-be-told advertisement for the November
2000 issue of *Racer X Illustrated.* The ad, featuring a photo of DC team riders Jeff Emig and Jimmy
Button in medieval-looking medical braces under the headline "Greatness Has a Price," was a poignant
portrayal of the risks resting beneath every motocross track's terra firma.

Motocross is a sport of chances. And while taking big chances throughout their legendary careers helped make
Jeff Emig and Jimmy Button international sporting heroes, laying it on the line also ultimately cost them their livelihoods.
Motocross is a poetic sport. Motocross is a magnificent sport. Motocross can be a wicked sport. Nobody knows that better than

*Dustin Miller at the Perris
Raceway, California, 2001.*

RICKY
CARMICHAEL
A LEGEND IN THE MAKING

BY DAVEY COOMBS

Supercross is big business in America. In just a few years, this stadium version of outdoor motocross racing has grown from a niche activity to a motorsports phenomenon in which top riders are featured on *The Late Show with David Letterman* and races show regularly on ABC's *Wide World of Sports.* On any given Saturday night, 60,000 fans pack the grandstands of the nation's big ballparks to watch supercross racers do battle on treacherous obstacle courses filled with double and triple jumps.

For years, supercross fans came to see a Southern California racer named Jeremy "Showtime" McGrath lead the charge, and McGrath did not disappoint: he won seven titles from 1993 to 2000 and a jaw-dropping seventy main events. So dominant was McGrath that many of the sport's insiders felt he would one day retire while still reigning as "King of Supercross," simply parking his bike before any of his rivals could grab the Number One plate from it.

Then along came Ricky Carmichael, a quiet, modest kid from Havana, Florida, who grew up with a McGrath jersey hanging on his bedroom wall, and riding motorcycles—constantly. While McGrath was building his legendary status, Carmichael was working on one of his own as the sport's fastest-ever minicycle racer. His motocross

Rich Van Every

Rich Van Every

Ricky Carmichael gets used to a new bike with a pointing whip on a newly built set of supercross triples at his two-hundred-acre training ranch outside Tallahassee. Florida, 2001.

R.C. rebuilds his training tracks at the beginning of each season—supercross in the early fall, outdoor in the early spring. Scenes from the ranch, including a hefty collection of Number One plates and his super-supportive mom. Tallahassee, Florida, 2001.

Ricky Carmichael whips it out alongside his inspiration/rival Jeremy McGrath on a parade run at the 2001 Anaheim Supercross Series in California.

. . . out on the track, where McGrath is a technical and precise rider, Carmichael's style is significantly more wild and explosive, in every aspect.

career began aboard a 50cc peewee bike on Valentine's Day when he was age five, then progressed through the 50cc, 60cc, and 80cc minicycle divisions to a record ten AMA Amateur National Motocross Championships. He grabbed his first professional title in the 1997 AMA 125cc National Championship as a seventeen-year-old rookie, a fearless age where physical strength was poised on the verge of fearless stamina. Carmichael seemed an excellent candidate to someday take over where McGrath would leave off.

"Someday" came a lot sooner than anyone expected. When the 2001 U.S. Supercross Series ended in early May in Las Vegas, the twenty-one-year-old Kawasaki/Chevy Trucks factory rider was the winner of a remarkable fourteen out of sixteen races. After just one season, Carmichael had defeated the greatest rider the sport had ever seen, which immediately positioned him as the best supercross racer in the world. The sport's foundation was rocked to its core simultaneously with the realization of a dream.

"Jeremy is one of a kind, a great champion, and a really good sport," says Carmichael of defeating his boyhood idol. "To be compared to him is quite an honor. We don't hang out, but we're always nice to each other."

Although Carmichael and McGrath are often compared, their similarities end at good results and the almost demonic desire to win. Throughout his tenure in the sport, Jeremy McGrath has welcomed the white-hot spotlight of supercross. Conversely, Carmichael is uneasy and somewhat shy in front of his adoring audience. Moreover, out on the track, where McGrath is a technical and precise rider, Carmichael's style is significantly more wild and explosive, in every aspect. Wherein was this track magic spawned?

Carmichael's meteoric rise to the top was preceded by a lengthy amateur career in outdoor motocross, the sport's more traditional form of racing. Beginning at age eight, and subsidized by the financial and technical clout of Kawasaki's Team Green amateur support program, he and his parents, Rick and Jeannie, began spending every weekend—and sometimes up to three races per week—on the southern motocross circuits of Florida and Georgia. "Those days were fun," says Carmichael. "That's when it was kind of stress-free. I think I put a little more pressure on myself than the other kids, but it paid off."

Indeed, Carmichael's amateur winning streak continued right into his professional career. During a three-year period, he won a record-tying twenty-five outdoor nationals in the 125cc class as well as three straight 125cc U.S. National Championships. And in 2000, when he moved into the premier 250cc class full-time, he won nine of the twelve races in the U.S. National Championships and a record-breaking fourth straight title.

"Outdoor racing just always came easy for me," says Carmichael, who started the 2001 season with thirty-four career national wins, just three shy of the all-time mark set by the Jeremy McGrath of outdoor motocross, Bob "Hurricane" Hannah. "I always feel like I'm in a groove out there."

Even with such outstanding results in outdoor motocross, a 250cc Supercross Championship seemed a long way off for Carmichael. After all, at five-foot-four he was the shortest man in the class, not to mention (at that time at least) the pudgiest. The very nature of supercross racing, with its long, washboard-style whoop sections and steep banked turns, requires long legs, strong arms, and excellent anaerobic endurance.

But what Carmichael gave away in height he made up for with heart. When his 2000 supercross season ended with only a single win—the motocross-like sand race at

Carl Hyndman

Sometimes his goats, Jack and Jill, are the only lucky witnesses to ultra–laid out tailwhip lookbacks while Ricky Carmichael trains at his ranch outside Tallahassee, Florida. 2001.

Paul Buckley

Simon Cudby

Paul Buckley

Simon Cudby

Daytona International Speedway—R.C. dug in. During the off-season, he put in time at the gym, hired a personal fitness trainer, and began reshaping his body. While many of his rivals were flying around the world making an easy paycheck on the international exhibition circuit, Carmichael was pounding out countless laps on the many brutal practice tracks that dot north-central Florida.

The 2001 supercross season kicked off at Anaheim's Edison International Field, and Carmichael was ready—perhaps too much so. He came out firing but soon found himself succumbing to nervous tension as he chased after the leader, McGrath.

"I think I worked and thought myself right out of that race," he says. "I was so ready and I wanted to win so badly that I couldn't relax. I didn't take my time, settle down, and let the race come to me. But I did learn a lot that night about how to race with Jeremy." McGrath won the race while Carmichael struggled to finish third behind Team Honda factory rider Ezra Lusk.

Carmichael stormed back to take the second race, held at San Diego's Qualcomm Field, from McGrath, then battled him straight-up in the second of three Anaheim races before losing once again. But beginning the following weekend at Phoenix's Bank One Ballpark, Carmichael embarked on a winning streak that would last through the rest of the season. From January 20 to May 5, the young man who was once thought to be too short, too fat, and too wild for supercross never lost a race. Along the way he clinched the series championship and became the first person to take the Number One plate away from McGrath.

Carmichael's string of successes guarantees him a place in supercross history as the sport's first $2-million-a-year man. His asking price for a multiyear contract has entered the economic stratosphere of stick-

(1) Ricky Carmichael airing it out for his fans in 2001. (2) Clinching his 250cc championship in Dallas, Texas: twelfth win of the 2001 season, eleventh win in a row. (3) Every win earns R.C. a fox and crossbones—you do the math. (4) Going down hard at Glen Helen Raceway, San Bernardino, California, 2001. (5) Podium shot for number one supercross champion, R.C. (6) Victory lap at Glen Helen Raceway, 2000. (7) A well-earned Number One bike at R.C.'s home in Florida. (8) It all comes down to this—R.C. and his mom sharing a victory moment.

1		3		5	6		8
2		4			7		

and-ball sports like the NFL and Major League Baseball. In fact, when R.C. adds in his factory bonuses, prize money, and sponsorship for riding gear, goggles, video games, and (ahem) shoes, he might actually be his sport's first $3-million-a-year man.

As a reward for realizing his lifelong dream of becoming a supercross champion, Carmichael recently bought himself a new house and a large parcel of land for his own private motocross and supercross practice tracks. He has long-term deals with major motocross players Fox Racing and Oakley, and owns his own company, RC Racing, which his mother and his girlfriend, Ursula, help run. That's a good thing for Carmichael, because it frees up time for the endless laps and hours at the gym necessary to thrive in the world of motocross and supercross.

"I'm willing to do whatever it takes to win," he says. "To be a legend in this sport, you've got to beat one or two. I'd like to think that I can break every record, but it will be tough. I think the competition is really tough right now and there are a lot of guys who want to be the best. That's why it was so important for me to beat Jeremy now, while he is still an active racer. If I had waited until he was gone from the sport to win, people would have said, 'But what if Jeremy was here?'"

McGrath was there. And so was Ricky Carmichael. After sixteen rounds and over three hundred laps of racing, the 2001 Supercross Championship was won in a straight-up fight. Factoring in skill and determination, supercross is, without a doubt, the type of sport in which the best man wins. In 2001, the best man was named Ricky Carmichael.

JEFF EMIG
TO THE TUNE OF 65,000 CRAZED FANS

BY ERIC JOHNSON

"You know, I've been having dreams about riding again," said Jeff Emig, standing atop a neon green bulldozer and watching his two riders train on the Kawasaki factory motocross test track in Corona, California. It was December 2000, and the opening round of the EA Sports Supercross Series at Edison International Field was less than two weeks away. Emig, who was forced to retire from the sport he loved after breaking his back in a training crash at Glen Helen Raceway in San Bernardino, California, on May 14 that same year, had taken on the role of team owner. Although he relished both the challenge of operating his own race team and working with the outfit's two riders, Michael Byrne and Casey Johnson, he hadn't been on a bike since his accident. He missed riding. He missed racing. He missed flying through the night air to the tune of 65,000 crazed fans. He missed the passion he'd first discovered on a frozen path behind the family home in Independence, Missouri, over a quarter century before.

For virtually his entire life, Jeff Emig has been a motocross racer. First introduced to the sport by his father, Gary, some four years after he was born on December 1, 1970, Emig quickly adapted to two wheels. He began racing every Friday night at Kansas City International Raceway and progressed rapidly, supported by an enthusiastic motorsports-loving dad—a renowned auto racing engine builder whose work graced the asphalt bullrings of the Midwest. By the time Emig was out of elementary school, he and his family were receiving motorcycles and travel expenses from the Yamaha Motor Corporation. By age twelve, the shy and demure rider—then struggling to overcome a severe stuttering problem—was already a multitime 60cc and 80cc minicycle national champion.

Emig possessed the natural talent and speed required to make it in the big leagues, and backed by Team Kawasaki, he turned pro at age eighteen. After a year spent acclimating to the fierce pro-level competition, he won his first pro race in 1990 at the Houston Astrodome. Two years later, Emig cracked his first major title: the AMA 125cc National Championship. Upon crossing the finish line that dreary, rain-lashed afternoon in Budds Creek, Maryland, he broke down in tears on national TV, an in-your-face testament to the emotional tension behind usually stone-faced world-class racing.

Paul Buckley

The day Jeff Emig won the 250cc National Motocross Championship for the second time and became the seventh rider in history to win the 250cc supercross and motocross championships in the same year. AMA Motocross Series/Broome Tioga. Binghampton, New York, 1997.

INSET PHOTOS (LEFT TO RIGHT): Moments from a career in motion: a hundred G's for winning the 1999 U.S. Open of Supercross in Las Vegas, Nevada—J.E.'s last professional win; sliding out during the 1993 Hangtown Motocross race in Sacramento, California; sobriety test photo shoot for Racer X Illustrated outside of Las Vegas, Nevada, 1998; taking the high road at the multinational Des Nations event in Europe, 1996; Shift ad on a private jet, 1997.

Chris Hultner

Racer X Illustrated

Racer X Illustrated

Racer X Illustrated

Winning the AMA championship, one of the most prestigious titles in the world, made Jeff Emig an international motocross star almost overnight. Rather than being galvanized by the success, however, Emig almost seemed to lose his way in the ensuing three seasons. He gave up the 125cc title in 1993 and placed an apathetic fifth in 1994. In 1995 he was bumped up to the 250cc

This DC ad ran in September 1999 motocross magazines during the scandalous Clinton administration, and in response to Kawasaki firing Jeff Emig after the "Lake Havasu incident."

class by his employer, Team Yamaha, and while he earned an impressive second overall in his rookie campaign, he was no match for class champion Jeremy McGrath.

Just prior to the 1996 season, Emig defected to Team Kawasaki, a switch that proved to be a deft maneuver. Not only would he disrupt Jeremy McGrath's astonishing thirteen-race-long supercross win streak at the Trans World Dome in St. Louis on April 27, he'd also defeat McGrath in a dramatic final moto showdown at Steel City, Pennsylvania, that summer, earning himself the AMA 250cc National Championship title.

In 1997, Emig won five of the fifteen AMA 250cc Supercross Series events to defeat Jeremy McGrath—now his bitter arch-rival—for the championship. He also defended his 250cc National

Championship title, becoming one of only a handful of riders in American motocross history to claim both titles in one year. He had also become the best motocross rider in the world—and the most popular.

A legion of enthusiasts cheered the champion's racing exploits, many of them donning poofy circa-1974 wigs to honor his new nickname, Fro (boiled down from Jeffry to Jeffro to Fro). The fans had flocked to Emig's side, not only because of his results but because he'd go that extra mile after races. In effect, Emig was able to shut the "competitor" off when not racing, and turn it on when he was. He was approachable and personable, cracking jokes, allowing kids to sit on his bike for photos, and letting his enthusiasm shine through.

But within a year, it would all go wrong. Emig loved being a star, perhaps more so than any other rider of his generation. He allowed fame, and the negative trappings that can often accompany it, to get the better of him and his results: parties, Learjets, and big-dollar contracts took the place of blood, sweat, and tears. Visibly out of sorts and riding with none of the electric smooth grace and precision that had come to define his professional career, Emig went, in the span of one year, from being a winner to banging about in the forgettable, midpack realm of lappers. His fall from grace was well documented and obvious to all; talk of the "distractions" plaguing him began to overshadow anything he managed to do on a racetrack.

On August 22, 1999, Emig, wandering around Lake Havasu City, Arizona, in the early morning hours with a small amount of marijuana in his pocket, was picked up by the local police, searched, and promptly cuffed. Although the possession charge was a relatively minor offense to the American court system, it was a public relations fiasco for Emig's sponsor, Team Kawasaki, and he was immediately fired.

Emig addressed the issue head-on by submitting a heartfelt letter to several motocross magazines in which he pledged to pull it all back together. On the advice of close friends, he checked into an alcohol treatment program, which left him rejuvenated and more motivated than he had been in years. He procured a motorcycle from Yamaha and cashed in on a number of favors from longtime

J.E. is rarely seen on the ground when out freeriding. Here he is in 1999 at Mike Cinqmars's house in California, waking up the neighborhood.

Derrick Swinfard

INSET PHOTOS (TOP LEFT TO BOTTOM RIGHT): Jeremy McGrath and Jeff Emig face off for a publicity poster hyping up the annual Paris-Bercy Supercross, smack dab in the middle of Paris, France, 1997; retirement banquet trophy; "Hey kids, start your day with a fat bowl of Emig O's cereal." Things were "out of control" when J.E. shot his cereal commercial on the set of the movie Fresno Smooth in 1997; J.E. celebrating with the coveted Number One plate; J.E.'s big crash, out cold at the Glen Helen Raceway, San Bernardino, California, in 2000: broken back and leg.

Jeff Emig's first DC advertisement, a tailwhip in Southern California, 1998.

(and loyal) sponsors, and just seven weeks after his arrest, Jeff Emig stunned the motocross world by winning the 1999 U.S. Open at Las Vegas's opulent MGM Grand Hotel and Casino. He had, for all intents and purposes, exorcised his demons and come full circle.

DC's straight-up advertisement with Jeff Emig and Jimmy Button. Greatness does have a price, 2000.

It would be the racing gods who smacked him down next. First he broke both wrists in a crash during training for the 2000 Supercross Series when he came up short on a jump. The following spring his throttle stuck during training at Glen Helen Raceway and he was launched off the back of his Yamaha. He ended up lying in a puddle of mud and water, an undignified heap with a broken back and shattered leg. That's when he realized that he had had enough. He retired from professional motocross to become a team owner.

Emig did his best to take a step back and channel his energy and enthusiasm into his fledgling team, Team EdgeSports.com, but his subconscious refused to cooperate. "I had this dream that I was riding on this incredible outdoor motocross track," he says. "The dirt was dark and real loamy, and the track had these radical berms where you could literally drag the bars all the way through the corners. It was just unreal. When I woke up, I said to myself, 'Man, I really need to go riding again. I really miss this.'"

Emig spent the early part of winter 2000 in physical therapy, and two days before Christmas, his doctor gave him the go-ahead to ride again. "I couldn't believe how much fun it was," says Emig. "There was no race, no pressure, no crashes. I was just going to ride and enjoy myself. I was going to do something I had loved doing so much as a kid."

He stood by his decision to retire from professional motocross, but Ken Block insisted that Emig (who had been a DC rider since 1998) remain a part of the team. Because Emig personified the winning attributes of other DC team riders such as Motocross des Nations champion Ryan Hughes, 125cc supercross champion Ernesto Fonseca, and the current number one rider in the world, Ricky Carmichael, DC stepped up to help sponsor Team EdgeSports.com.

DC also came up with an ad that mirrored what riders like Emig go through to achieve their goals and dreams. "At that point, there was a bad vibe about riding and racing," says Emig. "A lot of top guys, such as Jimmy Button and I, had been hurt. When we were talking about a potential headline, I spoke up and said, 'Greatness has a price.'" Emig's words became the ad's headline.

Spring 2001 brought with it another example of how professional motocross can be a cruel, "what have you done for me lately" occupation: Emig's primary sponsor, e-commerce firm The EdgeSports.com, collapsed under its own weight and ultimately filed for bankruptcy, resulting in the immediate disintegration of Team EdgeSports.com. But it is just these kinds of humanizing ups and downs that continue to make Jeff Emig a larger-than-life superstar in the world of motocross. He has openly risked it all— his savings, his emotions, and his humility—and still remains determined to give something back to the sport he loves, whether in the form of a team, or coaching, or simply continuing to inspire others. As Emig says, "It's a dangerous sport and sometimes you have to pay the price. You owe that risk to your fans and to yourself."

Emig was and always will be a crowd pleaser, going higher, farther, and faster than the pack on the road to motocross and supercross history. All those fans who wore wigs in his honor or craned their necks from the sheer amplitude of his glory can't argue: they've been paid in full.

"One of the funnest jumps of my life," says Jeff Emig of this Castillo Ranch, California, sequence taken in 1999.

Mike Balzer

MIKE**CINQMARS**
C O M M I T T E D

BY ERIC JOHNSON

When a topflight rider gets hurt, a deep, almost palpable shudder goes through the American motocross community. On January 22, 2001, twenty-two-year-old Mike Cinqmars, one of the most talented and technical freestyle motocross pilots in the world and a DC team rider, came up short on a huge, cavernous jump at Southern California's Sunrise Motocross Park. The result was a fractured L1 vertebra in his lower back and a frenzied Medi-Vac ride to the emergency ward.

Cinqmars, who knew immediately that he'd misjudged the ninety-foot double jump and was in deep trouble from the takeoff, jettisoned from his bike at the last possible second. "I saw that I was going to come up pretty short," he says. "I jumped off and landed on my feet on the back-side of the landing and felt my back fold over—I felt like I kissed my feet. I remember rolling back down the landing and feeling the tingling in my back. I knew my back was broken right away."

Mike Cinqmars, Indian air seat grab at his parents' home in Apple Valley, California, 2000.

Derrick Swinfard

Mike Cinqmars,
all whipped up in
his folks' yard.
Apple Valley,
California, 2000.

While freestyle motocross is somewhat difficult to define and categorize, a relatively accurate definition would be "the untamed, punk rock offspring of traditional motocross and supercross." Freestyle's roots date back to Evel Knievel and his double-decker-bus-jumping exploits of the mid-sixties, but its "sports" status took hold during the late nineties when iconoclastic videos such as *Crusty Demons of Dirt* and ad hoc SoCal-based freeride contests formed a critical mass that exploded into a cultural phenomenon. At the vanguard of the new "freeride movement" was Mike Cinqmars, a former professional motocross racer from Apple Valley, California, who'd been bashing out countless laps on the dusty, blue groove SoCal circuits since his *Sesame Street* days. Burnt out on the old format, Cinqmars refocused his sights on the burgeoning freestyle scene that was gaining momentum in the badlands of the Southwest, and quickly became one of the sport's biggest stars—completely by chance.

One afternoon in 1998, a friend had invited him to go dune riding. Some of Cinqmars's jumping exploits were captured on video that eventually made its way into the motocross video *Chrome*. That cameo appearance started a chain reaction of filming opportunities.

A natural showman with phenomenal technical skills, Cinqmars bagged a silver medal in the 1999 ESPN-produced X Games, and kicked in the year 2000 with a high-profile 197-foot leap over a sand dune at Dumont Dunes in Barstow, California, that ended up in the *Guinness World Records*. It was the lure of pulling off Evel Knievel–inspired stunts, however, that truly appealed to Cinqmars.

To that end, Cinqmars eventually found his way to the MTV network, which was having great success with its *Senseless Acts of Video* program. MTV execs discovered that nothing draws a crowd (or Nielsen television ratings) like a motorcycle jump over inanimate objects. Cinqmars became an instant celebrity by performing mind-boggling leaps over his parents' large home, a bus station in Fresno, California, and off a dock and over a bay in Cancún, Mexico. On top of the world and cashing in on his success, Cinq was living large.

In summer 2000, Cinqmars rolled out of Apple Valley and hit the road with a big mobile home and his Honda CR250s to produce a kind of Jack Kerouac *On the Road* narrative video for the freestyle set. Along with close friend Carl Harris and a few other pals, Cinqmars barnstormed across America for almost two months, dropping in on small towns, county fairs, and motorcycle dealerships to exhibit jumps for the thousands of fans who came out to watch him fly over their local airspace.

Then came Sunrise.

Cinqmars had returned home and was putting the finishing touches on *35/01 My Trip* with Harris when he suffered his back injury. Making the most of a devastating situation, the pair procured a doctor's

M.C., high-speed, low-drag portrait, 2000.

Markus Paulsen

Mike Cinqmars timed this Hart Attack over Tommy Lee's band, Methods of Mayhem, perfectly. The stage was two tour buses (or 130 feet) long. 2000 Ozzfest, Sacramento, California.

approval for Harris to remain in the operating room and video the surgery just hours before Cinqmars went under the knife.

After wading his way out of the deep, anesthesia-induced fog that followed his operation, Cinqmars followed his heart and included the surgery as the powerfully realistic conclusion to *My Trip*.

"I just wanted to show people who only see the good side of motocross what can happen," he says. "I wanted to show them it's a real deal. After a number of people watched the end of the video, some of them said, 'That's gnarly! I can't believe you put that in!' I didn't do it to gross people out. I did it to show them that this sport isn't always limos, parties, and glamour."

The public response to *My Trip* was so positive that the video became something of a word-of-mouth cult classic, which only made Cinqmars more hungry to ride again. "Every day I look outside and want to go out and ride," he says. "I have two new bikes just sitting there in the garage, and it's driving me crazy. I just want to get back on the bike and ride as good as I was before I got hurt. It all plays with your head mentally, because I keep thinking, 'Will I be as good as I was? I'm sitting here doing nothing while everyone else is out there progressing.'"

Thrilled, not intimidated, by the prospect of competing again, Cinqmars hopes to pull off a couple of contest wins before turning his attention toward an objective he believes will make him the undisputed king of freestyle motocross. "I have something big planned that is going to blow people out of the water," he says. "When people see what I'm going to do, they're going to be like, 'Jeez! This guy just doesn't care!' I'm going to show people that I'm back doing what I love to do best: jumping my motorcycle."

Stay tuned.

A gopher's-eye view of life according to Cinqmars. Indian air seat grab near Apple Valley, California, 2000.

Dave Norehad

SIGNATURE SHOES: DC'S CORNERSTONE

DC is based on the signature model strategy. During 1994 and 1995, its first four shoes—Danny Way, McKay1, Rudy Johnson, and Dyrdek1—set the stage for innovation in skateboard shoe technology. Since then, other non–pro-model shoes have been included in the DC line, but virtually every technical feature was, and is, introduced through the high-end, pro-designed shoes that remain the foundation for DC's continued success.

When BMX superstar Dave Mirra joined the DC team, he used his expertise to help create DC's first BMX-specific model, the Mirra, in 2001, continuing the trend of sport-specific models designed by the very best athletes. The high-performance shoes evolve as quickly as the tricks the athletes perform; their bold designs, colors, and materials showcasing a time line of style and function.

COZMO
MIKE**CARROLL**

HOWARD2
RICK**HOWARD**

HOWARD1
RICK**HOWARD**

RUDY3
RUDY**JOHNSON**

McKAY3
COLIN**McKAY**

WAY4
DANNY**WAY**

LEGACY
DANNY**WAY**
COLIN**McKAY**

DYRDEK2
ROB**DYRDEK**

DYRDEK3
ROB**DYRDEK**

MANTIS
ROB**DYRDEK**

McKAY1
COLIN**McKAY**

RUDY JOHNSON
RUDY**JOHNSON**

McKAY2
COLIN**McKAY**

RUDY2
RUDY**JOHNSON**

RAIDEN
COLIN**McKAY**

DANNY WAY
DANNY**WAY**

DYRDEK1
ROB**DYRDEK**

DANNY WAY2
DANNY**WAY**

DANNY WAY3
DANNY**WAY**

INFINITY
DANNY**WAY**

| 1994 | 1995 | 1996 | 1997 | 1998 |

MIRRA
DAVE**MIRRA**

WILLIAMS
STEVIE**WILLIAMS**

REASON
STEVIE**WILLIAMS**

RATIO
DAVE**MIRRA**

KALIS
JOSH**KALIS**

A.V.E.
ANTHONY**VAN ENGELEN**

SPECIFIC
ANTHONY**VAN ENGELEN**

EMBARKO
MIKE**CARROLL**

DEUCE
DANNY**WAY**
COLIN**McKAY**

SOLUTION
DANNY**WAY**
COLIN**McKAY**

VERDICT
JOSH**KALIS**

KOVAR
RICK**HOWARD**

ENDEAVOUR
ROB**DYRDEK**

TRUTH
JOSH**KALIS**

REALITY
DANNY**WAY**
COLIN**McKAY**

METRO
ROB**DYRDEK**

UNITED
ROB**DYRDEK**

EXACTA
ROB**DYRDEK**

JEWEL
ROB**DYRDEK**

RELAY
COLIN**McKAY**

AKIRA
COLIN**McKAY**

TEKRON
COLIN**McKAY**

CENTRE
COLIN**McKAY**

IOMI
RUDY**JOHNSON**

EVOLUTION
DANNY**WAY**

DIABLO
DANNY**WAY**

AEROTECH
DANNY**WAY**

1999   2000   2001   2002   2003

*Josh Kalis, frontside crooked
grind in Philadelphia, 1999.*

JOSH KALIS

FULL CIRCLE

BY KEVIN WILKINS

Imagine waking up one day and realizing that you are on the journey that is Josh Kalis.

You are the guy with his name on one of DC's best-selling kicks. You are the professional skateboarder born on April 27, 1976, in Grand Rapids, Michigan, but now living colossal in a three-bedroom residence in downtown Philadelphia because that's where you want to be, that's where you love to be. You are supporting a family; you're driving around in your own BMW (not the bank's); you take showers in your own shower (not your landlord's); and you are the self-appointed foot soldier keeping guard over your city's most famous skate spot, Love Park. On top of it all, and without which you'd be just another dude grinding out a life and making ends meet, you can skateboard with the surprising ease of someone whose conscious and subconscious are on a first-name basis.

"It surprises me pretty much every day," says Kalis. "When I wake up, hop in my car, and go buy my little girl *The Land Before Time* DVDs, that's when it really surprises me. I got this shit from skateboarding? I don't even look at myself as pro. I try to carry myself as if I am one of the kids at the demo. I'm just allowed to skate, you know what I mean?"

Kalis's first exposure to skateboarding happened as it does with most kids: a junior high pal had a board and let him check it out at school. One recess of tic-tacking and Kalis was hooked. He saved up money from a summer of mowing lawns between sixth and seventh grade just to buy his first setup. He progressed rapidly from seeing how long he could tic-tack to seeing how many 360 flips he could do in a row.

The only child in a single-parent household, Kalis spent most of his early teen years with his father in Grand Rapids, a place where skateboarding wasn't viewed as something fun for kids to do, but rather something that got kids into trouble. Bad kids skateboarded. Kids who did drugs and drank skateboarded. Kalis's dad

"JOSH HAD TRICK DYNAMICS WORKED OUT . . . HE WAS AHEAD OF HIS TIME."
– Jamie Thomas on a young Josh Kalis

held the same view. Says Kalis, "Every time I got in trouble, skateboarding was always the first thing to go. I'd get my skateboard taken away and my dad would lock it in his closet. He used to put Oreo cookie filling on one of the wheels, so if I ever rode it, he'd know. That's around the time when he would cut up my boards and microwave my wheels and stuff like that, too."

His parents had split up when Kalis was seven and in the years that followed he divided his time bouncing between his dad's residences in Michigan and Dallas and wherever his mom happened to be living at the time, usually Philadelphia or New York City. Though his parents didn't support his aspirations, Kalis saw skateboarding as a career path and he dropped out of high school at sixteen to set out on his own. It was the beginning of a year of sporadic moves spurred on by skateboarding, but soon enough the pressures of supporting himself as an underage adult made skateboarding a nonpriority. Making rent became the unfortunate reality.

He was seventeen and living in Dallas when a fortunate event rekindled the dying skateboarding flame. That's when established pro skater Jamie Thomas, whom Kalis had met in Philly a few years before, came to town on a demo tour with his then-sponsor Invisible Skateboards.

The touring pro and his friends were collecting footage for a video of their trip and asked Kalis if they could film him skating around the city. He agreed, and proceeded to blow everyone away. Thomas remembers it well: "Josh had trick dynamics worked out to where he could make them look really good. He wasn't trying extra hard; it's just the way they worked for him. He had backside flips over

Mike Blabac

*This 360 flip off a Love Park tile—
Philadelphia, 1999—became the box
top for Josh Kalis's first pair of shoes.*

Josh Kalis, switch crooked grind on a picnic table. You guessed it: downtown Philadelphia, 2000.

Mike Blabac

Soaking wet frontside
noseslide in New York
City in 1999.

Michael Ballard

hips and over pyramids, high and caught. No one else was really doing that back then. He was ahead of his time."

As far as Thomas was concerned, Kalis's innovative approach was up to the pro standard. He knew that some kid in the middle of Texas skating the way Kalis did could really shine if he skated with people at his level. Thomas flowed Kalis the two or three extra decks he had on hand and told him he'd try to get him a sponsor when he returned to the West Coast. He didn't have to try hard. After Thomas played the video for his equally awed teammates, Kalis received a full sponsorship from Invisible.

Six months later Thomas switched gears to ride for a new company, Toy Machine, and wanted Kalis on board. Thomas sent him a box of boards worth enough for a plane ticket and offered what turned out to be a bit of priceless advice: "Get your shit together and come out to California." Kalis did just that and the next thing he knew he was out West

A frame-by-frame stakeout sequence of a highly suspect switch backside tailslide used for a 1994 Josh Kalis/Droors ad at San Francisco's famous ledge: Hubba Hideout.

filming full-time for Toy Machine's first video, *Heavy Metal.* Shortly after that the word was out that Kalis had what it took to turn pro—his reputation built by pulling out the best-looking form of any trick.

Kalis's pilgrimage to the hub of skateboarding may have brought his other-level skills to the attention of the skateboarding world, but he wasn't a fan of California's southern expanses or suburban scene. Kalis preferred city life, so he headed north to San Francisco in 1996, a shift that coincided with a switch to his current board sponsor, the eclectic, Ohio-based Alien Workshop. Both moves proved worthy: San Francisco because of the exposure to a tight-knit skateboard scene and urban landscapes, and Alien Workshop because the company recognized Kalis's boundless talent and turned him pro at the ripe young age of twenty-one.

For the next few years Kalis continued his nomadic urban lifestyle, never holding an address for more than a few months. He remained focused on one thing: progressing real street skateboarding without fronting with an elitist street attitude. "You don't have to be a ledge skater or handrail skater," he says. "If you can just cruise down a street and flow through people in intersections, or skate down a busy sidewalk without stopping, then you're a true street skater."

When all true street skaters look at Kalis (and they all do look), they see those very aspects he holds in such high regard: strength, confidence, and commitment. There's a certain positive spring to his skateboarding; he bounces into and out of tricks that others lumber and contort through. His footwork and placement are spot-on and over-the-bolts faultless, whether he's coming off a sticky ledge or catching a flip trick three feet off the ground. He guides his frame through an encyclopedia of perfectly scooped, flicked, and driven skateboard trickery, punctuating his prowess with a style that won't quit no matter what or where he's skating. Pure precision.

The critical eyes of skateboarding took note. Kalis has graced covers of two of the sport's biggest magazines, *TransWorld SKATEboarding* (November 1996 and March 2002) and *Slap Skateboard Magazine* (February 2000 and June 2002), has been featured in a half dozen magazine interviews, and has had twice as many video parts, including his favorite, TransWorld's *Sixth Sense,* in which he shared a part with longtime friend and fellow DC teammate Stevie Williams.

Before and during nearly all of these stepping stones to fame, Kalis was adorned with DC shoes and clothes—the low-key support of a three-year ride (beginning in 1997) on DC's flow team. Kalis worked hard and

Josh Kalis and Stevie Williams, where they love to be
on a Sunday afternoon in Philadelphia, 2001.

Mike Blabac

Frontside heel shove-it at Love Park,
Philadelphia, Pennsylvania, 2002.

Mike Blabac

continued getting lots of exposure, yielding positive reactions via curb-level self-promotion. It became apparent that he was due for a pro deal with the company that had been leaking him footwear. In 2000, Kalis got his first pro signature shoe.

Certainly, Kalis's success has provided him with the elaborate trappings worthy of any professional athlete, skateboarding or otherwise, but never has he let his eyes stray from the prize: "I will never love any material thing, you know what I mean? From the heart, I will never love it. But from the heart, I love skateboarding."

Only a few short years from his hectic youth with its uncertain future, Josh Kalis is a skateboarding success story. He loves what he does. He helps others. He and his long-time girlfriend are the proud parents of a daughter, Jaelen, born in 1999. Kalis's father has accepted his son's career and now advises him on financial matters. There is a stable place to call home, only a short drive from his mother's Pennsylvania home where she lives with Kalis's half-brother. He's also actively trying to create a skate spot in Philadelphia, where he was inspired as a young skate rat, that will be like the one he experienced in San Francisco: a sturdy, established, and legal scene totally supportive of skateboarding.

Kalis believes that Love Park, with its endless marble ledges and wide-open city square expanses, should be that scene. But for now, it is illegal to skate at Love Park, for a number of arguable reasons that include misblamed vandalism and other stereotypes associated with skateboarders. Park rangers and cops constantly surveil the spot. Still, Kalis, Stevie Williams, and others skate there as a tribute to the past, when swarms of skateboard-

ers hung out and sessioned. It's worth the hassle to keep the city's—and some say the East Coast's—most famous spot in the limelight.

Not surprisingly, much of Kalis's affection for Philadelphia can be traced back to Love Park's early days, days when cops kicked skaters out of all the city's spots and told them to "go skate at Love Park." Days full of ten-hour sessions and a crew of skateboarders twenty deep. Fun days that forged strong friendships. "I got a lot of pride for Love Park, you know?" he says.

A diplomat for Philly skateboarding, Kalis has for years calmly explained to any cop, security guard, or city administrator who he is and what skateboarding and Love Park have done for the town and its skaters. It's worked. Said official types have gradually come around, easing up on the Philly pro and his contemporaries. Some of the undercover cops even sport his shoes. Kalis still gets the occasional citation, but he feels it's his duty to go ahead and pay the fine, reasoning that the money might go back to the city in positive ways, like getting drug dealers off the streets and skateboarders back into the park.

It's this focus that sets Kalis apart from other personalities. Not only is he a progressive force on the frontlines of technical street skating, he appreciates and loves skateboarding for reasons the rest of the world's skaters can relate to: friends and a vibe-free place to skateboard. He heard the siren song of California promises, yet steered his personal odyssey full circle, settling back into a place that offers him what he needs—family and stability—cultivated around a dream to see skateboarding legal in a place he holds closest to his heart, Love Park.

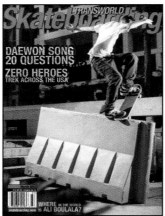

Kalis covers, clockwise from top: TransWorld SKATEboarding, *March 2002 (photo by Ryan Gee);* Slap, *February 2000 (photo by Mike O'Meally);* Slap, *June 2002 (photo by Mehring);* TransWorld SKATEboarding, *November 1995 (photo by Skin).*

Josh Kalis schools the class of 2000 with a high-speed switch backside tailslide on a table at Temple University, Philadelphia.

ACTION FIGURE EVOLUTION

MICHAEL LAU

It was only a matter of time before the generation of kids who grew up with action figures started making their own. Rather than mass-producing toys for children, however, these artists created small runs of collectible figures considered "twenty-first-century sculptures." At the forefront of this new art/toy hybrid is the Hong Kong–based artist Michael Lau. No one has fused Eastern and Western urban culture like Lau, who was originally an illustrator. His sculptures first appeared on an album cover of the Hong Kong punk group Anodized: he painstak-ingly sculpted each member of the band, complete with hand-painted, handmade, interchangeable DC shoes. He then began casting characters from his comic strip, *Gardener,* in thick, poseable vinyl. These were streetwise kids with the details Lau noticed on skate-boarders, graff artists, breakers, and DJs on the streets of Hong Kong: spiky hair, baggy cargo pants, chain wallets, and DC shoes. Lau's work gained popularity with the Crazy Children series, and his well-crafted, limited-edition figures have become increasingly sought-after.

MICROGROOVES

The desire to be a part of the action sports culture leads to some interesting product tie-ins, such as these DC key chains, made by Microgrooves Action Sports Replicas, which sell at skate shops and toy stores across the United States.

IMPERIAL TOY

The cultural tremors set off by skateboarders reached a frenetic peak in the mid-nineties, moving pros beyond the category of athlete into icon status. DC's athlete ranks are filled with cultural icons, the pinnacle of which is being cast as an action figure, like these Imperial Toy replicas of Danny Way, Rob Dyrdek, and Colin McKay, pictured from left to right.

ROB**DYRDEK**
BENEATH THE FACADE

BY ERIC BLEHM

"Rob Dyrdek, Professional Skateboarder" is what you'll hear if you're lucky enough to get the third original member (and first street skater, he'll remind you) of the DC Shoes skateboard team to answer his cell phone. That in itself is a challenge, considering his reliance on caller ID, a necessity when you're an international superstar covered in diamonds, transported by fast cars, and chased by persistent fans and hungry media.

Dyrdek has fit this, yet another interview, into his busy postmillennium schedule of, among other things: starring in DC's second national television commercial, baring his soul as guest editor for *Strength* magazine, posing with a cheetah for the cover of *Big Brother,* and recording a cameo voice interlude on Limp Bizkit's multiplatinum album *Chocolate starfish and the hot dog flavored water,* along with Ben Stiller and Mark Wahlberg.

All these public displays are indicative of the eclectic personality (and, of course, mind-blowing abilities on a skateboard) that has earned him widespread acclaim, such as being touted as the personification of urban skateboarding culture in a 2001 issue of *Playboy.* An editor "checking the facts" of this "exclusive story" brought up an $80,000 estimate for Dyrdek's Mercedes (plus $15,000 for the rims), a price well above the actual purchase price. Dyrdek confirmed the number anyway. "If someone is interviewing me and brings something up about my life that's cool and over the top, who am I to deny it?" he says. "It's not a lie, it's just a rumor, and they all blend together as truth eventually. Why slow the process?"

This coming from a guy who bought a time machine, or personal "hyper dimensional resonator," that he heard about on a talk-radio show for $350, a bargain too good to pass up. Make no mistake, though. Beneath the facade of this larger-than-life personality is an athlete who has been highly motivated since youth, and an entrepreneur who has helped shape modern street skateboarding and played a major part in building DC and other influential skateboarding companies into what they are today.

Let's pretend for a minute that Dyrdek's time machine really works and zip back to June 28, 1974, the day he was born. The town is Dayton, Ohio, and . . . well, actually, the subatomic particles of the time continuum get a little blurry here, so we might not be able to piece together all of Dyrdek's cryptic yet highly entertaining life. He says he doesn't want to bore you with irrelevant details.

Frontside flip. Rob Dyrdek at home in his "world-famous" training facility outside San Diego, 2000.

In a nutshell, Dyrdek received a skateboard as an early Christmas gift in the fall of 1986. After only one month of messing around on launch ramps and curbs, the twelve-year-old entered his first skate contest. The result of that event, like Rob D. himself, is a bit of a mystery, so we'll assume he either (a) won or (b) lost. Regardless, the fact that he entered an event, any event, after only one month on a skateboard spells three things: skills, prodigy, and supreme self-confidence.

Immediately following this debut contest, Dyrdek, a fan of Neil Blender, confronted the skateboarding icon as he climbed into a car packed with people. The amateur skater boldly said to the legendary professional, "I don't think there's room for that board in there." After a moment of contemplation, Blender responded, "Yeah, you're right," and tossed his skateboard to Dyrdek, who honored his hero's gift by skating the hell out of it.

Three months later, a local skate shop sponsored the fearless new kid, and five months after that he became the youngest member of the popular Gordon & Smith (G&S) skateboard team.

As Dyrdek grew into his early teens, he began to build his rep in the skateboarding industry with numerous regional and national amateur competition wins. These results, along with a part in G&S's first major video release, *Footage,* established him as one to watch. At sixteen, Dyrdek decided to forgo his final year of high school to turn pro for the newly formed Alien Workshop, a skateboard company that had settled in Dyrdek's obscure hometown of Dayton and whose founders included Chris Carter, Mike Hill, and, coincidentally, Neil Blender.

"PERSONALITY COUPLED WITH TALENT MAKES THE ULTIMATE CELEBRITY . . ."
– Chris Carter on Rob Dyrdek

Carter had previously been the team manager/talent scout for Tracker Trucks and G&S. One of his earliest memories of Dyrdek is of a mini-ramp session at a Dayton skate shop called Surf Ohio. "There were all sorts of visiting pros who were stoked on 'little Rob' and talking about how he was just beating roof on the place," Carter remembers. "Compliments like that are hard to come by." Years later, when it came time for Alien Workshop to build a team, "We wanted great eccentric skaters. Personality coupled with talent makes the ultimate celebrity, and Dyrdek had the ability to wrap it all into one incredible ball of energy."

Dyrdek catapulted into the professional ranks when he came out of nowhere to earn a shocking fourth-place finish in his first pro contest, the 1991 World Championships in Münster, Germany. Alien Workshop's groundbreaking first video, *Memory Screen,* premiered that same year and featured Dyrdek flowing through street terrain with technical wizardry beyond his years. In December 1992, Dyrdek was named, along with Danny Way and Colin McKay, one of *TransWorld SKATEboarding*'s twenty most influential skateboarders of the next decade. A month later, both *TransWorld* and *Thrasher* featured him with prestigious pro spotlights.

At eighteen, Dyrdek set out to enforce his position as one of the top street skateboarders in the world by moving to the proving grounds of Southern California. There he enjoyed constant magazine coverage by taking his cool and confident street dominance to a playground of palm trees and year-round skateboarding.

Rob Dyrdek's selfless blue-paint-on-the-head sequence, the most memorable Droors advertisement by popular vote. 1994.

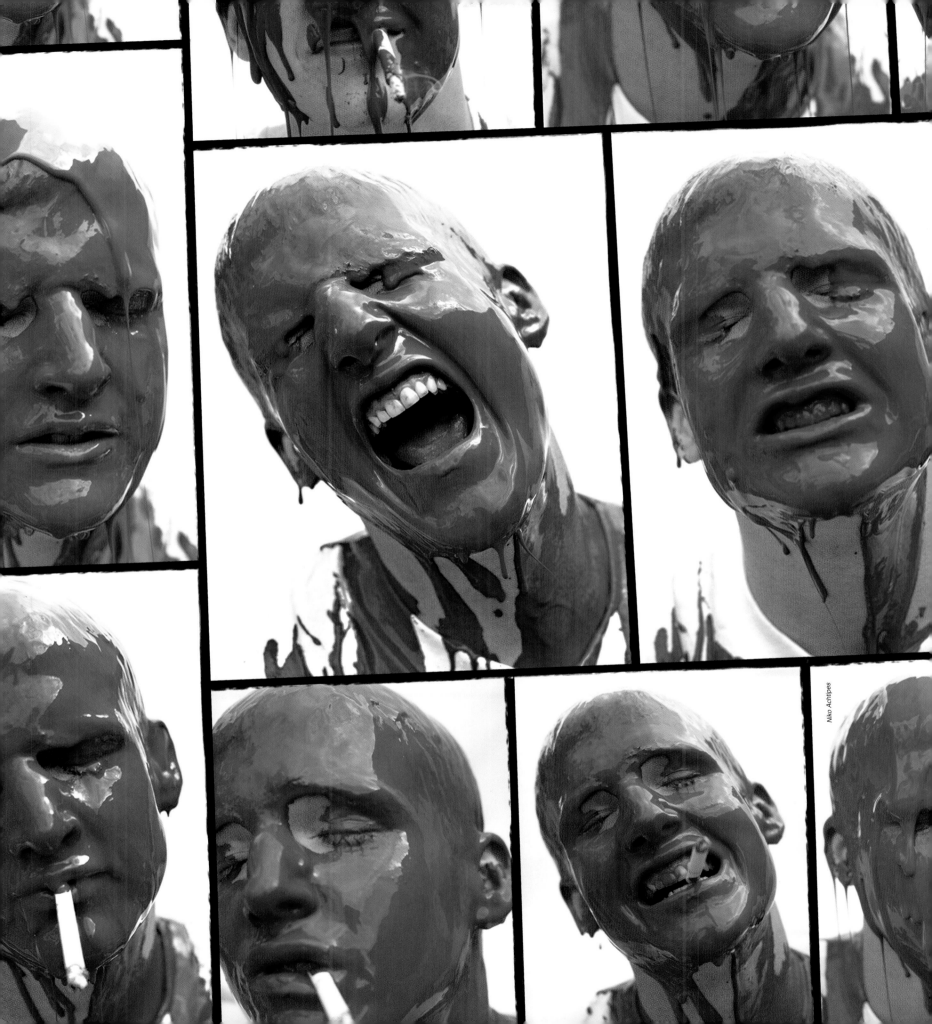

Niko Achtipes

Rob Dyrdek airing over Fred Durst and the boys while filming
the Limp Bizkit "Break Stuff" video (which won MTV's "best
rock video of the year" award) in Los Angeles, 2000.

While at the 1993 Back to the City skate contest in San Francisco, Dyrdek met Droors Clothing president Ken Block. "Rob and I got along right from the start," says Block. "He was, and will always be, a smart-ass, but somehow his comments come across in a likable way. He was innovative and dedicated to his skateboarding, but discovering his personality is really what got me sparked to sponsor him."

Over the course of the next three years, Dyrdek, Block, and Damon Way became friends, in part because of a collective desire to market the Droors label in a highly prolific manner that included

The caption for this February 1995 cover of TransWorld SKATEboarding *read: "Rob Dyrdek, switch-stance crooked grinding a monster ledge. Damn, did he make that?" (He did.) The issue also ran DC's first advertisement.*

Dyrdek's now-famous advertising campaigns. Dyrdek was photographed having blue paint dumped on his head, and being stuck to a brick wall with hundreds of feet of masking tape, bizarre antics that solidified his reputation as an incredible marketing tool with an unbridled sense of humor.

Meanwhile, Alien Workshop's *Time Code* and TransWorld's *Dreams of Children* were released. Dyrdek's strong segments in both made him the ideal choice to join Danny Way and Colin McKay on the

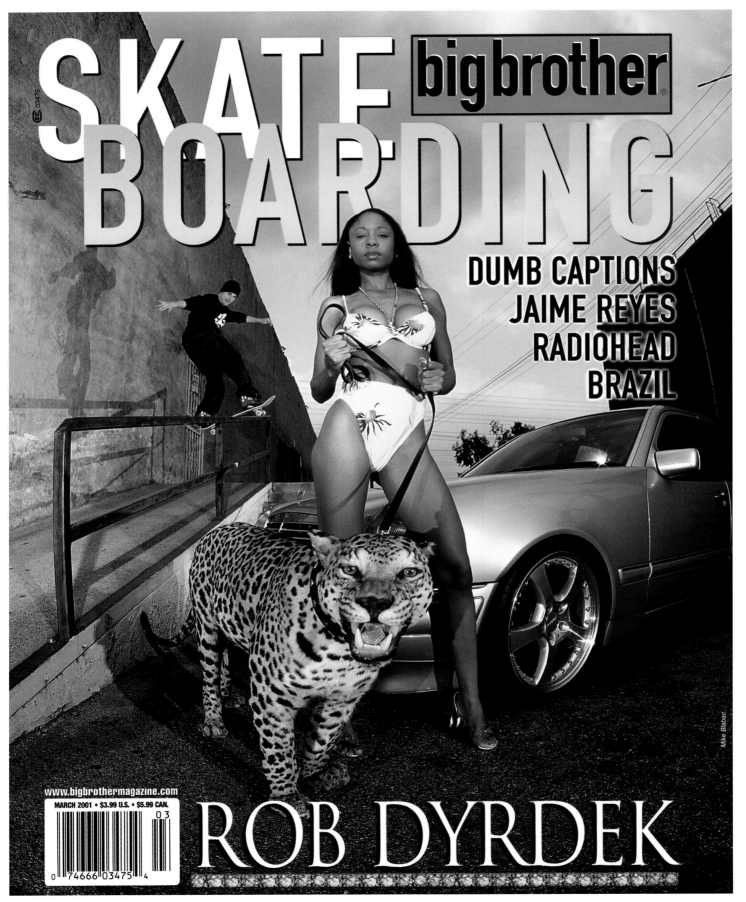

SKATE big brother
BOARDING

DUMB CAPTIONS
JAIME REYES
RADIOHEAD
BRAZIL

www.bigbrothermagazine.com

MARCH 2001 • $3.99 U.S. • $5.99 CAN.

03

0 74666 03475 4

ROB DYRDEK

Mike Blabac.

Rob Dyrdek on the cover of the March 2001
Big Brother magazine. Frontside boardslide in
the urban jungle of Los Angeles.

STRENGTH

skateboard culture

special issue!
celebrity guest editor
rob dyrdek

commuters
jason dill and
fred gall

colin mckay
transitions

september2001
$3.99US $4.99CAN

09>

radiohead+weezer

win turntables, crates of wax, skateboards, shoes, cds and more!

R.D. does a 360 kickflip in South Gate, California, for the cover of the September 2001 Strength *magazine.*

Mike Blabac

newly formed DC team, where he immediately started thinking of new skateboard shoe designs.

Skateboarders had always worn running or athletic shoes when they weren't skateboarding, so Dyrdek, along with Block, set out to create the first-ever skate shoe with sports appeal. His resulting signature shoe, the Dyrdek1, featured breakthroughs in skate shoe design—most notably, nylon lace loops.

As these shoes were being assembled by the thousands, Dyrdek contemplated his success. He had a signature model shoe and a signature model skateboard, two of the most sought-after career goals for a professional skateboarder. Yet he was experiencing nightmares. "When the shoes were being delivered to the shops, I had these dreams that all the lace loops broke, and the kids hated the design, and DC went out of business," he says.

Quite the contrary happened. The shoes sold out in record time, marking the moment when DC became known as a skateboard shoe innovator. Dyrdek credits much of the shoe's success to DC's advertising campaign, which primed the market with a never-before-seen trick (nollie nosegrind on a handrail) and never-before-seen shoe design sharing equal page space. The Dyrdek1 rocked the skateboarding community: shops, skateboarders, and other companies.

The Dyrdek2 continued the evolution with a switch to rubber lace loops and a more detailed, sporty look. Then came the Dyrdek3, which moved away from a traditional flat sole, another innovation that also became a skateboarding shoe standard with most companies.

With the success of his signature models backing him, Dyrdek asked DC and Alien Workshop to support his latest idea: Rob Dyrdek's World-Famous Skateboarding Training Facility, 3,600 square feet of warehouse space located outside San Diego and filled with a personally designed collection of street-skating obstacles. The finished product, completed in October 1998, had graffiti-covered walls, an eardrum-shattering sound system, and the freedom for Dyrdek and friends to do whatever they wanted behind the closed doors of a private skate mecca.

Dyrdek went on to found Reflex Bearings, an independent hip-hop record label named P-Jays, and the first-ever truck company, Orion Trucks, owned and operated by a small elite team that

Rob Dyrdek, midnight bluntslide.
Miami, Florida, 2001.

Frontslide bluntslide transfer on a big white wall near R.D.'s home in San Diego, California, 1996.

Michael Ballard

R.D., backside nosegrind in the San Fernando Valley, California, 2001.

Mike Blabac

Mike Blabac

Another Alien Workshop board falls victim to R.D.'s perfectionist frustrations. South Gate, California, 2000.

*Classic Rob Dyrdek kickflip
over a gap in San Diego, 1997.*

included fellow pros Eric Koston and Kareem Campbell. Despite all that was going on, this became a dark period for Dyrdek, whose focus on skateboarding faltered, thanks to chronic ankle sprains and the pressures of maintaining start-up businesses. The training facility sat empty for long stretches, and Dyrdek simply stepped out of the spotlight for a while.

As time went by, he realized that his break from the action was throwing him into a downward spiraling funk, so he took steps to regain his edge. In April 1999, he underwent orthoscopic surgery to remove calcium deposits and broken-bone chips that had lodged in his right ankle from repeated abuse over the years. By summer 1999, his rehabilitation was complete. He cleared his schedule of business dealings, rebuilt the training facility, and in his words "gave my life back to skateboarding."

Up to then, most street skaters, including Dyrdek, had shied away from contests. They dedicated their lives instead to the freedom, or lack thereof, found in illegal urban skating zones. Dyrdek hadn't entered a contest since his first two years as a pro, and saw this as a travesty. "There weren't any full-package street skaters," he says. "I wanted to offer up a pro package beyond the punk-ass kid, the party kid, the smart-ass, all the other elements of my image that were funny and all, but weren't even close to the epitome of the modern street pro I was striving for."

R.D.'s coveted Neil Blender board: used and abused, but never broken.

So Dyrdek put his reputation on the line by entering contests, a decision that many street skaters frowned on. At the end of his first season and only a year after his surgery, he placed sixth overall in the 2000 World Cup Skateboarding Tour. This "on demand" skateboarding only boosted his confidence and increased his skills in the more relaxed atmosphere of photo shoots, his training facility, and the streets of Los Angeles, where his weekend "skate house" is located.

His other home is a sort of art deco shrine dedicated to his heritage as a skateboarder. The spotless modern house in downtown San Diego is decorated with skateboarding-influenced art by the Gonz, Lance Mountain, and David Kinsey, and mementos from international demo tours to Europe and Japan. He has Christian Hosoi's last signature skateboard deck on the wall, but still considers the Neil Blender skateboard he acquired at age twelve his most prized possession.

This reverence to his skateboarding history is an apt example of the synchronicity of his success—really an elaborate plan carefully conceptualized by Dyrdek to keep everything about his life on a "major scale." Like the September 2001 cover of *Strength* magazine that showcases one of his supertechnical tricks, a backside 360 ollie kickflip. This showed up on newsstands everywhere, along with the *Big Brother* cover where he's frontside boardsliding a rail alongside a stuffed cheetah, a porn star, and his flashy car. Then there's the *Stance* cover on which he's holding his DC shoe like a gun and dripping in enough jewels to make a rapper

ABOVE: Rob Dyrdek, frontside half-Cab flip. South Gate, Calfornia, 2001.

ABOVE: R.D., switch tailslide. San Diego, 2000.
BELOW: R.D., switch 5-0, 180 out. Miami, Florida, 2001.

BELOW: R.D., nollie frontside noseslide. Miami, Florida, 2001.

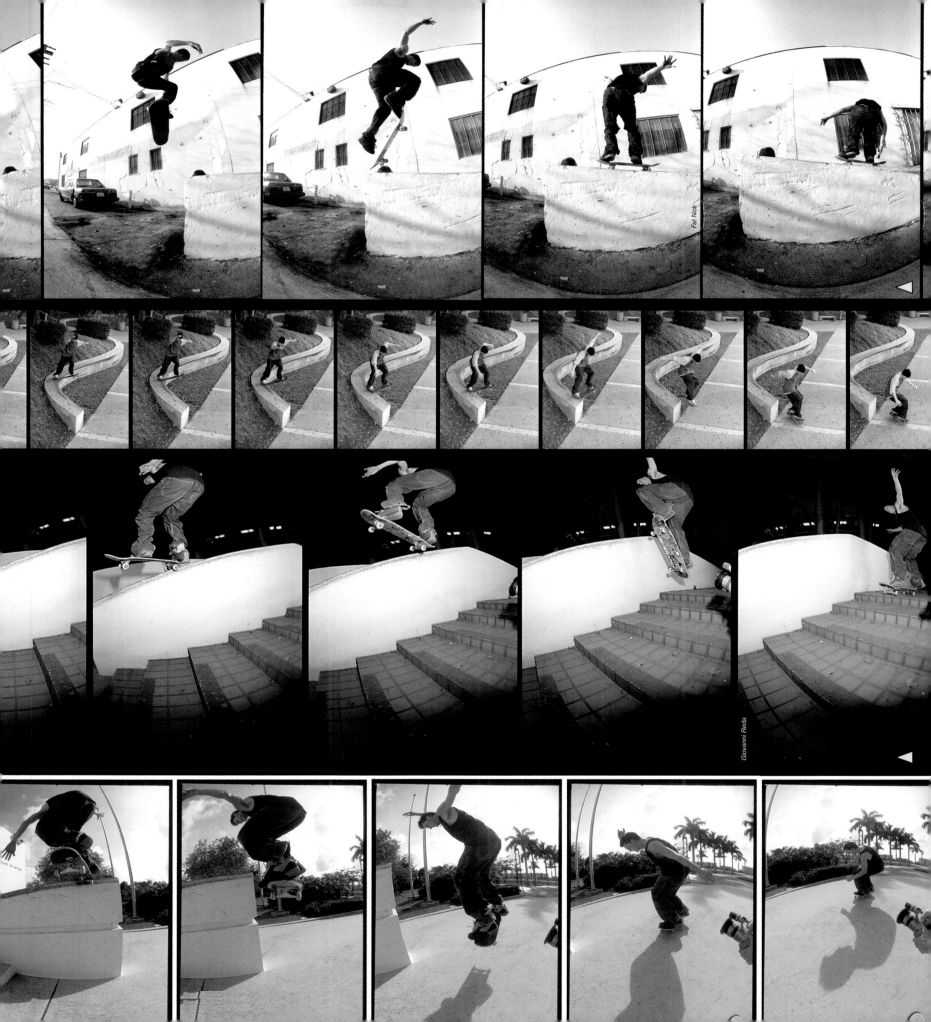

Fat Nick

Giovanni Reda

jealous, and the *EXPN Magazine* spread: he's standing on the hood of a Bentley, with a Learjet in the background, appropriate transportation for a skateboarder who is featured in *Rolling Stone, Playboy,* and every skateboarding publication on the planet.

It doesn't stop there. His skating and likeness have been replicated on video games and as action figures. His name graces random skate-oriented products like an electronic skateboard slot-racing game, skateboarder dog tags, trading cards, computer stat cards, and dozens of others. But perhaps the most fitting example is the national television commercial that introduced the nation to the DC Exacta, Dyrdek's 2001 signature shoe. In the commercial, he eludes a mob of fans by skateboarding through the streets of Los Angeles (see "The Chase" on page 176) and nailing death-defying moves like a twenty-stair rail grind, one of the hardest tricks he's ever attempted. He pulled it off on the second try.

The Hollywood lights and cameras, like the cheetah, the Benz, and the diamonds, are just a veneer. The truth is that Rob Dyrdek, Professional Skateboarder, wouldn't be here if it weren't for his skateboarding roots. And he'll be the first to remind you that "Image and personality aren't anything if you can't back them up on a skateboard."

Rob Dyrdek considered this genuine time machine, or "hyper dimensional resonator," a bargain at $350.

R.D., ollie over to a frontside crooked grind at a Philadelphia, Pennsylvania, playground in 2001

© Gee

SOLUTION FIRST RELEASED: FALL 2001

Danny Way and Colin McKay have earned a reputation for their relentless ability to push skateboarding to new levels. Their third combo signature model, the Solution, reflected their exceptional skating abilities and marked a major milestone in the history of DC, which became the first company to produce a laceless skateboarding shoe. The Solution's design includes a single adjustable strap that crosses over the tongue, providing solid support while completely eliminating the hassles of lace burnout—an issue that all vert skaters deal with.

For the Solution, DC created a two-part advertising campaign that ran in back-to-back issues of *TransWorld SKATEboarding*. The ads featured the tag lines "Laces Not Required" and "For Every Problem There's a Solution," catchy phrases that stuck in the minds of consumers. The skateboarding community's curiosity was piqued, and the Solution's popularity and reputation as a versatile, high-performance shoe have both continued to grow. From concept to reality, the Solution carries on DC's tradition of pushing the envelope.

KALIS FIRST RELEASED: SPRING 2000

Street skater Josh Kalis has an innovative talent that continues to dominate the skateboarding industry. The Kalis, his first signature model, was designed to be a highly durable skate shoe that would complement his technical skills and style.

At the time the Kalis was released to the public in December 1999, Josh Kalis was experiencing a tremendous amount of media coverage, including several new video parts, interviews, lots of dynamic photos, and DC's first television commercial, in which he had a starring role. Although the shoe wasn't featured in the commercial, it made its public debut at the same time. Ken Block explains: "It's really important that the pro gains exposure and supports the product before it comes out. The coverage that Josh had at the time, coinciding with the fact that the Kalis was a great shoe, made a complete package that sold really well."

The Kalis has secured a reputation of quality and performance that has far exceeded expectations. It has sold for over eight seasons and was available in ten different colorways, making it one of DC's most successful and longest-running pro models.

WILLIAMS FIRST RELEASED: **HOLIDAY 2000**

Because of his raw technical skateboarding style and electric personality, Stevie Williams is one of the most exciting and versatile street skaters in the sport. His debut signature shoe, the Williams, released one year after Stevie's 1999 induction onto the DC team, was designed to be like its namesake: rugged, versatile, and original.

The lightweight, high-performance Williams, which became one of DC's best-sellers, fuses skate shoe features like a PAL AB2000 toe cap and a revolutionary abrasion-resistant coating (applied to the ollie area on the lateral part of the midsole) with the flowing lines and support of a basketball shoe. This fresh design had an immediate impact on the skateboard industry, putting DC on the cusp of a trend that would be copied again and again.

LEGACY FIRST RELEASED: **SPRING 1998**

The Legacy, Danny Way and Colin McKay's first combo signature shoe, was the result of their combined talents and years of domination in the skateboarding industry. Its design incorporated elements that had never been seen before in a skateboarding shoe, including a visible thermo polyurethane arch in the midsole that provided added foot support and a shock-absorbing air pocket in the heel.

The design, according to Ken Block, "was spawned from the modern technical running shoe," with multiple layers of protective materials added to the upper to increase resiliency and versatility. The Legacy's place in DC's history as a high-performance skate shoe remains a legacy in and of itself.

ON AUGUST 3, 1997
VERT SKATING
CHANGED FOREVER

BY MIKI VUCKOVICH

On Sunday, August 3, 1997, I was witness to probably the most amazing exhibition of skateboarding in the history of the sport . . .

In this issue you will see and read about this achievement in detail. You, too, will be amazed, unless of course you are a skeptic like some of the jealous folks in the skateboard industry. The reason I say that is because a few of those types have already dismissed the validity of Danny's fabulous feat. Rumblings such as "were other people skating it?" and "of course he went that high—who wouldn't with such big transitions?" have been heard. All I have to say to those people is, "Wake up!" Would Evel Knievel invite every motorcycle lunatic he knows to jump with him? I don't think so.

In closing, I'd just like to congratulate Danny Way and the geniuses at DC Shoes on a job well done. Vert skating will never be the same again.

—Dave Swift, editor in chief, December 1997
TransWorld SKATEboarding, Gasbag column

Grant Brittain

Tim Payne was the architect and builder for the largest halfpipes in the world on two different occasions: in 1986 for the Powell Peralta Bones Brigade skateboard team during the filming of The Search for Animal Chin; and here, in 1997, at Brown Field in San Ysidro near the California/Mexico border. Danny Way stands atop the massive structure, ready to drop into vert skating history.

Grant Brittain

It could not be done by an ordinary skater. Nor could it be done on an ordinary ramp. In August 1997, just eight months after Sergie Ventura set the new high-air standard at eleven feet eight inches (topping Steve Caballero's 1988 world record of eleven feet), Danny Way dropped into DC's Super Ramp and stuck a sixteen-and-a-half-foot method air.

The world record for the highest air wasn't just broken, it was outright obliterated—albeit on a ramp built for that purpose. DC funded the thirty-two-foot-wide, eighteen-foot-tall halfpipe that had a drop-in tower standing thirty-five feet over the ground. The ramp, constructed in secrecy at an airfield near the California/Mexico border, was skateboarding's Tower of Babel.

Moments from the day that Danny Way changed skateboarding forever: August 3, 1997.

Photos by Grant Brittain, Skin Phillips, Dave Swift

To accomplish the task of building this immense structure, DC called on Tim Payne, the celebrated ramp designer who, before becoming architect and executor of the biggest halfpipe in the world, was better known for his 1986 masterpiece, the infamous Animal Chin Ramp. Built from a sketch scribbled by the Powell Peralta Bones Brigade skateboard team, the Chin ramp was an off-the-cuff plywood playground that, like the Super Ramp, had been assembled and dismantled by Payne in the course of a week—just long enough for the Brigadiers to film a segment of *The Search for Animal Chin.*

The Chin ramp was erected at a nondescript location in Southern California and kept secret to avoid interference from curious fans, allowing the film crew to accomplish its task under a tight schedule. Like Chin, DC's version was a covert forum for select superstars, in this case Colin McKay and Danny Way. While McKay proved beyond a shadow of a doubt that the ramp was totally skateable (his frontside pointer grinds were pretty convincing), the ramp was really made to order for Danny, who used the sixteen-foot transitions to their full launch potential.

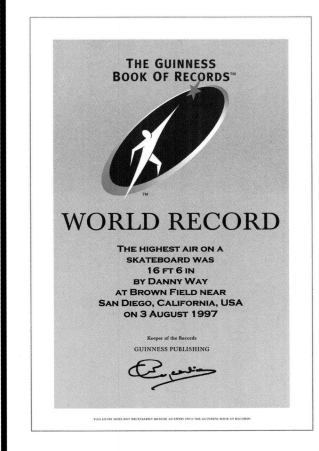

THE GUINNESS
BOOK OF RECORDS™

WORLD RECORD

THE HIGHEST AIR ON A
SKATEBOARD WAS
16 FT 6 IN
BY DANNY WAY
AT BROWN FIELD NEAR
SAN DIEGO, CALIFORNIA, USA
ON 3 AUGUST 1997

Keeper of the Records
GUINNESS PUBLISHING

THIS ENTRY DOES NOT NECESSARILY DENOTE AN ENTRY INTO THE GUINNESS BOOK OF RECORDS

With seven photographers documenting the event from various angles, including a nearby hovering helicopter, Danny lifted himself several times over the sixteen-foot post used to mark his height, but could be accurately measured only after an additional three feet were attached to this giant ruler. Video shot from the top of the roll-in deck

LEFT: Danny Way is the only person in the world who knows what it's like to bail a seventeen-foot-high backside air. Look at frames seven through ten and imagine what would be going through your mind.

This is the photo DC used to announce Danny Way's history-making backside air. The advertisement ran worldwide with the tag line: "If you never try, you will never succeed."

directly opposite the sixteen-foot marker revealed without a doubt that Danny's board cleared the height by six inches. The proper documentation was immediately submitted to *The Guinness Book of Records,* which included the feat in the "Extreme Sports" section of subsequent editions.

Initial goal achieved, Danny decided to have some fun before his $20,000 playground was dismantled. He managed a twelve-foot Indy flip, kicking the board off his feet and catching and replacing it after the deck had spun a full rotation. Danny's attention then focused on the helicopter DC had brought in as a photo prop and photographers' vantage point. It took some persuading by Danny, but the pilot eventually consented to aid in another first: a bomb drop unlike any other.

Christian Hosoi first coined the term "bomp drop" in the early eighties when he hopped off a rooftop adjacent to a ramp. Since then, many skaters have followed suit using railings and other stationary objects that are even with or a few feet above a ramp. But no one had ever bomb-dropped into a ramp from an aircraft hovering thirty-five feet off the ground, which is exactly what Danny—after several drops and spectacular wipeouts—pulled off.

The records were set. The photos and film were rushed off to processing. And Payne, the master stage builder, went back to work, picking apart what he had barely finished in time for the show. For onlookers, the structure had taken and lost shape seemingly overnight—an apparition that, like the Chin ramp of a decade before, was fleeting evidence of a magical occurrence best preserved by removing all tangible traces of what had gone down. Even as word began to spread about the structure, its possible location, and Danny's feats, trucks were hauling the dismantled sections of the Super Ramp to a top-secret warehouse. In keeping with the leave-only-footprints, take-only-photos philosophy of low-impact insanity, not a single nail was left at the site to indicate the ramp's presence.

The accomplishment quickly turned into a cover story for *TransWorld SKATEboarding* and several other international skateboarding and action sports magazines. MTV attempted to replicate the spectacle at the 1999 Sports and Music Festival, even going so far as to hire Payne as the ramp builder and extend a special invitation to Danny. He accepted.

Although Payne orchestrated yet another behemoth structure, the MTV high-air contest ended up being the diametric opposite of the original hush-hush DC version. It was staged (appropriately so) in Las Vegas, where a public industry-wide media circus was on hand documenting a line of competitors who climbed the Sin City ramp in an attempt to beat Danny's record.

Two days before the contest, Danny warmed up with a repeat of his helicopter bomb drop. He dislocated his shoulder in the process, but kept at it until he landed the stunt. The next morning he defended his high-air title, failing to break his own record but winning the contest with an admirable fourteen-and-a-half-foot air. This time around, a chorus of cheers and congratulations from fans and peers alike rewarded his feats. And those who had doubted his record were summarily silenced.

Some of your parents might not appreciate this thirteen-and-a-half-foot kickflip Indy, so explain that it's kind of like climbing Mount Everest. It's all about strength, focus, and determination at an altitude that could kill you, but when you stick the landing, you can honestly say you've been on top of the world.

Dave Swift

This bomb drop wasn't planned. The helicopter was supposed to be a prop, hovering above the ramp, and used for bird's-eye camera angles, but Danny Way saw things differently—and, with a whole lot of persuasion, so did the pilot.

The shot seen around the world: TransWorld SKATEboarding's *December 1997 cover—which means the magazine hit newsstands sometime in late October, which means these photos (taken on August 3) were literally squeezed in at the last possible moment. In magazine terms, this photo "stopped the presses."*

January 21st, 2002

DC Shoes Inc.
1333 Keystone Way Unit A
Vista, CA 92083

Dear Company President,

I am writing to tell you that I think DC is the best company ever and to say thanks. I always look for your products at the local skate/snowboard shop and I have only had good experiences with them. I currently have a pair of your DC Dash model and they are one of my more favorite pairs that I have owned.

Your products have all of the good qualities for skate/snowboarding such as durability, strength, comfort, pop, and style. I will always buy your products because they are the best for the price. I also have to compliment your team of skaters and boarders. I am always buying Transworld Skateboarding and Snowboarding magazines because I like the posters of your team. I especially liked the commercial when Rob Dyrdek did the 50-50 down the twenty-stair handrail. That was killer, Rob! And not only your pros but also I would like to thank your entire behind-the-scenes personnel, they make all the great stuff happen.

Hopefully some day I will have the opportunity to work as one of those people. I was also wondering if you could send me some stickers, posters, or pictures. I just want to say keep up the good work, and keep on truckin'.

Sincerely,

Zach Chase

Zach Chase

If it weren't for skateboarders like fifteen-year-old Zach Chase from Wisconsin, this book—in fact, DC Shoes—wouldn't exist. Thanks to everybody who has supported us throughout the years.

Ken Block
Damon Way
Clayton Blehm

CHARLES FAUDREE
INTERIORS

CHARLES FAUDREE
INTERIORS

CHARLES FAUDREE WITH M.J. VAN DEVENTER
PHOTOGRAPHS BY JENIFER JORDAN

GIBBS SMITH
TO ENRICH AND INSPIRE HUMANKIND
Salt Lake City | Charleston | Santa Fe | Santa Barbara

First Edition

08 09 10 11 12   2 3 4 5 6 7 8 9 10

Text © 2008 Charles Faudree
Photographs © 2008 Jenifer Jordan
Illustrations © 2008 Jim Steinmeyer

Published by
Gibbs Smith
P.O. Box 667
Layton, Utah 84041

1-800.835.4993 orders
www.gibbs-smith.com

Designed by Debra McQuiston
Printed and bound in China

Library of Congress Cataloging-in-Publication Data

Faudree, Charles.
Charles Faudree interiors / Charles Faudree ; with
M.J. Van Deventer ;
photographs by Jenifer Jordan.—1st ed.
p. cm.
ISBN-13: 978-1-4236-0209-5
ISBN-10: 1-4236-0209-9
1. Faudree, Charles—Themes, motives.
2. Interior decoration—United States.
3. Decoration and ornament, Rustic—France—Influence.
I. Van Deventer, M. J. II. Jordan, Jenifer. III. Title.
NK2004.3.F38A4 2008
747—dc22
2008012369

Jenifer, M.J. and I would like to dedicate this book to our talented and beloved friend, Nancy E. Ingram. She brought me into the spotlight thirty years ago when she was editor of *Oklahoma Home & Lifestyle* and later when she was working as a scout for a national group of design magazines.

She was the first to publish my work and was there with me on both of my previous books as a stylist, proofreader, and editor. She was not able to be with us on this adventure. We want her to know that we truly missed her talent, charm, and ability.

An antique Swedish secretary incorporates a tall painted clock. The Louis XVI–style armchairs are also Swedish and are covered in Brunschwig & Fils check. The engravings are antique and hand colored, *previous overleaf and facing.*

FOREWORD

Charles Faudree, perhaps more than any other American interior designer, has championed the Country French style. America is a relatively young nation, and we embrace design from all over the world. We are especially fond of classic European. But while Charles is a devoted Francophile, he freshens his interiors by incorporating other influences as well.

Taste can be acquired by exposure—visiting fine antiques shops, galleries, and museums and exploring high-quality design books and magazines. Elsie de Wolfe defined good taste as suitability, suitability, suitability. Your home must suit your personality and the way you live, and Charles is a master at achieving that. He believes that every room should be usable, and he takes that a step further by making the room comfortable, too. The wonderful thing about his interiors is that they appear to reflect years of collecting, as if each succeeding generation has added furnishings to the home. Indeed, his warm and cozy rooms are meant to last for generations.

I, along with countless others, analyze his rooms over and over, admiring his natural sense of style. His carefully selected antiques command attention, but so do the high standards he demands for fabrics and workmanship. And then there is that special spark from a bit of whimsy.

Books are the most revealing objects in a room, and Charles and I share a love for them. At photo shoots with him, we often discuss a book that I really admire but that I do not own. The next week, invariably, it arrives on my desk: a gift from Charles. His kindness and generosity are boundless, and he is always willing to share his knowledge and talent.

We have photographed six of Charles's houses for *Veranda*. One of my favorites is his own small lake house filled with treasures, including an antique Swedish painted *secretaire* and chair settled comfortably into the cabin with typical Faudree panache. Some might find this an incompatible juxtaposition, but when Charles, with his superb sense of scale and color, assembles an interior, it always works.

A particular room that stands out in my mind reflects the premise that favorite colors and hues repeated throughout an interior can produce a harmonious environment. Charles used the red bookbindings in a library as his cue and enlivened the room with a variety of patterned, solid and textured fabrics—even fresh flowers—in that vivid color.

Charles has a passion for all things beautiful, even when it comes to his choice of canine companionship: his adorable King Charles Spaniels, who are ever present. He is also an informed speaker who loves his subject, and he can be very persuasive. At one of his lectures, which was illustrated with glorious images of his work, I knew that most of the audience owned homes decorated in an English or contemporary style. By the end of his presentation, though, many were ready to explore the "Charles Faudree Country French" look. You, too, will be inspired after reading this book.

—Lisa Newsom
Founder and Editor-in-Chief, *Veranda*

An antique painted metal
sideboard from The Gray
Door in Houston lines a
hallway in the Pielsticker
home. It is accessorized
with Italian altar sticks and
a pair of tole-and-procelain
bouquets from the Paris
flea market. The Jonathan
Sobel painting completes
the vignette.

INTRODUCTION

MY DESIGN PLEASURES

All of my clients and friends are aware of my love for French
Country. I still consider it one of my strengths. But the winds
of change touch all of us and a sparer look is having its way.
So, that being said, this book has varied groups of homes, but
they still produce a mix of personal, comfortable rooms with
a sprinkling of modern, Swedish, and Asian furniture, and, as
always, our favorite fabrics. Each look is created with a mixing of special accessories, a jumble of prints, animal paintings,
sisal and animal-print carpets, and the unconventional use of
conventional things.

This year has been full of accomplishments and joy. My
new line of fabric for Vervain is being launched, as well as my
third book, which is a book on flowers and interiors with my
friend and favorite florist forever, Toni Garner. I turn seventy
—never did I think about being seventy—but on we go and
on we will decorate, with all of you to keep me company.

Italian heraldic sconces illuminate the family room space in the Pielsticker home. Directoire campaign daybeds from Dennis & Leen flank the fireplace. They are upholstered in Ralph Lauren "Piedmont Twill," *facing*. Draperies fashioned from Lee Jofa "Megan's Sheer" frame the über-chic iron doors and windows in the Pielsticker home. The Gustav IV–period sofa, circa 1810, is upholstered in Nancy Corzine "Silk Canvas." A small recycled library ladder from Paris and the Tibetan silk-and-wool carpet add to the ambience, *above*.

BAMBU VILLA, JAMAICA

Bambu Villa, owned by Gayle and Frank Eby, is truly a hidden treasure. Built high on a hill in the 1960s by Trinidadian architect Robert Hartley, Bambu enjoys breathtaking views of the Caribbean, the city of Montego Bay, and the rainforest. The original owners, Diene and Douglass James Cooper, enjoyed travel and were greatly influenced by Hadrien's Villa at Tivoli while designing their island get-away. The round pool and classic colonnade, as well as the fourth-century Roman statues, give this Jamaican paradise a decidedly European air.

In 2005, Gayle and Frank bought Bambu and wanted to retain the European elegance while keeping the relaxed "no problem" vibe that drew them to Jamaica. Gayle has a great eye and knew that a "few changes" could take Bambu from wonderful to spectacular. We began immediately, and the construction crews were there for more than a year. A new dining pavilion was built, the original pavilion was turned into a family room, all the bathrooms and kitchens were remodeled, ebony-stained teak floors were added, and the list of improvements goes on and on. The results speak for themselves.

What a delight it was to work on this sprawling home. Traveling to Paris, the south of France, Belgium, and Dallas to search for just the right antiques was a labor of love. I never tire of working with beautiful fabrics nor with clients who share my love for detail. Throughout the home are unusual chandeliers, an abundance of comfortable seating areas, and a recurring theme of seashells and coral.

My role in the design transformation was much more than cosmetic. I was very involved, with my assistant April Faudree Moore, in enhancing the interiors and making Bambu Villa a place where Frank and Gayle would love to live and entertain in this magical island setting.

dm Steinmeyer 2007

The villa's downstairs entry is a study in a range of textures. Cut-limestone tile covers the walls, while bricks anchor the floor. A French Directoire-style settee is accented with a quartet of etchings. An Italian *pantoliano*—for "trousers"—hand-painted commode is ca. 1810. The Napoleon III Empire Revival pier mirror is one of the few pieces original to the home, as is the nineteenth-century Dutch brass chandelier, *facing*. ❧ Greeting guests in the downstairs entry is a French 1940s-style bronze center table with a limestone top. A Chinese ceramic garden seat is placed nearby, *above*.

French-style iron garden tables serve as end

tables in this setting. Ralph Lauren crystal-column lamps cast a warm glow over the room. Italian altar sticks converted easily to unusual candleholders, *below left*. ❧ The living pavilion in the villa continues the arched doorway theme and provides a variety of comfortable settings that invite conversation. An extraordinarily large Dutch-style barnyard-scene oil painting is original to the home and makes a powerful design statement in this room. A Directoire-style child's *fauteuil* is nestled close to the table. The sofa fabric is Brunschwig & Fils "Villandry Linen Print," and the game chairs are covered in Pierre Frey "Toile De Nantes," *above left*. ❧ The Louis XIV–style armchair and *os de mouton* (mutton bone) ottoman flank an occasional table that features a bronze Bouillotte lamp with a striped tole shade. A sea-shell bouquet is housed under a glass dome. The armchair is covered in Pierre Frey "Sintra," *above right*. ❧ A walnut armoire from Dijon represents the Louis XV and XVI period. The slipper chairs are from Charles's chair line. The club-style chairs are from the Louis XVI era. Schumacher "Samarkand Ikat" covers the sofa, and the chairs are from Duralee . The ottoman, which doubles as a coffee table, is upholstered in Brunschwig & Fils "Cebre Woven," *facing*.

In the upstairs formal entry, a seashell mirror in the Napoleon III style makes a stunning first impression. Again reflecting the symmetrical theme that is a hallmark of Charles's designs, a pair of early-twentieth-century bronze blackamoor sconces frame the mirror. They

are probably by Jansen of Paris and are identical to a pair in the Duke and Duchess of Windsor's Paris hotel, Particuliers. The seventeenth-century French walnut commode is very rare, probably unique. The commode is accented with painted Directoire-style *fauteuils* and a rare

blackamoor Majolica jardinière. The chair fabric is Bergamo "Plantation Café," *above left*. A Country French painted pine clock now echoes a sea-life motif, complementing the numerous arrangements of seashells throughout the villa, *above right*. Nineteenth-century French iron

garden chairs flank the table in this area of the home. The 1940s French bronze table has a faux marble plateau that holds a pair of Chinese lamps and a porcelain seashell box. The wall above the table includes a collection of blue-and-white Chinese export pottery, *facing*.

One of a pair of multi-floral seashell bouquets in a Napoleon III style rests on a Louis XVI bronze ormolu pedestal, *above*. ❦ The indoor dining room is spectacular with its wall of bookshelves holding a variety of treasures. A beamed angled ceiling adds architectural interest to the room. The exquisite and rare inlaid dining table had its origin in Syria. The chair seats are covered in Cowtan & Tout "Tortola" fabric, while the backs are adorned with Beacon Hill "Fresco Stripe." Presiding over the dining table is a bronze, crystal, and seashell chandelier from Alan Knight, *right*.

T he outdoor dining pavilion overlooking the ocean is enhanced by the theme of arches that circles the room. A nineteenth-century carved base supports the massive round faux bois tabletop. The dining chairs are covered in Pierre Frey "Braquenié" fabric.

Included in the room are matching marble-topped French *tables de bouchier* (butcher tables). The chandelier is in the Italian-ate style, *facing.* An antique French *chateau* birdcage, with a modern bird, is an attractive conversation piece in the out-door dining pavilion, *above.*

Two starfish and a crab shell are part of the home's endless collection of crustaceans, *below left.* ❧ A French glass trophy dome is home to a rare Napoleon III seashell bouquet, *above left.* ❧ A Chinese export Ming-style vase serves as a backdrop for a seashell-ornamented box, *above right.* ❧ Antique iron and plush, oversized Country French furnishings provide comfortable seating in the television pavilion. The sofa is covered in Robert Allen "Chevron Row." The chairs are upholstered in Cowtan & Tout "Palmier," *facing.*

The master bedroom is anchored by

a custom bed. The sofa, original to the house, is covered with
Osborn and Little "Portavo." The club chairs are covered
in Greeff "Mecox Stripe." The painting is by the original
owner of the home, *facing*. ❧ An antique bronze Bouilotte
lamp with a striped tole shade is a handsome piece on the
end table in the master bedroom. It is one of a pair of lamps
with a dolphin motif that was original to the home, *above
left*. ❧ In keeping with the tropical theme so prevalent in
Jamaica, shells are used in several places throughout the home
as decorating accessories. Fresh flowers and family portraits
accompany the shell motif, *above and below right*.

M y love for symmetry is beautifully expressed in one of the guest bedrooms, which is decorated in Louis XV style. A trio of botanical prints separates the twin beds, with their unusual headboards. Matching pillows with a coral reef theme are colorful accents.

GEORGIAN HOME
IN VIRGINIA

After raising their daughter in Tulsa, Kathy and Bob followed their dream of owning a horse farm in Virginia. These empty nesters studied historic architecture at the University of Virginia and decided to pattern their house after a classic southern home. Their Mid-Georgian H-plan is a quintessential manor house, which, though new, feels centuries old, thanks to details such as 150-year-old beamed ceilings and period plaster mantels and moldings handcrafted by a local architectural sculptor.

Having known each other for nearly twenty-five years as clients and friends, we watched their house come alive with the extensive collection of French and English antiques acquired for the two other houses I had decorated for this family in Oklahoma.

Despite its grand scale, the home feels cozy and inviting, a fact appreciated not only by Bob and Kathy but by their friends, who tell them they love its warmth and never turn down a dinner or party invitation. Filled with wonderful collections, scrumptious fabrics, and restful colors, the house achieves a casual elegance that perfectly suits this couple's hunt-country life while providing plenty of romping room for their three young grandchildren.

An eighteenth-century English secretary houses the owners' partial collection of Staffordshire figures and English porcelain. Chippendale chairs covered in Clarence House "Velluto Flaminio" surround the game table, *below left*. ❧ Custom tufted loveseats upholstered in David Easton "Checquers Velvet" are overseen by an eighteenth-century English painting of a shepherdess. Antique gold leaf brackets flank the portrait, *above left*. A custom lamp made from an antique Napoleonic figure welcomes guests at the foot of the stairs. The second-floor landing is inviting with an antique demilune holding a wonderful tole lidded coal bin and a pair of bronze-and-brass candlesticks. Hand-colored engravings of trees complete the vignette, *above right*. ❧ The pivotal fabric on curtains and on the pair of Gainsborough chairs is "De La Chine" by F. Schumacher. The camel back sofa is in Lee Jofa "Soiree Damask." The painting over the mantel is by Francis Sartorius, *facing*.

Viking range with an iron fireback is decorated with a fabulous collection of French copper cookware and handmade baskets. The center island doubles as an eating area, with Windsor barstools, *left*. ❧ The sitting area makes this the ultimate in kitchen design. The loveseat is upholstered in Braquenié print from Pierre Frey, "Bougival." The club chair is covered in Fabricut "Parasol." Each end of the loveseat features a custom table from Bryce Ritter. The wall is decorated with Kathy's collection of majolica and a metal grape basket filled with antique garden tools, *above right*. ❧ A cozy corner of the kitchen has a built-in banquette covered in Colefax and Fowler "Eaton Check" and nestled next to an antique trestle table. An eclectic mix of toile pillows completes the picture, *below right*.

Detail of and English Welsh dresser with the owner's collection of Blue Willow prominently displayed, *above left*. ❧ The walls are papered in "Aviary" by Greeff. The draperies are Pierre Frey "Toile De Nantes," with fringe by Global House of Trims. Antique Windsor chairs are dressed in Brunschwig & Fils "Curzon Check." The dining room is illuminated by an antique brass chandelier, *below left*. ❧ The painting above the mantel is a late-seventeenth-century portrait of a hunter and his dog. This is flanked by a pair of Minton-Spidell mutton bone chairs, *right*.

The wood carving at the bottom of a crest reads "God and my right," which refers to the right of kings to rule, frequently used by British monarchs. The verse in the middle reads "Evil is to him who thinks evil"—the battle cry of Richard the First, *above.* This room is truly Bob's. His book collection, along with equine and military artifacts, lines the built-in bookshelves. The draperies are made from Duralee "Andover Stripe," and the sofa is dressed in Brunschwig and Fils "On Point," *facing.*

Kathy's sitting room is a place of calm and beauty. The camel back sofa is in Fabricut "Deloris," accompanied by two small wing chairs covered in Ralph Lauren "Molloy." The odd chair is upholstered in Nobilis "Leonie," while the round ottoman is dressed in Bennison "Feather," *left.* ✄ Velvet curtains from Brunschwig & Fils frame the antique English oil painting of a distinguished dog. The sofa in the foreground is upholstered in Ralph Lauren "Hampton Paisley," *above right.* ✄ The nineteenth-century pine breakfront has been outfitted as a bar as well as a home for the television (behind the lower doors). Two wing chairs are featured in "Kingsbridge" by Ralph Lauren, *below right.*

HOME IN THE ROLLING HILLS OF VIRGINIA

When Frank and Cathy Keating ended their tenure in state politics, they chose to enjoy a life in the rolling hills of Virginia. They discovered their new address nestled in the midst of mature trees on a quiet, secluded lane. Set back a distance from the street, the home's soft yellow exterior was very inviting. Cathy knew this was it. But imagine what a home that has been empty for thirteen years might look like inside: the first-floor ceiling had fallen in, and the kitchen cabinets were in the garage.

At first blush, the home wasn't much of an endorsement for the elegant lifestyle and gracious entertaining the Keatings had always enjoyed. But Cathy has always had design vision and knew this could become a gorgeous home for them and for special guests who would come to visit from around the country. Although she admits to being a do-it-yourselfer when it comes to interior design, Cathy asked me to "work a miracle" on the new house. I had done her mother's home and she liked what I had created there; additionally, we had worked together on the Oklahoma Governor's Mansion, so I already had knowledge of her likes and dislikes.

Jim Steinmeyer 2007

First impressions are lasting, and what an impression the Keating entry makes! The flowers on the William IV mahogany center table are from Royce Flowers. Also shown is a pair of Louis XV–style candelabra on marble pedestals, *above*. ❧ Each piece of a twenty-five-year collection of Battersea enamels marks a trip or special occasion, *facing*.

I integrated the Keatings' existing furnishings and antiques with new upholstery and beautiful fabrics to make them look fresh. While Cathy wanted her home to reflect their personalities, she let me have a strong voice in the design. In the formal entry hall, I relied on symmetry—pairs of mirrors and sconces and all kinds of things that look good in twos—to make a pleasing first impression. We used an abundance of blue-and-white porcelain, one of my favorite design accessories, throughout the downstairs. On an antique baker's rack, I showcased Cathy's Staffordshire figures that she had collected on their travels.

In the formal living room I culled much of the crystal she had collected, telling her, "I know what your next store will feature." I try to be honest and direct about things I don't think will work well in a room. I always soften such suggestions with a sense of humor. Most importantly, I find a way to showcase special treasures, such as Cathy's rose medallion and the couple's political memorabilia recalling their distinguished career in politics.

Together, we created a home that is a gracious place to live, entertain, and enjoy the fruits of a life that has always focused on community service.

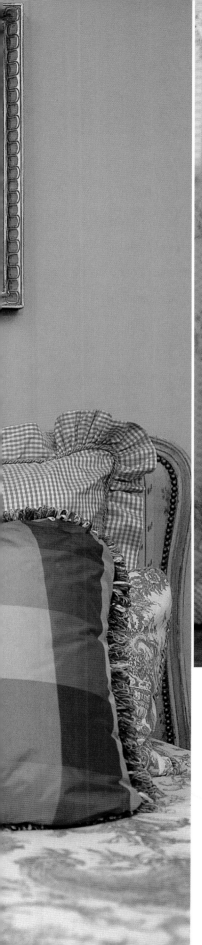

The Keatings' bed, a nineteenth-century-style headboard wearing fabric by Pierre Frey, enjoys a mix of silk pillows from Duncan Ticking. Framed botanicals and part of the owners' rose medallion collection finish the wall, *left*. ❧ The Louis XV–period fauteuil is not taking itself too seriously in bold silk check. A needlepoint pillow shows Cathy's philosophy, *above*.

A Louis XV–style center table features a Qing Dynasty vase lamp, a collection of silver picture frames, and a Tantalus set cleverly used to also hold a bouquet of flowers, *left*. A cast-limestone mantel overhung with Frank's Oklahoma gubernatorial portrait, by Kathy Walker Richardson, is the focal point of the living room. The symmetry of the room is shown with a pair of Louis XV bergères and a pair of Chinese export vases, *facing*.

A Louis XV–style buffet is transformed into Cathy's lavatory. The flower arrangements are by Royce Flowers of Alexandria, Virginia. The dressing table, which belonged to Cathy's mother, now wears a new skirt of Pierre Frey fabric, *above left*. ❧ The powder room is dressed in a beautiful wallpaper by Scalamandré with a Louis XV commode converted into a sink. This is a perfect spot for part of Cathy's collection of ruby overlay glass, *above right*. ❧ Cathy and Frank's library is not only filled with books but also with western art. The painting over the Louis XV Provincial buffet is by Richard Thomas, and the smaller painting is by David Bodelson. A bronze, *Standing Bear, Chief of the Ponca Tribe,* shares the buffet with a custom Staffordshire lamp. The painting on the bookcase is by Cathy Keating, *facing*.

HIGH-RISE IN FLORIDA

Gena and Bob Franden have been clients of mine for many years. I have worked on their home in Tulsa for a number of years, refreshing and refurbishing, updating interiors, and adding new accessories and furnishings. It was a pleasure to help them with their second home, a high-rise in Florida overlooking the Atlantic Ocean. They have a spectacular view. Sunsets are a joy to watch; nature is always one of the best accessories.

I must say, we all had our work cut out for us when they purchased the property. The high-rise was of 1960s vintage and had been lived in since then by the same person. It doesn't take a lot of imagination to visualize the paltry condition it was in.

Gena started from ground zero, you might say, installing new hardwood floors and building an entirely new kitchen. We worked on the project for a year, having all the work done in Tulsa and then shipping everything to Florida. We went on shopping sprees when necessary to find just the right accessories, like the wonderful starburst with the dove "Holy Ghost" above the sofa.

In the kitchen, I used open shelving, quite similar to what is in my kitchen. The shelves are filled with Gena's eclectic mix of serving pieces for entertaining. The kitchen is very low maintenance; it's small and compact yet easy to work in—even for entertaining large groups—with a beautiful small seating area.

Jim Steinmeyer 2007

A faux stone wallpaper by Brunschwig & Fils serves as a quiet backdrop for the entryway in the Frandens' Florida high-rise. A Louis XV commode is the anchoring star for the entry. An antique French trumeau mirror is accented by a pair of flat-back altar sticks that I had redesigned as custom lamps with custom silk shades. The entry sets the tone for the rest of the condo and is a beautiful introduction to gracious living for the couple's guests, *left*. ❧ Equally as striking in the entry is the four-panel French *paravent* (folding screen) mounted on the wall. An almost life-size terra-cotta *santo* of St. Joseph appears to welcome guests. A Directoire padded bench sits beneath the screen, *facing*.

The condominium has a light and open contemporary feeling, balanced with some of the couple's more traditional period antiques and collectibles. Books are important in their lives and there are plenty of shelves filled with engaging reading material. The books are interspersed with some of their favorite collectibles.

All my signature design touches are here—pairs of lamps, fauteuils, an antique French trumeau mirror and, always, luxurious fabrics for chairs and sofas.

I was especially pleased with the formal entry to the condominium. It features a traditional Country French theme of a commode and a trumeau, but I love the sophisticated surprise of the unusual French screen and the St. Joseph *santo*. I think these elements provide a dramatic first impression.

Working with Gena has always been a great pleasure. She has impeccable taste and style. She understands design so well. She really should have been an interior designer herself.

Perfect for this classic setting in the
living room is this eighteenth-century European Verdure tapestry.
The tapestry is fronted by a wrought-iron garden table housing a
Provence artisan glazed jar and paired with large Chinese export
vases, *below left.* ✤ This sofa, which is covered in Brunschwig &
Fils, is accented by a symmetrical display centered with an antique Holy Ghost starburst—a religious fragment—surrounded by
antique engravings. The pillows are dressed in antique Aubusson,
above left. ✤ This charming vignette in the living room features
a hand-painted fabric on an antique French Louis XVI fauteuil,
accented by an Italian side table with a Spanish stretcher base,
above right. ✤ The living room is a subdued setting for entertaining. A Louis XVI carved-limestone fire surround is accented by an
eighteenth-century *plaque de cheminee*—an iron fireback. Two display
cases reveal more collections. The comfortable seating areas feature
Louis XVI *bergère oreilles*—wing chairs with pillows—and a Louis XVI
club chair covered in Pierre Frey "Petit Parc." The ottoman is in
Nancy Corzine "Cavallo," *facing.*

A coral fan and Chinese export jars mix well with the Lucite table and the Gustav daybed, reflecting how comfortably contemporary materials can be right at home with Country French. A lead crystal column lamp adds interest and the Lucite side table lends a contemporary touch, *facing*. ❧ The handsome striped painted *lit de repos*—daybed—features a 1940s-style gueridon. Louis XVI club chairs are companions in this setting, *above*.

The Niermann Weeks Avignon chandelier is an incredibly unusual light fixture, adding dramatic interest to the dining room setting. The chandelier is styled in a custom silver gilt finish with crystal swags. The French 1940s table is accented by period chairs covered in "Petit Genosse" fabric by Pierre Frey *left*. ❧ The Chinese console and Louis XVI pier mirror—both one of a pair—provide a surprising contrast. An ornamental iron pineapple rests under the table, *above right*. ❧ The Frandens' diverse collection of antique pewter shows off in an eighteenth-century fruitwood faux *palier*, a style of kitchen étagère. The palier is a grand stage for this collection. It is flanked on both sides by Louis XVI—style dining chairs, *below right*.

A Louis XVI–period ornate mirror and painted commode look fabulous against the elegance of the "Latrobe" wallpaper by Brunschwig & Fils. A handsome terra-cotta statuette becomes the towel bearer, a nice piece that enhances the mirror and commode, *above left*. ❧ Even a small rectangle of Lucite can add a modern look to a traditional tablescape, especially if it's topped with a piece of antique coral on the library table, *above right*. ❧ A collection of books makes a classic statement in this alcove that features a sofa covered in Stroheim & Romann and accented by decorative pillows. The antique painting of a military figure, which I like to call "an instant ancestor," is accented by a pair of wall sconces with custom lamp shades. The armless chairs are covered in "Chinoiserie" by Travers. The Victorian ottoman is covered in Clarence House and sidles up to the Napoleon III low table, *facing*.

he open étagère-style shelving has long been popular in French design. I've used open shelving in all of my homes and love the way it allows me to display my collections. The granite farmhouse sink is perfect for the design of this kitchen, as is the wallpaper, "Oakwood" by Colefax & Fowler. The prints balance the myriad collections on the shelves, *left.* ❧ This cozy seating area in the kitchen is a perfect place for settling in with a savory cookbook or sharing early morning coffee. Two Directoire-style fauteuils are covered in "Leonie" by Nobilis. The nineteenth-century *rafraîchisson*—wine and cheese table—is featured as a side table. It features a custom lamp made from an antique seltzer bottle. The side-panel draperies are Duralee fabric with Biran fringe, *above.*

HUNTING LODGE HOME

I've known Steve and Shelly Jackson for more than twenty years and have helped them renovate and redecorate their Tulsa home several times. It has always been a joy to work with these longtime clients.

Seven years ago, Steve found this wonderful wetlands property on a hunting trip in southeastern Oklahoma, which is a beautiful area of the state with abundant trees and rolling grasslands—a picturesque setting for a ranch house that serves a dual purpose as a hunting lodge. He just fell in love with the countryside and bought two thousand acres, comprised of fourteen hundred acres of wood and pasture and six hundred acres of hardwood wetlands, two bass lakes, and a care-taker house.

I welcomed the opportunity to help the Jacksons design a large ranch house—more than 6,500 square feet—on the property. I call it a French ranch house but admit it is an eclectic mix. It was a design challenge I so enjoyed. Because the location is three hours from Tulsa, I helicoptered in for every meeting, saving time and the stress of driv-ing. There was certainly plenty of room for landing.

Jim Steinmeyer 2007

The entry to Steve and Shelley's ranch home reflects the hunting theme that is central to their lives. I used a Gustavian tall clock as the centerpiece for a collection of hunt trophies, balanced with two small paintings.

Also in the entry is a uniquely carved commode, accented by a pair of matching custom lamps and antique engravings of pinecones, which have frames made from pinecones—a perfect touch for this ranch setting.

It was a two-year design project, and Steve and Shelly were hands-on during the total process. The result is a warm country style with beautiful fabrics, animal and Oriental carpets, and lots of antiques from shopping in North Carolina, Mississippi, and, of course, Tulsa. The completion of the project was wonderful. To see a home rise from the earth and become a place where people love to live has to be one of the best feelings a designer could ever enjoy.

There is nothing pretentious about the ranch. The architectural design is very open and the home has a great traffic flow. It's a terrific house for the kind of casual entertaining that Steve and Shelly enjoy. The kitchen has a huge center island, where guests always congregate. The kitchen, living room and dining room appear as seamless spaces, making the Jacksons' style of informal, casual entertaining easy.

This ranch home is much more than a hunting lodge. Now, it is a weekend retreat—Steve is there almost every weekend, Shelly almost twice a month—and it has become a special place for family holidays and entertaining.

Steve and Shelly have two daughters: one lives in New York, another in South Carolina. Shelly says the girls love bringing their friends from the East Coast to this ranch in Oklahoma, showing them a side of comfortable, rural life they might otherwise never see.

The Belgian server in the entry hallway, with matching lamps and custom shades, makes a grand statement. The mirror reflects another vignette: a pair of bird prints in a charming wood frame, *left*. ❧ Every good ranch needs a well-stocked library. This one is magnificent and has a great fireplace. The library provides a relaxing place for early morning or late-evening reading in English leather chairs. A Barley Twist drop-leaf table is an important feature in the room, as are custom lamps with unique wood shades, *right*.

W hen you walk into this living room, your eye is immediately drawn to the mantel. It is spectacular! The painting of Black Bear sets the stage for the living room. Walking in the front door, there is no question that the ancient sport of hunting is part of this couple's lifestyle. Among the special features are wing chairs flanking the fireplace, covered in Pierre Frey "Sologne," and an antique oak biscuit barrel. The ottoman is covered in Hinson "Raj Chenille," *left*. ✎ The Jacksons' beautiful Boone is in repose. Of course, he is resting on a sofa covered in a fabric by Brunswig & Fils, "York Chenille." I think Boone looks fabulous in this setting, just as Nicholas and Ruby love to rest on one of my sofas, snuggled up to French Aubusson pillows. I believe most dogs have very good taste in home furnishings, *above*.

his luxurious and spacious bedroom provides a relaxing oasis. The paneled ceiling is dramatic, with beams layered in a pyramid-style vault. The draperies are "Tristan" Greeff and the coverlet is from T.A. Lorton in Tulsa, *above*. ❧ In another view of the master bedroom, a Victorian painted-pine chest of drawers anchors the assemblage, with a charming mirror above. The ladder-back chair is covered in Lee Jofa "Mayfair Stripe" and the club chair is in Duralee. An antique cricket table and a coaching bench are at the foot of the bed, *right*.

GEORGIAN HOME IN TULSA

When John and Julie Nickel decided to purchase the 1920 Georgian house they now call home, they knew there was much to be done. The estate was far from its glory days and the Nickels were determined to return it to its former beauty in every detail—and all in just twelve months.

The house itself is elegant. The large rooms, intricate plaster moldings and beautifully detailed woodwork cried out for a more formal decor than Country French. Their previous country home in Tulsa was a yellow stucco Country French house that they purchased from me fully furnished. We began their new Georgian home with only a handful of pieces from their previous home: Three wonderful antique commodes, a baby grand piano, and a few special accessories are all we had to start with; the rest of the furnishings were destined for the guest house.

Tradition reigns in this home filled with elegant chandeliers, formal window treatments, and antique mirrors that reflect the gracious furnishings. This is a haven of traditional elegance for John and Julie's family as well as for lavish entertaining. Throughout the home there are cozy seating areas combining period furnishings and custom fabrics along with touches of Louis XIV and XV.

This project was a rare and wonderful accomplishment for all involved. In order to complete the home and meet the deadline of one year, John, Julie, April, and I traveled to New York, Los Angeles, and Dallas, shopping for all of the furnishings, chandeliers, artwork, and accessories that make this Tulsa jewel sparkle.

Jim Steinmeyer 2007

An 1812 painting by William Bradford is flanked by a pair of antique tole altar sprays on giltwood baskets. The Medici sofa by Minton-Spidell has 24-karat gilt trim. The fabric is "Bellagio" by Fabricut. The French chairs are from Old World Weavers in "Florian Stripe." A Regency tortoiseshell tea caddy, ca. 1810, adorns the coffee table. The fauteuils are from the Louis XVI period, *left*. ❧ The painting over the mantel is by former Tulsa artist Leonard Wren. The trellis-pattern woven carpet is by Edward Fields. The two coffee tables are from Minton-Spidell's Warwick Collection. French wing chairs accenting both sides of the fireplace are upholstered in "Marquis" by Scalamandré, *above right*. ❧ The "Hampton Sofa" is from George Cameron Nash and is upholstered in Travers "Melo." The Louis XIV–style giltwood table—one of a pair—displays an outstanding collection of precious and rare antique tortoiseshell objects that are conversation pieces at any gathering in this home, *below right*.

The Georgian painted alder wood fire surround is complemented on the mantel with an Empire ormolu clock, *facing above.* Antique silver and crystal epergnes are beautiful companions, accenting the formal dining room table. The flower arrangements in the epergnes are by Toni Garner, who can create fabulous fresh bouquets on a moment's notice. Merci. The dining table was custom made by Carl Akin and is accented with Minton-Spidell's Louis XV–style "L' Avant Dining Chairs" covered in Glant "Wisteria Orientale." The rock crystal–and–bronze Louis XV chandelier is from Villa Melrose. The draperies are "Delamont Weave" by Nina Campbell. The custom rug is by Edward Fields, *left and facing below.*

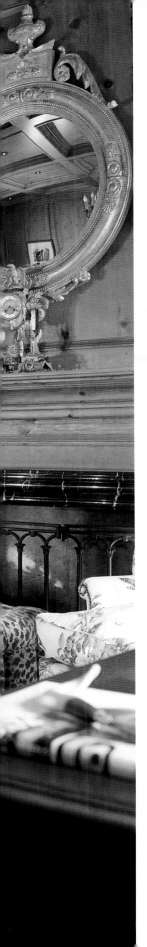

I believe every home needs a library—a place to relax, a literary hideaway where one can savor the pure pleasure of reading a good book. A St. Germain sofa by George Cameron Nash is covered in Cowtan & Tout "Blanford Check." The comfortable club chairs are wearing "Forrester Velvet" by Schumacher. The draperies are "Heathfield Paisley Velvet" by Lee Jofa, *left.* ❧ Ralph Lauren "Malloy" was the perfect fabric for the banquette upholstery and the draperies. I chose Brunschwig & Fils "La Seyne Check" for the reproduction Country French dining chairs, *above right.* ❧ I used a variety of unusual accessories in the spacious kitchen. Two of my favorites are an iron *plaque de cheminée,* placed over the cooktop for visual interest, and a lead rooster found in London; he was an ideal conversation piece for the kitchen counter, *below right.*

What young girl would not love this room as her special teenage retreat? With its antique chair and a painted armoire—both accented with Brunschwig & Fils "Sonnet" fabric—and a dust skirt appropriately titled "Silk Treasures" by Pindler & Pindler, McKenzie has to love the grown-up design features of this room. In this setting she could feel cosseted in an atmosphere of beauty and elegance, *above.* A guest room should contain all the amenities a visitor to your home would want: a great place to sleep, relaxing sofas and chairs, a writing desk, adequate lighting, and treasures from the homeowner's collection that add interest to the haven's "get away from it all" atmosphere. This room has it all. From a bed designed by Patina to the antique French sofa and beautiful accessories, a guest will feel very comfortable and pampered in this room, *right.*

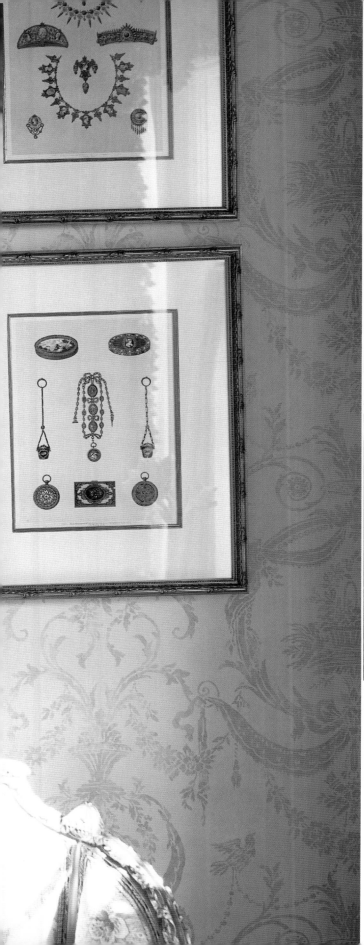

Colored engravings of jewelry surround an antique Venetian clock in Julie's dressing room. The settee fabric is Stroheim & Romann "Surfeit Silk Brocade." The draperies are Scalamandré "Napoli Stripe."

GUEST HOUSE

Many would consider the Nickels' guest house over the top, or at least up there with any small five-star hotel—and that makes John and Julie very happy. Ever the gracious hosts, they want guests to have every amenity at their fingertips.

In order to create a home away from home for John's grown children and few lucky friends, a complete remodeling was necessary. Elegant marble bathrooms were added, as well as a new miniature gourmet kitchen, a living room complete with a vaulted and beamed ceiling, a limestone fireplace, and a television that hides behind an oil painting.

I loved this charming and inviting space even without furnishings. Since most of the furniture from their previous home was not grand enough for the main house, we began with a treasure trove of fine Country French antiques to work with. We added antique chandeliers, beautiful custom draperies, new upholstery, and some accessories and viola! Now the only problem is guests don't want to leave, including me.

Jim Steinmeyer 2007

A sofa covered in Lee Jofa "Tuxedo Linen Velvet" is an inviting place for conversation in the living room. The side chairs and draperies are covered in Bennison's "Song Bird" pattern, while the ottoman is dressed in "Velvet Butterfly" by Clarence House. A trio of antique Italian altar sticks have been converted to candles on the coffee table, *above*. ❧ A painted antique lantern from an abbey in France sheds light on a collection of small paintings that line the stairway leading to the landing in the Nickel guest house. Bailey's favorite napping place is beside a 1920s blackamoor, *facing above left*. ❧ A Napoleonic figure accents a side table in the living room. An antique console features temple jars, *facing above right*.

A very rare mistletoe chandelier presides over the dining table in the guest house. The *bonboniere* (candy jar) on the table is from T.A. Lorton. The chairs are covered in Travers "Nimoise" and the side panel draperies are "Dogwood 2177 Sesame," *below left and right.*

A scalloped canopy in a guest bedroom is dressed in Bennison's "French Twist" fabric, matching the bed coverlet, *facing above left.* An antique French chair rests beside a French commode, accented with a symmetrical arrangement of lamps and wall sconces, *facing above right.* A Louis XV--style table accents a window in another guest bedroom, and classic shelving arrangement features Napoleonic figures, *facing below left.* A small nightstand nestles between the twin beds, featuring a miniature oil-painted bust on ivory in a bronze frame, *facing below left and above.*

A painted commode serves as a lavatory in the guest house bathroom. It features a marble top and a sculpted marble sink. The wallpaper is "Petersburg" by Thibaut, and the space is highlighted with bronze Louis XVI–style appliqués, *left.* This chair has a place of honor in one of the guest bathrooms. It is a wonderful and rare provincial Consulate walnut chaise—a side chair, vintage 1790, with a carved *dossier* (back), *above.* This giltwood mirror could be of Italian or French heritage. It features *parecloss* (mirror panels) and a beautiful carved bouquet surmount, *facing.*

FAMILY HOME IN MIDLAND, TEXAS

Kate and Stuart Beal are a young couple who invited me for a return engagement when they bought a new home in Texas. Like many of my clients, I had helped them with design projects on a previous home. I knew their tastes, their lifestyle, and how they wanted their home to look for friends and family. And I knew this home would represent a changing lifestyle for a busy, growing family with three boys.

Kate is an inveterate collector, and I wanted the décor in this new home to reflect her great taste and her love for displaying the family's many unusual collections.

Throughout the home, the look is traditional Country French, with beautiful antiques and sumptuous fabrics in upholstery and draperies. I filled the home with subtle decorating surprises. Vintage altar sticks were turned into custom lamps. In the entry, an antique paysage oil painting is featured in a distinctive trumeau mirror.

A miniature French wood cart became the dining room centerpiece.

In the den, a small antique ladder was used as an end table and a French milk bottle carrier was repurposed as a vase on a tole tray. I always think it's fun and interesting when I can assign new uses for furnishings and accessories in surprising ways. The old objects are comforting, but to see them used in a more contemporary way adds design excitement.

Throughout the home, the collections make a statement, especially when displayed in settings that feature antiques.

The real star of the house is the Beals' "super dog," Woolsely, who is a Cavalier King Charles Spaniel and a brother to my new dog, Ruby, named for my late mother. Ruby is a companion to Nicholas, who is the love of my life. I love that our King Charles Spaniels are a special bond Kate and I share.

Jim Steinmeyer 2007

Collections are plentiful in the

family's den and are arranged for visual design impact. The painting is by Patricia Wilkes. Comfortable furnishings make this a favorite gathering place for friends and family. The coffee table is a Victorian-style convex storage ottoman, with fabrics by S. Harris and Pucci. The lamps are custom made from Spelter figures, *below left*. ❧ A painted Louis XV–style commode is flanked by two Louis XVI–style side chairs. Tole flower pockets on the wall accent the trumeau and lamps, *above left*. ❧ The living room coffee table, by Neirmann Weeks, houses books, flowers, and candlesticks. The wingback chair is upholstered in Brunschwig & Fils "Walnut Tree" cotton print, *above right*. ❧ Symmetry was definitely a guiding principle in this living room setting. A Leonard Wren landscape painting sets the stage for art appreciation. The sofa is covered in Stroheim & Romann "Vintage Chenille." The "Patrice" chairs are from my custom line of CHF chairs and are covered in Brunschwig & Fils "Bayberry," *facing*.

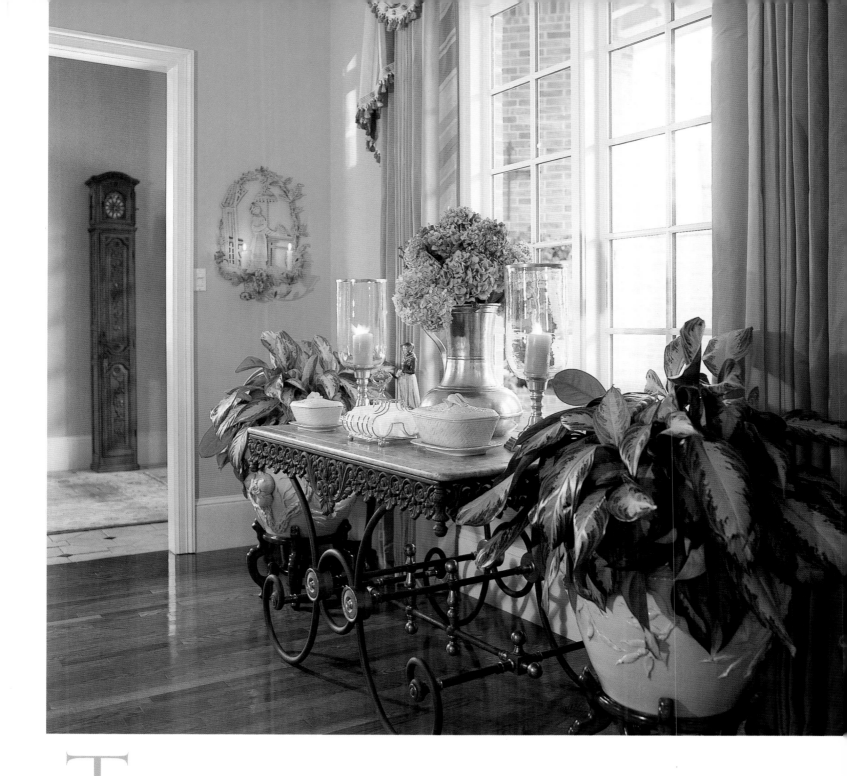

The reproduction French dining table and chairs are paired with an antique French sideboard featuring crystal lamps with custom shades by Sew & Sew. The period painting is by C. Carian, *facing*.   Tole Chinese wall sconces accent this corner vignette in the dining room. The French baker's table is home to an antique porcelain figure of the "turnip lady," pewter and crystal hurricane lamps, and an antique creamware game dish, part of Kate's extensive collection. The draperies are of silk loom taffeta and the swags and cascades are Duncan Ticking, *above*.

Kate's Victorian ironstone

serving pieces are artfully arranged above a painted
gateleg table. An old tobacco jar serves as a cache pot
for an orchid, *left*. ❧   The antique French walnut
table is from Mary Corley, circled by English-style
ladder-back chairs. The centerpiece on the table is a
pewter tureen by Kayserzinn Germany, coupled with
Kate's collection of creamware game pots. The chic
draperies and valances are in counterpoint, *above*. ❧
The antique daybed, of American origin, is upholstered in S. Harris "Bristol Mink." The small wing
chair, "Francoise" from my chair line, is dressed with
a Schumacher toile, "Le Meunier." The wing chair
in the foreground is covered in Brunschwig & Fils
"Beisteque" cotton print, *facing*.

The furnishings in the master sitting room, adjacent to the master bedroom, are in the Louis XV style. The daybed is covered in Bergamo "Maris," while the chair is covered in Nina Campbell "Delarmo." The patterned carpet is from T.A. Lorton, in Tulsa. The iron-and-brass low table is a French 1940s style. The painted end table houses a custom terra-cotta lamp with a custom shade, *left*. This is a favorite napping place for Woolsely, *above*.

SOUTHERN HILLS COUNTRY CLUB

When Nick Sidorakis, the general manager of Southern Hills, called to ask it I would be interested in taking on the interior design portion of a massive addition and renovation project the club was planning, I balked. After all, I was busy with clients and my first book had just been published, so I was traveling for book signings every week. I could think of many reasons why I should not begin such a lengthy commitment; and yet I said I would think about it. Southern Hills' unique history and importance to Tulsa, as well as the wonderful members and staff, were a big part of my deliberation. In the end, it was my assistant, April Faudree Moore, whose encouragement and total support (plus her promise to be in charge of the budget, deadlines, and enough paperwork to sink a small ship) convinced me to agree to such an enormous long-term project.

Southern Hills is truly a jewel in Tulsa's crown. Built in 1936 on land donated by local oilman Waite Phillips, the club was to be a place for sportsmen and families in a vast open area of south Tulsa. In the beginning, there were polo fields, stables, a skeet range, four tennis courts, and a swimming pool. The golf course was added last, with much of the membership being against it; today it is ranked fifteenth in *Golf Digest*'s list of the top one hundred courses and has been home to fourteen major golf championships.

In the small hallway leading to the living room, hangs a chandelier of Italian origin. The Dutch confidante benches are covered in Lee Jofa "Checquers Velvet." The bird engravings are from Dennis & Leen, *above*. As members and guests enter Southern Hills Country Club, they are greeted by a grand 1940s French-style iron-and-limestone center table from Grandeur Imports. A Louis XV cherry country buffet is another welcoming design piece in the entry, accented by a Louis XVI pier mirror and Louis XV–style side chairs with leather upholstery, *facing*.

The clubhouse was originally designed by architect John Duncan Forsyth in his signature European country house style, with vaulted and beamed ceilings, huge windows, wood floors, and large, welcoming fireplaces. These are all design elements I enjoy working with today, and they were my inspiration for the areas of new construction. It was very important to me that the new areas of the clubhouse echo the feel of the original architecture, so we vaulted the ceilings, added custom hand-hewn beams and corbels, copied original doors and ironwork, added three new fireplaces, and searched for chandeliers with an old-world aesthetic.

Now that it is all behind me, I can honestly say that it was worth the effort. After three years of meetings with the construction managers, architects, and the small members design committee, we completed our task on schedule, just in time for the 2007 PGA Championship. The membership seems to like what I've done and I am proud to have played a part in the history of Southern Hills Country Club.

A mirror framed by a series of antique botanical copper engravings is a backdrop for this seating area in the club living room. Custom wrought-iron and painted low tables are accented with the classic touch of blue-and-white export porcelain, *facing*. ❧ As guests enter the main living room at Southern Hills, they are captivated by the elegant bronze-and-crystal chandeliers that have been fixtures at this country club since World War II. A limestone-and-wrought-iron low table enhances the setting. All fabrics in this room are from my new Charles Faudree Collection for Vervain, *above left*. ❧ A Directoire *lit de repos* (French daybed) is an accent piece in the living room. The fabric is "Monderville" from my collection. The facing wall features a symmetrical arrangement of art and engravings over two banquettes. The trumeau is original to the club, *above right*. ❧ Nicholas and Ruby are cozy and contented in a Louis XV confessional wing chair.

A Belgian-inspired low table is the centerpiece of this setting, accented by books, a crystal bowl, and a beautiful blooming orchid, *left.* ✂ "Ghost Chairs" by Kartell create a perfect setting for conversation in the ladies' locker room. The chairs are paired with Louis XV–style end tables. All of the fabrics in this room are by Fabricut, including the draperies, in the "Spearmint" pattern, *above right.* ✂ Osborne & Little "Medlar" wallpaper sets the stage for elegance in the ladies' restroom. A Spanish-style console is highlighted with a Louis XVI–style mirror, framed by mirror botanicals. The tête-à-tête is richly upholstered in Cowtan & Tout "Irina Embroidery," *below right.*

A Lucite game table is the focal point in this area of the lounge, teamed with four Ralph Lauren chairs dressed with Ralph Lauren fabric. The banquettes are covered in Pindler & Pindler chenille. Stone tables are accented by Orkney chairs. The rug is Odegard and the draperies are fashioned of Brunschwig & Fils "Swing Time Stripe," *above left.* ❧ The wine cellar features an inset of an exquisitely carved German wine keg end. The cellar displays a monumental hunt trophy with a huge reindeer rack. The Louis XIV–style dining chairs mix leather seats with Robert Allen "Paisley Velvet" upholstery for just the right masculine look one would expect in the club's wine cellar, *below left.* ❧ The limestone mantel in the membership lounge features a soaring trumeau by Dennis & Leen and leads the eye to the arched bookshelves, which hold a collection of Chinese export porcelain and majolica. The bronze low table in front of the fireplace is by Dennis & Leen and features a stone top. The sofas are covered in Kravet chenille; Minton-Spidell French chairs are covered in Travers "Chevallier," *right.*

WEEKEND RETREAT

After a two-year sabbatical from country life, I purchased my third cabin at Cedar Crest Country Club, a gated community on Spring Creek in northeastern Oklahoma, just an hour's drive from Tulsa.

Many of my clients and readers will remember the photograph in my first book, *French Country Signature*, on page twenty, that showed my welcome sign, "The Roost—C. Faudree." My new cabin is named The Roost Number Three.

Cedar Crest Country Club was originally built in the 1920s by oil scion J. W. Skelly as a place for his hunting and fishing buddies. Today, it is a weekend haven for a number of Tulsa families, most of whom are friends and began the weekend migration to this setting almost a decade ago.

In The Roost Three, which was originally a one-room cabin, the interior is fashioned of dark logs. Needless to say, I made some significant and necessary changes to the original floor plan. I added a new bedroom so I would have a wonderful view of Spring Creek, which meanders like a ribbon of blue-green water through this beautiful wooded setting. I also added a new bath and enclosed a small side porch to give it new life as the dining room.

Jim Steinmeyer 2007

Nicholas and Ruby have such exquisite taste. They love to nap next to the Aubusson pillows on the living room sofa. An antique horn table seems the perfect setting for this antique Black Forest lamp, *left*. ❧ The fireplace mantel is a real conversation piece in the cabin's living room. Carved into the mantel is the phrase "Good books, good wine, good friends." It seems quite appropriate for the things that are so important in my life, especially good books and good friends. The coffee table is an English reproduction accessorized with an old pine boat and a box with a needlepoint dog on top, *facing*.

My clients and readers are familiar with my love for decorating with chickens, roosters, and blue-and-white Chinese export porcelain, but I've stepped out of that design mode a bit for my new weekend retreat.

Like the other "Roosts," it's still a small, cozy cabin, but in this one I've stretched my color palette to the autumn hues of green, brown, and beige. The bedroom is light and cheerful, with a pure neutral palette of beiges, a little brown, and just a touch of black. I have used natural linens to create a quiet mood and complement the restful view of the creek. I've created a very warm and relaxing setting in the bedroom.

Throughout the cabin, I show my great love for dogs and nature through the interplay of fabrics, textures, and artwork—the kind of mix that I consider to be the signature of my design style.

I am so thrilled to be back at Spring Creek in a wonderful cabin that is my favorite weekend getaway, one I love to share with friends and my two treasured canine companions, Nicholas and Ruby.

A painted pine bookcase is the design star of the cabin kitchen. It features a collection, gathered over time, of old and new white ironstone. The open shelving is a design feature I love to use in kitchens. The table is an antique French garden table, and the custom chair, from my furniture line, is upholstered in Brunschwig & Fils "Grilly Print." The rooster, executed here in a custom lamp, is a familiar Charles Faudree signature. The draperies are "Orkley," from the Stout collection. Nicholas and Ruby are close by, waiting for a treat, no doubt, *above left*. ❧ A painted *vaisellier* is tucked under an antique pine shelf that is home to a collection of black-and-white hard-paste porcelain and antique pewter. The antique bible box keeps the host's linens out of sight, *below left*. ❧ Guests dine under the glow of an Italian-style chandelier while seated on Swedish dining chairs covered with "Herring Ticking" from Duncan ticking. Bird prints from the David Easton auction adorn the walls. The curtains are Lee Jofa "Cranborne Chase," *right*.

A cozy fire crackles under the antique Louis XIV limestone mantel, while a Black Forest dog, a special gift from special friends, keeps watch. Louis XVI-style bergère chairs, covered in natural linen from Fabricut, are favorite spots for Nicholas and Ruby to catch a nap. The trumeau over the mantel was made from French wood fragments, *left*. ❧ A Napoleon III faux bamboo desk has a new life as a bathroom lavatory. The antique bamboo cabinet was one of my first purchases after graduating from college. It has moved with me to every one of my homes. A Black Forest mirror above the lavatory represents "the mix" that always will be a hallmark of my designs, *above right*. ❧ Rare salt-glaze vase lamps sit upon a painted Louis XV-style commode. A Louis XVI fauteuil is covered in Nancy Corzine "Cavallo." A fabulous canine oil painting, after Landser, dominates the south wall of the bedroom, *below right*.

CONTEMPORARY HOME IN TULSA

Sally and Tom Hughes are wonderful longtime clients. Having worked on two previous homes, Sally knew exactly what she wanted even before the building began. She envisioned something more contemporary, a new look for both of them. The Hugheses sought guidance in interpreting their vision by choosing nationally renowned architect Michael Mahaffey, of Oklahoma City and Santa Fe. The result is a mix of old and new that is highly edited and very refined but still comfortable and welcoming.

Sally and Tom wanted a space that would be appropriate for entertaining large groups yet still comfortable for smaller family events. The living room features two carved-limestone fireplaces paired with custom mirrors to accentuate the high ceilings. Contemporary striped upholstery, gleaming glass coffee tables, and unusual accessories add a modern feeling to the design.

The ultimate goal for the Hugheses' home was to mix antiques with contemporary architecture and furnishings to create a home that is light, airy, and inviting. The home is a perfect example of a favorite expression of mine, both in life and design: it is the mix, not the match, that keeps things interesting.

Jim Steinmeyer 2007

Above a limestone Louis

XIV fireplace from Dennis & Leen hangs a custom trumeau.
Four Rose Tarlow chairs are covered in Groves Brothers "Lucy,"
facing. ❧ A contemporary square glass vase filled with flowers,
a large candlestick, a vase on a silver tray, and a bowl of fruit make
for a pleasing arrangement on the living room coffee table, *above
left*. ❧ A contemporary theme greets visitors to the Tulsa home of
Tom and Sally Hughes. Lucite—a transparent acrylic—is the material
of choice for the modern table in the entryway. It is dressed with
Italian polychrome altar sticks and an antique cast-iron urn with a
copper leaf bouquet. A contemporary painting complements the
modern look, which has the counterpoint of a Louis XVI armchair
covered in Pierre Frey upholstery, *above right*. ❧ The stool in the
left foreground is from Dennis & Leen, as is as the sofa, covered in
Fabricut "Bellagio." A pair of French chairs re-covered in Zimmer
and Rhode "Dauphine," *right*.

The silver leaf dining table is by Bob Phillips. Regency-style chairs are covered in Groves Brothers "Fortuny," *above*. ❧ The striking low ebony table serves the club chairs, which are upholstered in Zoffany "Rayure Chinee." The bolection molded stone fire surround is by Dale Gillman, *right*.

Appropriately, an oil painting of a colorful French butcher presides over this area of the kitchen. The high ceilings, expansive windows and French doors add design interest as well as light. The French farm table is a reproduction from "Woodland." The Gustavian-style painted breakfast chairs are covered in Peter Fasano "Brompton," while the four club chairs are attired in Zoffany "Rayure Chinese." The love seat features Cowtan & Tout "Livingstone," *left.* Much like candleholders that stretch the length of a table, this double-sided floral arrangement makes a striking centerpiece on the kitchen table. Toni Garner was the artisan for this bouquet, *above.*

$\mathcal{L}$ouis XV Provincial *bureau plat*—
writing table—rare in chestnut, holds
a bronze soldier. A modern-palette oil
painting of a Parisian cityscape hangs
above the marble mantel. The chair
fabric is "Traditions," from Cameron
Textiles.

A n antique Louis XV writing table with Louis XVI bench and armchair make a comfortable place for planning or journaling. The custom headboard wears "Shila Leopard," by Randolph and Hein. The draperies and dust skirt are Dedar "Leonia," *left*. ❧ Sally's dressing room chair is Regence style, with custom lamps made from antique Italian altar sticks, *center right*. ❧ Fresh flowers by Toni Garner and unusual silver and glass antiques add to the beauty of this dressing area, *below right*.

The Hughes' powder room is finished with a Swedish-style Bombe commode for the lavatory. A charming, small Belle Epoque trumeau with église panel hangs above the mirror, *left*. ❧ A Louis XV *fauteuil d'enfant*—a child's armchair—is a charming accessory in the guest bedroom, *above*. ❧ The guest room has wrought-iron beds with bronze medallions on the headboard. A Louis XVI—style Provincial mirror hangs above the Louis XIV petite buffet, *right*.

LIGHTER AND BRIGHTER IN TULSA

The home of Gayle and Frank Eby was originally built by John Duncan Forsyth, a well-known architect of the 1920s who left his mark on many Tulsa homes and even Southern Hills Country Club. Mr. Forsyth created a wonderful family home, and the Ebys have worked to make it even more gracious and inviting.

My assistant April and I began this project with the mission of making it lighter and brighter. Having just put the final touches on the Ebys' home in Jamaica, we knew just what to do. Our favorite painter came in and gave us a light ivory backdrop to showcase all of Gayle's wonderful collections of majolica, antique engravings, crystal, horns, and more. We rearranged, repurposed and reupholstered everything and then shopped for more. Gayle is a wonderful traveler and has impeccable taste, so a trip to Los Angeles and a trip to Paris filled out the rest of our needs.

This home beautifully showcases some of my favorite design elements. Collections are important; they give personality to the interiors. Books are essential, in bookcases and on tables, where they add interest and sometimes inspiration. Antiques, of course, bring warmth and a sense of history to a home. Most of all, wonderful fabrics create drama or tranquility, depending on the owners' wishes. We mixed all of these together, added the Ebys' gracious hospitality and dedication to detail, and created a home they treasure.

A nineteenth-century Provençal commode from Arles features eighteenth- and nineteenth-century elements and carving that was specific to the Arles region in France. The Louis XVI-style mirror is accompanied by twin lamps and a wonderful antique blackamoor, *above*. ❧ The entry chair is a Louis XVI–period walnut *fauteuil* with eighteenth-century *animalier* tapestry covers. The antique English terra-cotta chimney post is a fine place to stash umbrellas, *facing*.

The centerpiece of the living

room is a rare Regence table with deer-hoof legs and a Breche
d'Alep marble disked top. A rare Louis XVI–style *rafraîchissoir*
is in the background. The wing chair, from Dennis & Leen, is
covered in a Highland Court fabric. The period French *bergère*
is covered in Bennison "Chinese Pheasant," *facing.* ❦ The
Minton-Spidell sofa is covered in Brunschwig & Fils "Crystallo
Velvet." Behind the sofa is a Louis XV *bibliothèque* with wired
doors, called *grillage* in French. A collection of crystal candlesticks adorns the table, *above left and right.* ❦ Nineteenth-
century French paysage oil paintings accent a Louis XV walnut
commode, which features a pair of rare nineteenth-century
majolica vases. Antique tole lamps and a lacquer tea caddy
complete this vignette. The Louis XVI *fauteuil* was hand
painted by Janet Davies, *below right.*

The centerpiece on the dining table is a nineteenth-century English Masons ironstone footbath, accompanied by a pair of Georgian silver candlesticks, *left.* Gustavian-style dining chairs circle an oval table. The chairs are covered in Schumacher "Etienne Moire Check." The unusual chandelier in the Napoleon III style is fashioned of deer antlers, *above right.* A painted Louis XV–style enfilade is featured on the French-style chest, accented with a Belle Epoch giltwood mirror and a pair of Italian polychrome urn custom lamps, *below right.*

A focal point in the library is the painted Louis XVI game table. The backs of the French 1940s *guilloche* game chairs are covered in Lee Jofa "Sundance Velvet." The ottoman is wearing Cowtan & Tout "Livingstone," *above left.* ❧ The Stroheim & Romann "Lausanne" draperies provide a pleasant backdrop for the furnishings in the upstairs sitting room. The sofa is covered in Old World Weavers "Argento," and the Louis XVI Provence *fauteuil* is covered in Jane Shelton fabric. The room includes a rare walnut Directoire table, *below left.* ❧ The Louis XV canapé—a love seat—is upholstered in Hinson "Holyoke Chenille." Cozying up to the love seat is a Louis XIV-style *os de mouton* (mutton bone-shaped) low table. The Dennis & Leen wing chair to the left of the sofa is covered in "Duchess," from Clarence House. The draperies are Lee Jofa "Arbre," *right.*

MODERN AND TRADITIONAL BLEND

Kaye and Ernest Pickering had previously lived in two contemporary homes, which they loved. When they decided to build a new home in an established Tulsa neighborhood, they asked me to blend their modern furnishings with more traditional antiques and accessories.

They gave me carte blanche throughout the home, from the choices of fabrics to the colors of paint, and even the trio of colored bricks we used in the entryway and exterior casual areas.

A series of arched ceiling beams in the living-dining area continues the high-pitched drama. The first impression is of wide-open space, brought to scale with the artful placement of furnishings, accessories, and art.

I used a cast-stone fireplace and mantel to anchor the end of the living room and placed an antique French armoire nearby to contrast with the modern furnishings.

Jim Heinmeyer 2007

A faux fur throw by Ralph Lauren accents a subtle ottoman. Pillows by Greeff are in shades of mustard and seafoam.

I wanted to make a statement with the upholstery in this room and found two fabrics that expressed the contemporary theme. One has a 1950s retro design in brown and cream squares, appropriately titled "Hypnotic," by Calvin. It is an eye-catching piece of upholstery that garners comments from visitors. The club chairs are paired with two smaller chairs covered in "Akoni" by Harlequin, a stylized leaf pattern . The mix makes for a cozy and comfortable seating area.

Kay and Ernest love contemporary art and they like an eclectic look, especially in the main living areas. Above the mantel is an abstract painting by Gwendolyn Matson. A highly detailed painting of an Oriental rug by Kali Marquardt, formerly of Oklahoma and now of Italy, accents a similar painting by Marie Kash.

From fruits to flowers, the Pickerings' art collection is bold and expressive—brightly colored works of art that are bound to bring a smile to guests' faces.

Moving from the main living areas into the master suite is a study in design transition. I wanted the master suite to be restful, so I created a sea of pale aqua. The iron four-poster bed is elegantly dressed, facing chairs, a footstool and two tall windows draped in soothing, restful fabrics. A painted French *bibliothèque* hides the television. The adjacent master bath reflects a complementary design theme.

From a dramatic first impression to an island of quiet repose, this home provides everything the Pickerings wanted in a new home that mixes old with the new in a pleasing way.

The spacious living area blends old and new. Conversation areas are centered on a Neirmann Weeks oblong coffee table. The love seat is upholstered in Gaston Daniela's "Argentina." The cast-stone mantel was designed by Dennis & Leen.

An island with a granite top from Midwest Marble—"Purple Dunes"—is the centerpiece of the black-and-white kitchen. Behind the range is an antique fireback. Old tea tins adorn the top of the hood. A lead rooster from England presides over the kitchen setting, *above* The square dining table is an Italian reproduction, surrounded by Country French–style chairs by Sedersi Inc., and upholstered in fabric by Duralee, Number 41803. The design of the table makes conversation easy when the Pickerings entertain. An antique French buffet houses linens and other necessities for entertaining, *facing*.

or the Pickerings'
guest bath near the master
suite, I converted an Asian
table into a sink. The tole
triple mirror, accented
with tole sconces, seemed
perfect for this small room,
left. ❧ An unusual poster
bed and a painted French
Directoire secretary set the
tone for this quiet master
bedroom retreat. The
curtains of Lucia linen are
by Stroheim & Romann.
The small ottoman is from
T.A. Lorton. The fabric on
the twin chairs is "Simlar"
by Fabricut. The bed's
dust skirt is Scalamandré
"Chevalier," *right*.

TUSCAN FARMHOUSE STYLE

I have worked with Toni and Roy Bliss on two other homes in Tulsa and one in Crested Butte, a pattern of repeat clientele that has been such a joy in my design business. This home we began together when they decided to build, literally, from the ground up. I would call it Tuscan Farmhouse style architecture furnished with a wonderful mix of French, English, and contemporary pieces and artwork. It was fun to work on this home because Roy prefers contemporary and Toni loves traditional; it was a great mix of styles and personalities working together.

When we were close to finishing the home, they said, "You finish it," and went to Crested Butte for six weeks. They had planned a house-warming party for the week of their return and let me have free reign to accessorize and add all the finishing touches so they would be ready to have guests. That is pure trust indeed, and I so appreciated it.

Jim Steinmeyer 2007

The carved-limestone Louis XV-style fireplace with *trumeau* complements the arched French doors in the living room and unifies the whole room. Centered on the mantel is a French *regule* clock, paired with plated polished iron urns. The Louis XIV–style giltwood tabouret is an unusual piece, *left*. ❧ A Louis XVI commode, accented with a Baroque mirror, is a traffic stopper in the Blisses' entry hall, which leads into the dining room. The two-tiered wrought-iron chandelier is from Dennis & Leen. The draperies are Vervain "Chapelle," *above*.

A Louis XV–style walnut commode is accented by a duo of Louis XVI–style side chairs. French gilt altar sticks and a massive Chinese lidded jar sit in front of a painting by Hellen Yo, from Royce Meyer Gallery. A polished-iron garden table comes in from the outside to accent the setting, *above left*. ❧ The Louis XVI–style daybed is covered in Fabricut linen. A wrought-iron and glass low table faces the daybed. Export porcelain accessories add a touch of old-world tradition to this room, *below left*. ❧ Flanking the fireplace in the Bliss living room is a pair of chairs by Dennis & Leen, covered in Fadini Borghi's "Orta" pattern. The two handsome club chairs are dressed in Brunschwig & Fils "Boris Woven." The unusual gilded bench is from Grandeur and is upholstered in Nancy Corzine "Cavallo," *right*.

The Louis XVI–style painted *desserte*—side table—is accented with tole lamps featuring custom shades. The 1930s-style parqueted mercury glass reflects the fantastic wrought-iron chandelier, *above left*. ❧ The dining table features a monumental stone baluster base and a top of faux marble that is painted and parqueted. The ultra chic 1940s-style dining armchairs are covered in a sophisticated silk—"Colbrook Stripe" by Ralph Lauren—*below left*. ❧ The custom *bibliothèque* with open grille doors (from Dennis & Leen) creates a conversation piece in the sitting area of the kitchen. The love seat and club chairs are covered in Hodsoll McKenzie "Palm," adding a garden look to the room, *right*.

The custom headboard continues the arch theme and is covered in Chivasso. The dust skirt is fashioned of Brunschwig & Fils "Modern Stripe." Osborne & Little "Chicane" covers the bench. The French commode is by Amy Howard. Crystal lamps with custom shades accent the pair of nightstands, *left*. ❧ Three colors of silk were used to create the draperies accenting the arched French doors. The fabric is "Majesty Silk" from Fabricut. The club chair is by Zoffany, upholstered in "Brocatello Cineglia," *above*.

ACKNOWLEDGMENTS

My first thanks are to my clients, who, for more than thirty years, have allowed me to create and decorate their homes. Without their faith and trust, we would not be able to express our talent.

My special thanks to those clients who appear in this book. Among them Kate and Stuart Beal, Toni and Roy Bliss, Gayle and Frank Eby, Genna and Bob Franden, Sally and Tom Hughes, Shelly and Steve Jackson, Cathy and Frank Keating, Kathy and Bob Kucharski, Julie and John Nickel, Kaye and Ernest Pickering, Carol Pielsticker, and Nick Sidorakis at Southern Hills Country Club.

Hopefully, the book portrays our clients living in comfort, joy and with style.

I wish to acknowledge April Moore, my assistant, who is my right hand, my memory, my friend, my cousin, and who has been a great part of every project in this book. She also gives me that extra nudge to take on special assignments, always with her support. I also want to acknowledge and thank all my staff for their ceaseless efforts on my behalf.

As always, a big thank-you to my wonderful friend Jenifer Jordan for her countless hours of photography. She brought to this book warmth and her gift for wonderful, creative composition.

After the photographs are taken, the information passes on to M. J. Van Deventer. She does a great job of making my half sentences and notes scribbled on Post-its into an engaging story about a home.

Jimmy Steinmeyer, my longtime dear friend, deserves thanks for sharing his fabulous talent at renderings—making the title pages a great introduction to each home.

Special thanks to Dale Gillman, my brother-in-law, my historian and source of furniture styles and periods.

To Toni Garner, my dear friend and the best florist in all the world, thanks for delivering beautiful bouquets and cut flowers at a moment's notice.

Thanks to Madge Baird, my editor and friend, for her ever-patient demeanor; she has expertly guided me through anxiety and confusion to achieve my vision. Thanks to all the staff at Gibbs Smith who helped in the process of putting the book to bed.

I must express my heartfelt appreciation to all those behind the scenes who contribute to my success as a designer. They are as follows: trompe l'oeil painter Janet Fadler Davie; special finishes painter Bob Phillips; drapery aficionados Pat Warnock, Tim Gillean, and now-retired Linda Morris; master cabinet builders David Hollingsworth and Craig Gill; custom lamp shades girls at Sew-n-Sew, Ltd.; pillow finishers Evelyn Bruton and Yvonne Stringfellow; custom furniture builder and upholsterer Ron Thayer, who has done beautiful work for me for the past thirty years; Beller's of Tulsa; expert paper hanger Russell Smith; and carpet designer Steven Montamat. Without these people, none of my rooms would have come to completion. Thank you again.

Last, but not least, I'm grateful to my sister, Francie Faudree Gillman, and partner, Bill Carpenter, whose stability, love, and support are truly gifts to treasure.

And to all of you, I cannot thank you enough.

Merci,
Charles

RESOURCES

CALIFORNIA

ANN DENNIS
2915 Red Hill Ave, Suite B 106-7
Costa Mesa, CA 92626
714-708-2555

TERRA COTTA
11922 San Vicente Blvd
Los Angeles, CA 90046
310-826-7878

VILLA MELROSE
6061 W 3rd Street
Los Angeles, CA 90036
323-934-8130

TOM STANSBURY ANTIQUES
466 Old Newport Blvd
Newport Beach, CA 92663
949-642-1272

JEFFRIES LTD
852 Production Place
Newport Beach, CA 92663
949-642-4154

LYMAN DRAKE
2901 S Harbor Blvd
Santa Ana, CA 92704
714-979-2811

KATHLEEN STEWART
338 N La Brea Ave
Los Angeles, CA 90036
323-931-6676

HOLLYHOCK
817 Hilldale
West Hollywood, CA 90069
310-770-0100

LIEF
646 N Almont Drive
West Hollywood, CA 90069
310-492-0033

COLORADO

THE SHAGGY RAM
210 Edwards Village Boulevard
Edwards, CO 81632
970.926.7377

GORSUCH LTD.
263 East Gore Drive
Vail, CO 81657
970.476.2294

GORSUCH LTD.
138 Beaver Creek Place
Avon, CO 81620
970.949.7115

NEW YORK

GEORGE N. ANTIQUES
67 East 79th Street
New York City, NY 10021
212.861.2222

HERBERT DEFORGE
220 East 60th Street
New York City, NY 10022
212.223.9007

JOHN ROSSELLI
523 East 73rd Street
New York City, NY 10021
212.772.2137

ROYAL ANTIQUES
60 East 11th Street
New York City, NY 10003
212.533.6390

PIERRE DEUX
D&D Building
979 Third Avenue, Suite 134
New York City, NY 10022
212.644.4891

TREILLAGE LTD.
418 East 75th Street
New York City, NY 10021
212.535.2288

JOHN DERIAN
6 East Second Street
New York City, NY 10003
212.677.3917

KINGS ANTIQUES
57 East 11th Street
New York City, NY 10003
212.253.6000

NORTH CAROLINA:

DOVETAIL ANTIQUES
252 Highway 107 South
Cashiers, NC 28717
828-743-1800

A COUNTRY HOME
5162 US Highway 64 East
Highlands, NC 28741
828-526-9038

NEAL JOHNSON
601 S Cedar Street
Charlotte, NC 28202
704-377-1099

RUSTICKS
32 Canoe Point
Cashiers, MC 28741
828-743-3172

RYAN & COMPANY
384 Highway 1075
Cashiers, NC 28717
828-743-3612

THOMAS HOKE ANTIQUES
WAREHOUSE
125 Lane Parkway
Salisbury, NC 28146
704-377-1099

VILLAGE ANTIQUES
755 Baltimore Ave
Asheville, NC 28803
828-252-5090

VIVIANNE METZGER
ANTIQUES
31 Canoe Point
Cashiers, NC 28717
828-743-0642

OKLAHOMA

THE ANTIQUARY
1323 E. 15th Street
Tulsa, OK 74120
918-582-2897

ANTIQUE WAREHOUSE,
DALE GILLMAN
2406 E 12th street
Tulsa, OK 74104
918-592-2900

BEBE
6480 Avondale Drive
Oklahoma City, OK 73116
405-843-8431

COLONIAL ANTIQUES
1740 S. Harvard
Tulsa, OK 74112
918-743-6700

COVINGTON ANTIQUES
7100 N Western
Oklahoma City, OK 73116
405-842-3030

EMBELLISHMENTS
1345 E. 15th Street
Tulsa, OK 74120
918-585-8688

POLO LODGE ANTIQUES
8250 E. 41st
Tulsa, OK 74145
918-622-3227

ROBERT'S ANTIQUES
8270 E. 41st
Tulsa, OK 74145
918-582-1058

ROYCE MEYERS GALLERY
1706 S. Boston
Tulsa, OK 74119
918-582-0288

SAM SPACEK
8212 E. 41st
Tulsa, OK 74145
918-627-3021

T.A. LORTON
1345 E. 15th Street
Tulsa, OK 74120
918-743-1600

TONI FLOWERS
3525 S. Harvard
Tulsa, OK 74135
918-742-9027

TENNESSEE

CATHERINE HARRIS
2215 Merchants Row
Germantown, TN 38138
901-753-0999

FRENCH COUNTRY
IMPORTS
6225 Old Poplar Pike
Memphis, TN 38119
901-682-2000

JIMMY GRAHAM INTERIORS
3092 Poplar Ave
Memphis, TN
901-323-2322

LITTLE ENGLISH
713 S Mendenhall
Memphis, TN 38117
901-682-2205

MARKET CENTRAL
2215 Central Ave
Memphis, TN 38104
901-276-3809

THE PALADIO MARKET
2169 Central Ave
Memphis, TN 38104
901-276-3808

TEXAS

BRIAN STRINGER
2031 West Alabama
Houston, TX 77098
713-526-7380

CHATEAU DOMINGUE
3615-B W Alabama Street
Houston, TX 77027
713-961-3444

COUNTRY FRENCH
ANTIQUES
1428 Slocum Street
Dallas, TX 75207
214-747-4700

THE GATHERING
955 Slocum St.
Dallas, TX 75207
214-741-4888

GRAY DOOR
1809 W Gray
Houston, TX 77019
713-521-9085

INESSA STEWART'S
5201 W Lovers Lane
Dallas, TX 75209
214-366-2660

1643 Dragon Street
Dallas, TX 75207
214-742-5800

JOSEPH MINTON
1410 Slocum Street
Dallas, TX 75207
214-744-3111

JOYCE HORN ANTIQUES
1008 Wirt Road, Ste. 326
Houston, TX 77055
713-688-0507

KAY O'TOOLE ANTIQUES &
ECCENTRICITIES
1921 Westheimer Road
Houston, TX 77098
713-523-1921

THE MEWS
1708 Market Center
Dallas, TX 75207
214-748-9070

NEAL AND COMPANY
4502 Greenbriar
Houston, TX 77005
713-942-9800

PIERRE DEUX
415 Decorative Center 125 Lane
Parkway Salisbury, TX 28146
704-467-3546

UNCOMMON MARKET
2701 Fairmont
Dallas, TX 75201
214-871-2775

WATKINS & CULVER
2308 Bissonnet
Houston, TX 77005
713-529-0597

THE WHIMSEY SHOP
1444 Oak Lawn Ave
Dallas, TX 75207
214-745-1800

WHITE & DAY ANTIQUES
6711 W.F. M. 1960
Houston, TX 77069
281-444-3836